The Frontier in Perspective

THE FRONTIER
in PERSPECTIVE

Edited by Walker D. Wyman

and Clifton B. Kroeber

MADISON

The University of Wisconsin Press

1965

Published by the University of Wisconsin Press
Mailing address: P.O. Box 1379, Madison, Wisconsin 53701
Editorial offices: 430 Sterling Court, Madison

Paperback edition, 1965

Printed in the United States of America
Library of Congress Catalog Card No. 57-9403

To the Memory of

LYMAN COPELAND DRAPER

Founder of the Draper Collection, builder of the State Historical Society of Wisconsin, and contributor to the climate of scholarship that made frontier studies important at the University of Wisconsin.

Preface

IN the history of frontier studies, the year 1954 is of special significance, for it was just a hundred years before that Lyman Copeland Draper came to the State Historical Society of Wisconsin. When he assumed the duties of corresponding secretary (without salary), there was a library of fifty books housed in the office of the governor; when he retired four decades later, there were one hundred and ten thousand titles in the library that now occupied most of one wing of the state capitol building. That fact alone entitled Draper to special consideration by the historical profession in the centennial year of his coming to Wisconsin.

Draper came from Yankee stock that had settled New York State. Having heard family stories of the adventures of his ancestors, he acquired a thirst for frontier history at an early age and spent the rest of his life quenching it. Long before he came to Wisconsin, he was a collector of pioneer reminiscences and frontier lore and had a considerable library that he hoped to use for writing history. His biographer, William B. Hesseltine, in *Pioneer's Mission* (Madison, 1954) calls him a "romantic antiquarian" who amassed documents with the zeal of a missionary in order that his beloved pioneers—George Rogers Clark, Daniel Boone, and others—might not suffer the fate of oblivion. In the fullness of time, these items became the Draper Collection, 478 volumes of source materials, which caused many scholars of the Trans-Appalachian frontier to make pilgrimages to Madison. This collection has long given the department of history at the

University of Wisconsin a strong interest in frontier history, and a steady stream of students deeply conscious of the pioneer period has flowed from there into American society.

When Draper died in 1891, he had written no biographies of his pioneers, but he had rescued them from oblivion through the legacy of his life's work. As Hesseltine says in the closing paragraph of his biography:

And the Historical Society with its library carried on Draper's work and fulfilled his prophecies. Through the years he had asserted again and again that libraries and books were the foundation stones upon which the democratic spirit in America must build. Even before his death, a group of young scholars in the University of Wisconsin were utilizing the resources of the Society's library for new investigations into the nature and operation of American society, bringing the techniques of historical research to bear upon social and economic and governmental problems. Frederick Jackson Turner was preparing to assert, as Draper's whole life had asserted, the significance of the West in the flowering of American democracy. Within a decade, a political reform movement, capitalizing upon the investigations of the University's seminars, and based securely upon the Society's library, was to startle the world with the democratic reforms of the "Wisconsin Idea." The trees that Lyman Draper planted were to bear rich fruit in the state and in the nation. The library, which was his enduring monument, was the state's most precious asset.

In 1954 the University of Wisconsin Summer Session sponsored a series of lectures in honor of Draper's memory, under the title "Wisconsin Reconsiders the Frontier." The department of history and other departments invited a number of lecturers from within the University and elsewhere, and from this series of lectures thirteen have been chosen for inclusion in this volume.

In gathering these essays to form a volume, the editors urged the authors to take the Turner thesis of the significance of the frontier in United States history as a reference point, to keep documentation to a minimum, and to accompany their essays with selective reading lists rather than full bibliographies.

We would like to acknowledge the initial contributions and enthusiastic support of this project by Professors Robert L. Reynolds and William B. Hesseltine of the University of Wisconsin. The success of the summer program was due in large part to the generous assistance of John Guy Fowlkes, then dean of the School of Education of the University.

Walker D. Wyman
Wisconsin State College
River Falls

Clifton B. Kroeber
Occidental College
Los Angeles, California

Contents

Part I. The World Frontier

Part II. *The American Frontier*

Introduction

MAN has been a wanderer, and alone or in groups he has moved restlessly into new lands and against the border of other men's domains. The farthest limits of his advance have been called the frontier, a term describing so many situations that its meaning has become vague. To some the word may mean the border, the political boundary between sovereign states, the outer limits of national defense. However, in history the term has been used in numerous informal situations describing the expansion of a people.

Considering the great variety of frontiers, it is small wonder that historians have no fixed meaning of the term. They have considered it a place, or a process, or a situation. A frontier may mean a primitive people that live beyond a settled society, the movement of an aggressive people into the lands of a simpler folk called barbarians, military or trading posts in the borderland, or even the time and place where institutions are adapted to new conditions. The term may indicate either a stable front of settlement or a movement of people; it implies the existence of a vacuum beyond the outer limits of military and political power of organized states. It brings to mind the enchantment of distance and isolation, frontiersmen of heroic size, an ideology on the part of the advancing people that makes the movement something to cherish. Frontier history has been written largely by those who came and conquered, not by the native people who were pushed aside, enslaved, or destroyed.

New cultures have risen as people have wandered into strange lands, and many remember that moment when their pioneers broke the trail and made the first settlement. The Bible records the frontier experiences of the Chosen People as they left Egypt:

And thou shalt say unto him, The Lord God of the Hebrews hath sent me unto thee, saying, Let my people go, that they may serve me in the wilderness. . . . And the children of Israel journeyed from Rameses to Succoth, about six hundred thousand on foot that were men, beside children. And a mixed multitude went up also with them; and flocks, and herds, even very much cattle. . . . And it came to pass the selfsame day, that the Lord did bring the people of Israel out of Egypt by their armies. . . .[1]

In the extension and diffusion of culture, the frontiersman, in organized groups or as an individual wanderer, rich trader, landed colonist, or uprooted refugee, has been a prime agent. The culture of a new land could be fed from at least three sources: the milieu from which the frontiersman came, the components of that way of life he managed to bring with him and maintain there, the new environment that he entered. From ancient times to the present, scholars have given different weights to these varying factors, depending upon the basic sympathies of the writer and the type of frontier involved. The protection of the borderland from encroachment by enemies of the same cultural level is a different matter from the experiences of humble folk who hew out a home in an uninhabited wilderness. Thus a pioneer may be pictured variously as a protector of old values such as Christianity, as a creator of new institutions such as democratic government, or as a destroyer of old ways of life to make way for progress. The essays in this volume suggest different answers to the question of the influence of the frontier in history.

The thirteen scholars who have written on these experiences in the realm of their specialized interests—some of them thinking in these terms for the first time—have produced essays illustrative of a wide variety of frontiers. Paul L. MacKendrick shows that the Roman legions, organized for both imperial conquest and border settlement, planted outposts and colonies that softened the barbarian resistance at the edge of that world. Caesar's "All Gaul is divided into three parts" becomes a frontier document, a memoir

[1] Exodus 8:16; 12:37; 12:38; 12:51.

and manual of instructions for the task of pacifying primitive peoples and the settling of a Roman society among non-Roman people.

In medieval times, as Robert L. Reynolds points out, European expansion was often over the sea, on distant islands and coasts not easily controlled from home. From these frontiers travelers like the Polos brought back news of other Eastern lands beyond the boundaries of man's account. Some of the medieval frontiers in Europe were overland advances by large numbers of settlers, and sometimes they involved the settlement of the new, uninhabited or "raw" land. Repeatedly, these people pioneered important techniques of business, missionary, and colonial administration. This experience paved the way for the later expansion of Europe into the outer reaches of an unfolding world.

A static rather than a moving frontier is discussed by Eugene P. Boardman in his essay on China. In that remote land two different cultures impinged on each other for hundreds of years. Some of the other essays discuss the cultural borderland and the processes of acculturation that take place when two peoples live near each other. It seems clear that on a static frontier a different set of factors are at work than on a moving one.

If these essays indicate diversity, they also suggest some common features of frontier history. Several indicate that the frontier moment has been brief in the life of a people, and that the pioneers soon establish a type of society similar to that from which they have just seceded. These essays challenge the uniqueness of the frontier influence. Paul W. Gates bridges the gap, in the American Midwest, between the first "cutting edge" of settlement and the next generation and shows that the pioneer characteristics faded fast. Walter R. Agard further shows that the pioneer stage soon passed and that the long hand of the classical world reached to Mid-America to help mold it. These essays suggest that caution is necessary in generalizing about the beginnings of a civilization.

Distance and isolation are important elements in the history of frontiers. The influence of the national or central government in directing the process is important, not only in explaining purpose but also in determining the institutions erected. The Russian example, discussed here by A. Lobanov-Rostovsky, shows that the early part of that eastern expansion was carried out in isolation by successive waves of people of different ways of life who had little contact with European Russia. It also shows that the central government was extremely important in the latter days of the Russian expansion to the Pacific. Thomas P. Abernethy also illustrates the diversity of the American development by showing that both the masses and the classes occupied the southern frontier. These essays deal with the factors that will be familiar to the student of modern, state-sponsored settlements far from the centers of national life, such as the American experiment in Matanuska Valley, Alaska.

Most of these essays point out that the world frontiers have had some influence in history. Henry Nash Smith shows how the experiences of Mark Twain in the Far West influenced the well-known book *Roughing It* and left its stamp upon our literature into the twentieth century. Frederic G. Cassidy traces the development of the English language after it migrated here, where it lost its guideposts and was confronted with limitless new objects and situations and also came into contact with the liquid languages of other groups. A. Irving Hallowell's essay about the influence of the Indian on American civilization also indicates the variegated contribution of the native. The word frontier has a loose but still adequate meaning when referring to Mark Twain's mining camps, the frontier of English language in America, and the land where a primitive people have lived as they retreated before the impact of another civilization.

Until quite recently, many of these situations that are herein called frontiers, with their various cultural aspects, were not described as frontiers. Indeed, many writers still do not cast the expansion of an ancient people, for instance, into the frontier mold. In early medieval times, the distant parts of the world were dimly known through the faulty descriptions of Ptolemy's geography and such manuals as St. Isidore's *Etymologies*. Beginning as early as the Crusades, however, the idea of sustained contact with non-Christian peoples outside Europe increasingly became a part of Western thought. Questions relating to pioneer settlement and overseas trade among "barbarian," "heretic," or "pagan" people recur in European literature. Long before the opening of the New World, Europeans had begun to express their opinions of both the nature of pagan, non-Christian peoples and the role of the Christian intruder in such societies.

During the late Renaissance, and as late as the latter eighteenth century, the discussion of Europe's expanding frontiers concentrated on their natural environment and the nature of the "savage" inhabitants. "In the Golden Age," says one writer, "the Blessed Isles, the *Germania* of Tacitus, the scholastic distrust of learning and the mystical aversion to sophistication, we discern tendencies which go toward building up the complex figure of the Noble Savage. These traditions were part of the intellectual baggage of the men of letters who read the explorers' narratives." [2] Absorbed in learning and in glorifying the realities of worldly life, men of the Renaissance were intrigued by the new stories of the unknown lands and peoples. At the same time, they also shrank from the implication that the lack of human population on some frontiers might argue the absence of the Lord's hand in those wild new worlds.

With the establishment of sixteenth-century empires, the treatment of non-Christian peoples became an important moral problem. Some writers of the late Renaissance used the primitivistic theories of medieval times to prove that aborigines were simple children of God, living in happy relationships according to the Lord's design. Others looked on the aborigines as inferior people whom God had long since condemned to life in the outer darkness, far from the consolation and hope of salvation offered by the Roman Catholic Church.

The advent of seventeenth-century rationalism, coming with the growth of French and English overseas empires, had a dampening effect on the more idyllic view of the aboriginal world. In matter-of-fact style, some rationalists classified primitive society as a kind of dangerous anarchy correctable only by European discipline of government, religion, and property control. The Indian was seen as a hopeless primitive, both a foe and a problem for Protestant or Roman Catholic Christianity. The writers of the eighteenth century retained, however, the older idea that primitive society reflected the virtuous life of the original Golden Age. The eighteenth-century cult of Nature reinforced this view. Life in Nature was understood to resemble the earliest and best stages of human history—"a certain rude simplicity and native innocence which, when contrasted with the numerous vices and disorders that spring up

[2] Hoxie Neale Fairchild, *The Noble Savage, a Study in Romantic Naturalism* (New York, 1928), 8.

in a more advanced stage, merit a decided preference." [3] These two conflicting ideas, derived from rationalism and primitivism, remained typical of metropolitan thinking about overseas frontier people. They are still to some extent reflected in historians' and social scientists' writings about world frontiers. Nature was, and is, synonymous with both danger and innocent simplicity.

Thus eighteenth- and early nineteenth-century Europeans and Americans often understood their world expansion in terms of both wealth and moral concern. Travelers of the time left us, in their descriptive books, a large part of the existing literature of frontier history. Their minutely detailed accounts of remote places and peoples and their habit of close observation can be accounted for partly because they were so bent on finding the ultimate significance of what they saw. They gave high value to the native and unspoiled character of new lands and peoples, but they also looked forward to changing those natural conditions in accord with their rational spirit and its embodiment in the Idea of Progress.

The persistence of distinct views on frontier society is seen in the contrasting opinions of two eighteenth-century Americans. In 1784, Benjamin Franklin wrote:

The vast quantity of forest land we have yet to clear, and put in order for civilization, will for a long time keep the body of our nation laborious and frugal. Forming an opinion of our people and their manners by what is seen among the inhabitants of the seaports, is judging from an improper sample. The people of the trading towns may be rich and luxurious, while the country possesses all the virtues, that tend to produce happiness and public prosperity.[4]

By contrast, Hector St. John de Crèvecoeur, who also knew the frontier at first hand, wrote in the same period:

Now we arrive at the great woods, near the last inhabited districts; there men seem to be placed still farther beyond the reach of government, which in some measure leaves them to themselves ... the reunion of such people does not afford a very pleasing spectacle. When discord, want of unity and friendship; when either drunkenness or

[3] Hugh Murray, writing in 1808, as quoted in Lois Whitney, *Primitivism and the Idea of Progress in English Popular Literature of the Eighteenth Century* (Baltimore, 1934), 290.

[4] Franklin to Benjamin Vaughan, Passy, France, in Jared Sparks (ed.), *The Works of Benjamin Franklin* (10 vols.; Chicago, 1882), II, 450.

idleness prevail in such remote districts; contention, inactivity, and wretchedness must ensue. There are not the same remedies to these evils as in a long established community.... He who would wish to see America in its proper light, and have a true idea of its feeble beginnings and barbarous rudiments, must visit our extended line of frontiers where the last settlers dwell.... In all societies there are off-casts; this impure part serves as our precursors or pioneers....[5]

The trend of nineteenth-century science strengthened the Idea of Progress, quickening the desire to civilize the outlying fringes of the populated world and bring them within the scope of urban, industrial society. In this mood, some writers reconciled primitivism with the Idea of Progress. If early man and the first forms of society had been the best, perhaps it was still possible to return to that earliest state and, employing all of man's wisdom, to build a new and finer society. This view was attractive to New World writers who felt the hope of human perfectibility and the thrust of national pride. Frederick Jackson Turner could write, in 1893: "American social development has been continually beginning over again on the frontier. This perennial rebirth, this fluidity of American life, this expansion westward with its new opportunities, its continuous touch with the simplicity of primitive society, furnish the forces dominating American character." [6]

In Turner's generation, as Silvio Zavala suggests, there were some Americans who found different meanings in the overland movements of population. One of the essayists, Walter Prescott Webb, places the expansion of Europe in the frontier mold, finds that the experience had great influence in the homeland, and accepts the basic hypothesis that Turner laid down for the American westward movement. Other essays sustain, modify, and repudiate the Turner thesis and in so doing indicate the need to reconsider the expansion of people throughout history. For the editors, the significance of Turner's propositions is that they have been so widely held as assumptions about the American past. It is now time to reconsider the frontier in the perspective of world history, to lay

[5] J. Hector St. John de Crèvecoeur, *Letters from an American Farmer* (London and New York, Everyman's Library ed., 1912. Orig. pub. London, 1782), 46–47.

[6] "The Significance of the Frontier in American History," as reprinted in his *The Frontier in American History* (New York, 1920), 2–3.

the numerous frontiers against the Turner hypothesis to test its validity, and to search for valid elements in the non-Turnerian history areas.

Such a comparative approach to the study of world frontiers is but little more than suggested in this volume of thirteen essays. Each writer explores his niche of history seeking either common elements that may have existed in some phase of the frontier experience or the absence of such factors. This approach to a reevaluation of the frontier influence in history may appeal to the adventurous historian as strongly as the borderland appealed to the hardy frontiersman of the past.

PART I

THE WORLD FRONTIER

PAUL L. MACKENDRICK

Roman Colonization and
the Frontier Hypothesis

The Turner hypothesis on the American frontier proves fruit-
ful to Professor MacKendrick, a classical scholar, as he views the
expansion of ancient Rome. He observes similarities with the
American experience in the over-all geography of expansion, in
the type of colonies and colonists, and in the influence which this
experience had upon the central government. As Rome set up posts
and built roads throughout Italy, she provided a pattern of settle-
ment that was to prevail when the demands of the land-hungry
and requirements of politics led to the establishment of colonies
abroad. As seen here, men like Cato and Marius were the Lincolns
and Jacksons of that day, frontier types that emerged in the process
by which the city-state became a great empire.

Besides the similarities, there are also differences when Rome's
city-state expansion is laid side by side with the American frontier
process. There are questions of comparison that cannot yet be an-
swered. However, Professor MacKendrick believes that this seg-
ment of an ancient world frontier can be better understood when
looked at through the eyes of Frederick Jackson Turner.

WHEN Mussolini in 1932 opened the grandiose Via del' Impero
between the Piazza Venezia and the Colosseum, a part of the
symbolism of his dreams of empire was a series of four black and

white marble maps set in a wall beside the street. They depicted the expansion of Rome from a little village of mud huts beside the Tiber to the marble metropolis of a million souls, mistress of Mare Nostrum, that she became in the reign of Trajan. How far is it helpful to regard this expansion as the exploiting of a frontier, with a reciprocal reaction of the frontier upon the mother city? Can we isolate typical physical and personal characteristics of the colonies and the colonists which created that empire? Are the effects of that colonization—military, economic, cultural, political—illuminated by looking at them through the eyes of Frederick Jackson Turner? These are the questions this paper sets itself to answer.

The expansion of Rome on Mussolini's marble map began, the Romans believed, almost as soon as the Republic was established, in 509 B.C. But Roman history, like George Bancroft's, was written under certain delusions of grandeur, as an unfolding of the Deity's grand design to further Rome's manifest destiny. The fact seems to be that Rome, at her beginnings and for more than four centuries after, was a good deal less important than her historians wanted her citizens to believe. At Rome's beginnings, Greeks, Etruscans, and Latins were all more important than she; the Latin League, with its early hilltop settlements, was far more powerful than Rome till after 338 B.C.; Rome at her origin and for years after was nothing more than a shepherd's village, herself a primitive frontier post on a river ford controlling a salt route. It was under her Etruscan kings that Rome advanced in power and civilization, she acquired paved streets, her market place became a civil and religious center, and her boundaries were extended to include some 350 square miles; but under her foreign overlords she remained essentially a Latin city, and agriculture remained her chief industry.[1]

With the expulsion of her kings and the setting up of an aristocratic republic, Rome embarked on 250 years of interlocked struggle—one part internal, a class war; the other external, war with her neighbors. The result was the forging of the Roman constitution and the establishing of Roman supremacy as the head of a confederation of all Italy. We call this struggle "interlocked"

[1] H. H. Scullard, "Rome, History," in *Oxford Class. Dict.* (1949).

because some of the discontented, the oppressed, the land-hungry, the ambitious, the restive, dissatisfied with the way Roman political institutions were tipped in favor of men of property, went out into the colonies whose land they, as soldiers, had helped to wrest from Rome's neighbors. Once arrived in the colonies, they became men of property themselves. Perhaps the continuing conservatism of Rome's political institutions may be attributed to the siphoning off of the more radical elements into the colonies. Certainly, legislation congenial to the frontiersman, actual or potential, i.e., the redistribution of land and the cancellation of debts, provided the two main planks in the platform of such reformers as Rome can show from the Gracchi to Julius Caesar.

Tradition records eleven Roman colonies planted between 509 and 382 B.C.[2] Of these, all but two are in Latium, and only two are more than twenty-seven airline miles from Rome. These colonies are nearly all hilltop towns, impregnable, and girt with beetling polygonal walls of gray limestone. Only two of them are less than 750 feet above sea level, and one towers over 2,200 feet. Military motivation was obviously paramount in their planting, but economic reasons, i.e., land grants to the landless, are alleged six times—twice, perhaps significantly, in conjunction with the names of Roman colonial commissioners.

At this point, we should notice that the planting of Roman colonies was always a state-controlled, never a private, enterprise —admittedly a fundamental difference from the origins of our own frontier. Our earliest description of a formal *deductio* (leading out of colonists) comes from the age of Augustus,[3] but that monarch's well-known penchant for antiquarian revivals to serve his political ends makes it extremely likely that the practice of his time reflects earlier procedure. The *deductio* had a strong military flavor: the colonists marched out under a standard, in serried ranks, commanded by the senior of the three elected colonial commissioners. The fact that only two sets of commissioners are attested for the first eleven colonies, plus the consideration that Rome before the end of the Latin War (338 B.C.) was not as important as later historians preferred to believe, leads to the now

[2] E. Kornemann, "Coloniae," in Pauly-Wissowa, *Real-Encyclopädie* (Stuttgart, 1901), IV. For full citation, see list of readings below.

[3] Varro, *De lingua Latina*, V, 143.

prevailing opinion [4] that Roman colonies of this early period were not founded solely on Roman initiative but in coöperation with, and often in inferiority to, the Latin League.

The century 338–241 B.C. sees the planting of at least thirty-two colonies, of which the farthest from Rome, Brundisium, in the heel of Italy, the port for Greece, was almost the latest founded. Some (Luceria, Alba Fucens, Cosa) are of the old Latin hilltop type; others (Aesernia) are ridge colonies, like the favorite Etruscan sites (Marzabotto; compare Fort Laramie); still others (Ariminum, Interamna Lirenas; compare Fort Leavenworth) are flatland types, controlling rivers, roads, or ports, and possibly are as much economic as military in motivation. Some (Antium; compare Harper's Ferry) were fortified with earthworks; others were *castra* (Ostia, Castrum Novum Piceni, Castrum Novum Etruriae; compare forts Pontchartrain and Dearborn) with fortlike walls square in plan, resembling the familiar Roman camp of Polybius' day. For only two (Cales, Saticula) are the names of colonial commissioners recorded; for one of these two a "safety-valve" motive is alleged: *"ut beneficio praevenirent desiderium plebis."* The source is Livy: when he ascribes motive, some scholars smell rhetorical, not sober annalistic, sources; such motives are alleged to be a projection back into the past of motives prevailing in a more sophisticated period of Rome's history. In short, the "safety-valve" motive for expansion is as much quarreled over for Rome's frontier as for America's.[5]

Since this was a century of wars, colonies were planted where military need dictated: against the Samnite hill tribes to the south and east, against the Etruscans and Gauls to the north, against the seafaring Carthaginians. More than half the colonies of this period are on the seacoast. By 241 B.C., Rome had a chain of six colonies down the Adriatic seaboard, from Ariminum to Brundisium, and a dozen down the Tyrrhenian coast from Cosa to Paestum (the two on the ends of the chain were founded in the same year, 273 B.C.). Inland, the colonies controlled the Apennine passes; some were in rich farming country, and all were connected with Rome by roads: the Appia, the Valeria, the Flaminia, which served both a military and an economic purpose.

[4] E. T. Salmon, "Rome and the Latins," *The Phoenix*, VII (1953), 93–104, 123–135.

[5] P. L. MacKendrick, "Roman Colonization," *ibid.*, VI (1952), 139–146.

The third period of the Roman frontier embraces only forty-one years (218–177 B.C.) and includes at least twenty-three colonies. Rome now extends her influence into the toe of Italy (Thurii, Tempsa, Croton, Buxentum, Vibo, where Greek influence had been strong) and into the Po valley (Placentia, Cremona, Bononia, Parma, Mutina), these colonies linked by the long straight stretches of the Via Aemilia. The most distant colony, Aquileia, in the marshes beyond where Venice now stands, 450 miles from Rome, was connected by road with the gold mines in the back country and grew to be one of the first cities of the late Empire. For mining as a motive, we may compare Virginia City and Leadville. The experience of previous colonization is drawn upon, bureaucracy increases (twenty-five sets of commissioners are attested); with the founding of Luca, near Pisa, in 177 B.C., the great age of Roman frontier expansion ends. Italy was unified politically and culturally; Rome was a world power; the formative period of the Roman national character, when life was simple and austere, the age of the pioneers, was over.

Henceforward, Livy is lacking as a source and our detailed knowledge of Roman colonization becomes spotty. The free land in Italy is exhausted; capital is concentrated in vine and olive culture; Rome expands overseas, raising fundamental questions of the relations between the political machinery of the small city-state and the greater complications of empire; and in politics, radicals begin to question the aristocratic monopoly of the state. This combination of circumstances, which Turner thought he saw in the United States in 1890 when the frontier had vanished, is precisely the situation Rome confronted in the age of the Gracchi (133–123 B.C.). The Gracchan attempts at solution involved overseas colonies (e.g. at Carthage) and, in Italy, surveys and allotments (centuriation) of land acquired from owners or squatters. Air photography during World War II revealed one such area near Luceria, not far from the RAF base of Foggia, which later excavation has dated in the Gracchan period.[6]

In succeeding generations, Roman generals demanded land in Italy for their veterans. Homestead acts are difficult when the land is already occupied, but Sulla, Caesar, and Augustus were able to settle their men on lands confiscated from their political op-

[6] J. S. P. Bradford, "The Apulia Expedition; an Interim Report," *Antiquity*, XXIV (1950), 84–95.

ponents, and these cadres of Legionnaires proved useful in curbing subversive activities and encouraging loyalty up and down the peninsula.[7] Caesar and Augustus were great colonizers: a recent study[8] identifies thirty-one Caesarian and seventy-four Augustan foundations, all in the provinces. The result of Rome's experiment with over three centuries of colonization was that Rome expanded from a geographical concept to an idea of social and political status, and colonization became a device for the gradual evolution of provincial communities to the level of Rome herself. The idea that what Rome called *Latinitas* was a commodity which can be exported, beyond the Alps, outside Italy, is the germ of an idea that held the Roman Empire together in a cultural unity—one world-wide family, all akin to Rome—even after the *pax Romana* was crumbling.[9]

The colonies had certain physical characteristics in common. The mushrooming of these outposts on the marches makes, as we have seen, an exciting story: first the posts in Latium, their walls rising on the hilltops and the headlands, then the pushing on to the gateway to Etruria and into the Greek and Oscan south. By the beginning of the Second Punic War, Rome had a foothold in the valley of the Po, and by 177 B.C., when the pioneer age of Roman colonization apparently ends, these planned communities with their walls, their neat crisscross of streets, their forums and basilicas and temples, and their pattern of surveyed allotments stretching away from the foot of the wall into the surrounding country, were to be found from Aquileia in the north to Thurii and Vibo Valentia in the south, testifying already to the might and majesty of the Roman name.

The likeness of Roman frontier posts to one another, with which the government surveyors, the Daniel Boones of the ancient world, had much to do, is most apparent from the air. A typical

[7] R. Syme, *The Roman Revolution* (Oxford, 1939), 88: "A hundred thousand veterans, settled on the lands of Sulla's enemies, supported his domination, promoted the Romanization of Italy, and kept alive the memory of defeat and suffering."

[8] F. Vittinghoff, *Römische Kolonisation und Bürgerrechtspolitik unter Caesar und Augustus* (Wiesbaden, 1952).

[9] This is the core of the argument of A. N. Sherwin-White, *The Roman Citizenship* (Oxford, 1939).

Latin hilltop colony like Norba is approached by an easily defensible winding mountain road with horrendous hairpin turns. On the summit, the *arx,* or citadel, with its temples, is plainly visible, and the colony is girt by a polygonal wall, built of blocks irregularly shaped and fitted together without mortar. At sites where stone was not readily available, as at Antium, an earthwork sufficed. Antium became under the Empire a favorite beach resort: Nero had a villa there crammed with *objets d'art,* some of which survive. A typical ridge colony is Anxur, with its temple on the *arx;* the colony is a seaport, and its position on the Appia (though, as often, the colony was there before the road) meant that it commanded communications between Rome and Naples.

In the Samnite wars of the fourth century B.C., hilltop colonies were still necessary and the *arx* of Luceria rises on the site later occupied by the castle of Frederick II; Charles of Anjou's wall probably follows the footings of the wall built by the Roman engineers at the founding of the colony in 314 B.C. Ariminum, another seaport colony, was walled on the landward side; it became the terminus of the Via Flaminia as Independence was the head of the Santa Fe Trail (though again the colony came before the road); and it was the starting point of the Via Aemilia. It was an important assize town; Julius Caesar presided over the court here between campaigns of the Gallic War, and the fateful Rubicon is only nine miles to the northwest. Augustus repaired the Flaminia and built a monumental arch at the point where the road enters the town. Another typical ridge colony is Aesernia, controlling a road junction in the Apennines 1,600 feet above sea level. Here, as elsewhere, Roman engineers showed themselves creatively imitative in adapting their plan to the site as the Etruscans had done elsewhere centuries before. A flatland layout is Placentia, at the western end of the Aemilia, whose other terminus is Ariminum: the colony controls both the River Po and the road, and it became economically very important. A beachhead type is Pyrgi, built on the Tyrrhenian coast below Centumcellae (Civitavecchia) to hold three hundred colonists. The lowest courses of the thirteenth-century castle wall on the northwest side are Roman polygonal construction. Finally there is Naples, a puzzle, because we cannot say whether its plan is Greek, Etruscan, or Roman. At any rate, the checkerboard grid is typical of Roman colonial layouts. One plausible explanation of the origin of the grids connects them with the rectangular street blocks laid out in the fifth century B.C. at the Etruscan site now known as Marzabotto, in the hills on the River Reno fifteen miles south of Bologna.

We know most about three colonies of the late fourth and early third century B.C.: Alba Fucens, Minturnae, Cosa. The evidence as to their layout may be taken as typical and perhaps as suggesting a master plan. Alba, in the Apennines on the Via Valeria, which connected Rome with the Adriatic, was isolated enough to serve as a detention place for prisoners of state. Alba has the familiar polygonal wall, an impressive three-mile circuit; it had an *arx,* destroyed by the earthquake of 1915; its civic center had a basilica presenting its long side to the Forum (compare the governor's palace in Santa Fe) and involved with a complex of shops and circular market: features to be matched by colonies as far apart in space and time as Cosa and Lepcis Minor in North Africa.

Minturnae (colonized 295 B.C.) is on the Via Appia at the mouth of the Liris. Later it had a polygonal wall rectangular in plan; to this on the west was added another wall of ashlar tufa. The colony provides valuable evidence of how the Romans contrived to live peacefully side by side with native peoples on a live-and-let-live basis—as long as the natives behaved. A series of twenty-nine inscriptions of the early first century B.C., found in re-use in the podium of a temple here, provides a valuable list of colonial names. They are nearly all Greek, their station in life is humble, they include both men and women, and they have full status in the religious life of the community. The melting pot is at work; "have-nots" are striving to be "haves," and apparently are succeeding.

Cosa is the best known of the three sites. It stands on a headland above the Via Aurelia; it overlooks a fertile hinterland. Its wall, a mile in perimeter, is polygonal; there are three gates, as at Alba, and three temple areas; the *arx* has a three-celled Capitolium; in short, its triplicity is striking. Recent campaigns have centered in the Forum area, entered through a monumental arch, the earliest known in Italy (about 150 B.C.). The basilica presents its long side to the Forum, as at Alba; in the early Empire it was metamorphosed into a theater, as governmental functions grew less absorbing and the colony degenerated into an amusement center. The rectangular blocks of public housing are built to a uniform pattern—the welfare state at work in 273 B.C. The Capitolium, though built at a time when Greek influence was creeping in, remains firmly Etruscan in inspiration; it rises out of the native soil, with Tuscan terra-cotta revetments and Tuscan terracotta sculpture: the architects, resolutely old-fashioned and conservative, cling to the tried old ways, as they did when they built Greek revival houses and churches in the Middle West. But there is archaeological evidence of the decline of Cosa as a community: the ten thousand colonists felt cramped within their thirty-three acres of walled town and went to live on their allotments outside, coming in to the city only for festivals and market days; the temples, the public buildings, fell into disrepair, and at the fall of the Empire the colony was deserted, never to rise again.

The mention of allotments brings us to a brief discussion of centuriation: [10] the laying out by the surveyors of great areas outside the walls of a colony in sections seven hundred meters on a side. Air photography has recently revealed centuriation in so many parts of Italy and the provinces that it is safe to assume that it was standard practice in all the colonies. The plots of land were assigned to the colonists by lot, working from the outside in, so as not to leave the outer edges prey to the enemy. The size of the allotment varied from colony to colony, depending on the desirability of the site, the quality of the land, and the rank of the colonist. Roman slum dwellers were glad to give up the dubious blessings of Roman citizenship to go out to a Latin colony and till land of their own. In some areas, veterans were given homesteads (viritane assignments) not tied to any planned urban center; in one case, the veteran got two *iugera* (1¼ acres) for every year he had served in Spain. This system was branded by the conservatives as the beginning of demagoguery and decline for the aristocratic Roman Republic. One of the largest centuriated stretches known in Italy (220 square miles) is in the fertile *ager Campanus* near Naples; it may have been laid out as early as 209 B.C. Another fine example lies next to the Augustan colony of Zara on the Dalmatian coast.

These are the physical characteristics of the colonies. Did they produce recognizable frontier types? The best examples are Cato

[10] P. Fraccaro, "Agrimensura," *Encic. Ital.* (1929).

the Elder and Marius, who came not from colonies proper but from hill towns near Rome. Cato, born in Tusculum, was so much a self-made man that his grandfather had not even been a Roman citizen. We know what he looked like: red hair, gray eyes, prominent teeth, a ruddy complexion; a foursquare peasant type. We know his personality: a stern Puritan, opposed to luxury and frills; a cultural isolationist, a Greek hater, assuming a hillbilly pose in the midst of his cultivated fellow senators; a hard taskmaster, a grim apostle of the religion of eat-it-up, wear-it-out, make-it-do. We know his interests: he wrote a farmer's handbook, formless, old-fashioned in style, but an up-to-date account based on his own knowledge and experience of the new techniques of capital farming. Arpinum produced both Marius and Cicero, the latter being a more complicated frontier type whose ambition, driven by an inferiority complex, brought him to the highest office in the land. Marius was a G.I. general, bluff, uncultured, with all his wounds in front; a poor boy, little used to the decadence of cities, who rose from the ranks by merit and opened the way for others to do so; who was known for temperance and endurance, was popular with his men as sharing their hardships; a hater of aristocrats; a great and unorthodox frontier fighter in forest and mountain and desert.

Roman history is full of men like these, and the frontier bred them—they are the Lincolns and the Jacksons of the ancient world. "That coarseness and strength combined with acuteness and inquisitiveness; that practical, inventive turn of mind, quick to find expedients; that masterful grasp of material things, lacking in the artistic but powerful to effect great ends; that restless, nervous energy; that dominant individualism, working for good and for evil, and withal that buoyancy and exuberance which comes with freedom—these are the traits of the frontier, or traits called out elsewhere because of the existence of the frontier." The words are Turner's; the description may be guilty of "cultural monism," but it perfectly suits the hard-faced men who made the Roman Empire.[11]

These are the typical physical and personal characteristics of

[11] On the Roman national character see R. H. Barrow's *The Romans* (Pelican Books: Harmondsworth, 1949).

the Roman frontier. What were the effects of that colonial expansion? They were first of all military. The names of Forts Dearborn, Dodge, Laramie, and Leavenworth recall Roman colonial names like Castrum Novum Piceni and Castrum Novum Etruriae, outposts against native tribes, established on military roads, or attracting military roads to them. The colonies were planted to meet military needs; sometimes these needs create jump-colonies, beyond the frontier, as happened in the Spanish founding of Santa Fe. Once established, these colonies were both military outposts and centers of Romanization: the colonies in the Po valley Romanized Cisalpine Gaul in less than forty years.[12]

But what Rome won by the arts of war, she consolidated by the arts of peace. Some hill colonies moved down into the plain; Roman colonists lived on the whole in amity with the natives; in the market place of a Po valley town, you could hear six languages and hobnob with Celts in plaids and breeches. So the economic motive grows, the military roads become arteries of commerce, mines are exploited; the new landowners acquire the property qualification which will admit them to service in the old-style pre-Marian Roman army, with all its promise of booty. Agriculture and the marketing of farm products are all-important: etymologically, a colony is a place where men till the soil. Placentia is in wheat country; Beneventum is a place where six roads meet. The colonists did not regard themselves as soldiers only: they brought their wives and families with them. The colonies rehabilitated Italy after wars, as has been done in the Sila since 1950.[13] The peak of colonization in the Republic came at a time when imperious military necessity was past. Cato's book on agriculture tells us which colonies were important for the manufacture of a farmer's tools and equipment.

A third effect of Roman frontier experience in colonization is cultural. The traditional date of the founding of Rome is 753 B.C.; the earliest extant Roman literature appears over five hundred years later. What the Romans were doing in the interval was exploiting their frontier, and men so engaged have no time for

[12] G. E. F. Chilver, *Cisalpine Gaul* (Oxford, 1941), 80, 146.
[13] Sean O'Faolain, *An Autumn in Italy* (New York, 1953), 164–207. This work appeared at London, 1953, as *South to Sicily*.

literature and the arts. Yet the colonies had their reciprocal effect
upon the development of Roman literature when it came. Tne
father of Roman epic, Ennius, learned Latin in the colony of Brundisium and acquired citizenship through the founding of the colonies of Pisaurum and Potentia in 184 B.C. The dramatic poet
Pacuvius came from Brundisium, his fellow poet Accius from
Pisaurum, and the satirist Licilius was born in the colony of Suessa
Aurunca. These are old-fashioned authors, and we may suppose
that old ways of life, old ballads, an antique dialect, long persisted
in the out-of-the-way colonies as they have in the Tennessee and
Kentucky mountains. Later, in the Empire, the provincial frontier
deeply influences Roman literature: Seneca, Lucan, Quintilian,
and Martial came from Spain to seek their fortunes in the metropolis; Apuleius and Augustine came from North Africa. In architecture and art the influence is reciprocal. The Tuscan plan, the
terra-cotta *décor* of temples at Luna and Cosa had their effect
upon the capital; Rome does not become a city of marble until
Augustus, and when it does, the influence is Greek, not indigenous. The dictator Sulla's settling of his veterans in colonies was
the signal for grandiose architectural plans at Praeneste, Tibur,
and Terracina: symmetrical precincts daringly perched on beetling crags, all possibly inspired by the same architect. Under
the Empire, provincial art both is influenced by the capital and
barbarizes the art of the capital itself.

But perhaps of all the influences, the political are the most
striking. It is the present fashion [14] to criticize the Roman constitution of theoretical checks and balances, on which our aristocratic founding fathers based our own, for failing to expand the
administrative mechanisms of the city-state to suit the needs of
empire. Yet the Roman Empire grew not as a federation but as a
set of municipalities: the core of loyalty was the colony or
municipal town, and it is not too sweeping to claim that the
colonial constitutions, little models of Rome's own, were the
cement of the whole structure.

We possess the charter (which comes late in the history of
Rome's frontier) of a colony of Caesar in Spain.[15] On internal

[14] M. Hammond, *City-State and World State in Greek and Roman Political
Theory until Augustus* (Cambridge, Mass., 1951).
[15] E. G. Hardy, *Three Spanish Charters* (Oxford, 1912).

evidence, it may be taken as typical and as embodying older practices. Some at least of the colonists are freedmen from Rome's proletariat. The *deductor* becomes the patron of the colony, and his position is hereditary, but the local senate may coöpt others, provided they are Italians and not military men. The colonists hold allotments of public land, confiscated from the previous owners, who had had the bad judgment to support Pompey; however, some of the natives still live in the colony and hold land there. The new landholders are eligible for membership in the colonial senate and for election to office: there are stiff fines for bribery in elections. The lands are inalienable. The colonists are liable for five days' *corvée* a year (an archaic provision long in abeyance in Rome). The highest magistrate, the *duovir,* is entitled to a retinue of ten; senators and magistrates have reserved seats at the theater. They give games at their own expense, dedicated to the Capitoline triad, the official gods of the Roman state, and to Caesar's patroness, Venus. They are required to live within a mile of the colony. If they set up a pottery or tile factory, the output may not exceed three hundred items a day. In lawsuits, relatives of the accused are not required to give adverse evidence; the time allotted for the defense is twice that for the prosecution.

The colony then is a little old-fashioned Rome, and the charter is intended, in minute detail, to turn "have-nots" into "haves," and to give them the property owner's sense of a stake in the nation. There is little originality or radicalism, but Suetonius tells us [16] Caesar settled eighty thousand colonists (perhaps 10 per cent of the population of Rome), and if most of them were previously landless, the end product is a small social revolution, at the expense of those provincials who had bet on the wrong side in the civil war. (History is repeating itself today in South Italy, with American help, through the Opera per la Valorizzazione della Sila; the *latifondisti* are being compensated.) These colonists could be depended on to be loyal to the central government in times of crisis. Little of Turner's postulated rugged independence can be expected under Rome's paternalistic system, but that these colonists exerted a political effect there can be no doubt. Nor can there be doubt that the effect was conservative;

[16] *Divus Julius,* 42.

Caesar's aim apparently was to set up a rival conservative bloc as a counterweight to his opponents in the civil war. These frontiersmen, some of whom were Caesar's own veterans, could be trusted to be loyal to the regime which had given them status.

Charters of earlier colonies do not survive, but certain archaic provisions in this one entitle us to extrapolate back, and to suppose reasonably that earlier Roman colonies of the Republic operated under similar charters with similar conservative aims. The evidence of the names of early colonial commissioners confirms the hypothesis: the commissioners are drawn quite evenly from the left and the right in Roman politics; both sides are interested in extending the frontier, in creating men of property, and in rallying them to their banner.

Colonies of the early Republic were one of two kinds, Roman or Latin. The Roman colonists had full citizenship rights; the Latin were regarded as having reached a stage on the way to full citizenship. Roman citizens in Roman colonies had the right to vote, but only in Rome; Roman citizens who went to Latin colonies lost the franchise but presumably felt compensated for this loss, more apparent than real, by the enhanced status they enjoyed as landholders and local magistrates in the new colony. A Roman citizen who joined a Latin colony would presumably have been, in Rome, a "have-not," a slum-dweller, a partisan of the left. To send him out to a colony relieved the pressure on the conservatives in Rome. Left-wing political leaders would favor the planting of colonies as plums for their partisans, and also because the public land granted to the colonists would be kept out of the hands of their political enemies, the large landowners of the senatorial class. And we have seen that left-wing politicians tended to favor homesteads (viritane assignments) without fixed urban centers, presumably in order to avoid creating the kind of *nouveaux riches* fostered by the charter of Caesar's colony in Spain.

In the colonies, we see a series of political paradoxes working themselves out. A new privileged class is created, but the proletariat achieves equality. An authoritarian government assumes the benevolence of a welfare state and grants home rule on the local level. The concentrated power of the Roman Empire results from the dispersal of powers through the colonies and the municipalities. And an empire based on a city-state governs half Europe by multiplying city-states in all its provinces.

We may conclude with a few miscellaneous comparisons between the Roman and the American frontier.[17] In the disposal of Roman public lands a limit was put on individual acreage (but the poorer the land, the larger the allotment). Land grants were made inalienable as a hedge against speculation. Veterans were given preference. Homesteads harmed the slave-owning economy of the plantations (*latifundia*). Land was disposed of for settlement or for revenue, not both. Cicero prophesied a reign of terror at the hands of the surveyors marking out the quarter sections. Agrarian law bulked large in Rome; in America 25 per cent of all federal legislation down to 1882 had to do with the public lands.

The Winnebago Indians, moved five times before 1863, have their ancient counterpart in the forty thousand Ligurians transferred against their will to the Samnite country in 180 B.C. The enormous land grants to railroads justify the query whether the discrepancy between the amount of land available along the Via Aemilia and the amount actually assigned conceals enormous reserves granted to the road builders. Absentee ownership defeated the purpose of the American grants: 65 per cent of the lands claimed were not occupied by the original entrant. Was this the case with the broad acreages in Aquileia, and did the evil of tenant farming therefore increase? Rectangular survey proved bad for arid lands. Was unscientific centuriation in part responsible for the rapid desertion of some Roman colonies? The most successful land commissioners were those familiar with the area of the grant. How many Roman colonial commissioners knew the ground? The American public domain was about equally divided among settlers, speculators, and government reserves. What was the proportion in Italy of the Republic, and how great a menace was the speculator?

In the present state of our knowledge we cannot answer these questions, but it is by looking at Roman history through Turner's

[17] See P. L. MacKendrick, "Cicero, Livy, and Roman Colonization," *Athenaeum* (Pavia), new series, XXXII (1954), 247–249.

eyes that we are able to raise them. To look at the Roman frontier
as Turner would have done is a salutary and refreshing experience. The many differences revealed between the development of
Rome's and America's frontiers may be due to defects in Turner's
hypothesis, but they may equally well be due to the difference between the political philosophy of the Roman Republic and that
of the American democracy. Certainly there are striking likenesses
in the sheer geography of the expansion; there are certain physical
and personal similarities of colonies and colonists, ancient and
modern. And the military, economic, and cultural effects are as
instructive in their differences as in their likenesses, but the
differences might not have been observed if Turner had not
pointed the way. In politics the differences seem most profound,
but some of Turner's soberer critics have pointed out with justice
that American frontier constitutions were not so innovating, nor
frontier society so fluid, as Turner had believed.

Turner himself was in his youth an assistant to an ancient
historian; he concludes his great essay of 1893 with a parallel from
the colonial experience of the early Greeks.[18] The application of
his hypothesis to the colonial experience of Rome appears to one
observer at least to promise fruitful results. Such hypotheses are
seminal, rare, and valuable. This investigator salutes in Turner a
historian great in a power of synthesis that has apparently been
denied to a majority of his critics.

SELECTED READINGS

Barrow, R. H. *The Romans.* Harmondsworth: Pelican Books, 1949.
Brown, F. E. "Cosa I." *Memoirs of the American Academy in Rome,*
    XX (1951).
Fraccaro, P. "Agrimensura." *Enciclopedia Italiana.* 1929.
Kornemann, E. "Coloniae." Pauly and Wissowa (eds.), *Paulys Real-
    Encyclopädie der classischen Altertumswissenschaft,* new ed. (Stutt-
    gart, 1901), IV, coll. 511–588.
MacKendrick, P. L. "Roman Colonization," *The Phoenix,* VI (1952),
    139–146.

18 I have used throughout with profit G. R. Taylor (ed.), *The Turner
Thesis Concerning the Role of the Frontier in American History* (Boston,
1949).

——. "Cicero, Livy, and Roman Colonization," *Athenaeum*, XXXII, new series (1954), 201–249.

MacLean, H. A. "Studies in Roman Colonization." Unpublished Ph.D. dissertation, University of Wisconsin, 1954.

Salmon, E. T. "Rome and the Latins," *The Phoenix*, VII (1953), 93–104, 123–135.

Scullard, H. H. "Rome, History," *Oxford Classical Dictionary*, 1949.

Sherwin-White, A. N. *The Roman Citizenship*. Oxford: Oxford University Press, 1939.

Taylor, G. R. (ed.). *The Turner Thesis Concerning the Role of the Frontier in American History*. Boston: D. C. Heath, 1949.

Vittinghoff, F. *Römische Kolonisation und Bürgerrechtspolitik unter Caesar und Augustus*. Wiesbaden: University of Mainz, 1952.

ROBERT L. REYNOLDS

The Mediterranean Frontiers,

1000-1400

In the expansion of Europe into the Mediterranean between 1000 and 1400, Professor Reynolds sees a frontier experience that is quite different from the expansion of Rome. These frontiers were not static; they moved over great distances by water. Since the European expansion into the Mediterranean took place before the emergence of the well-developed nation-state, it assumed forms that in some respects were unique.

Professor Reynolds observes that population pressures drove many people out to the frontier. He shows that young adventurers had to leave the family nest to find fame and fortune out at the edge of their world. These adventurers, going as individuals or as companies, established outposts not among barbarians or against barbarians, but among peoples of their status in the ladder of civilization. They traded, planted sugar cane, and mined silver and lead. The Mediterranean frontier provided opportunity for many and created the trading company as an instrument of colonization, but otherwise it had little influence upon the older societies. Perhaps it might be called the frontier founded by individual and corporate initiative.

THE peoples who established the first frontiers of European civilization in the New World had much experience in colonization before Vasco da Gama sailed to India or Columbus discovered the West Indies. Their experiences have often been overlooked by those who focus upon that which came after 1492. There were at least four chronological and geographical frontiers between 800 and the time of Columbus (who started his career in the field of Mediterranean colonization), and of these, the Mediterranean proved a lodestone for more adventurers than any of the others.

The Norse, often portrayed erroneously only as Vikings, had their own frontiers of trade and settlement in Russia, in the British Isles, along the coasts of France, Iceland, Greenland, and elsewhere. They colonized areas of empty land, established posts for trading with the natives, and introduced cattle, much as did the Americans as they moved westward. These frontiers generally flourished until around 1000, when the Norse lands became just a part of Western Europe.

The eastward movement of the Germans between the tenth and thirteenth centuries was another vast frontier. It was James West-fall Thompson of the University of Chicago who first interested himself in this frontier advance largely from the Elbe toward the Vistula and the region of Vienna. Influenced by Turner's thesis, he studied the "land boomers," or promoters, the organization of colonization prior to the actual advance, and the establishment of blockhouses for protection, which in turn became nuclei for settlements. He found that this expansion could in part be explained by using the criteria that Turner had developed for the American frontier.

The Iberian frontier, which Professor Silvio Zavala discusses elsewhere in this volume, was another medieval experience that trained Europeans for the task of colonizing the New World. It was the reconquest of that peninsula, followed by the re-establishment of Christian law, order, and religion, that gave to the Spanish and Portuguese both the ideology that served them in their conquest of the American Indians and the experience they needed to colonize Latin America. Zavala likewise has found that Turner's hypothesis explained in part the Spanish frontier advance.

The Irish and Welsh are quite reluctant to recognize that what happened to them between the eleventh and seventeenth centuries was roughly what later happened to the Iroquois and Chippewa. In both cases, it was Englishmen who pushed in on them from an area of greater wealth and population, either subjugating or engulfing the native people. This type of historical experience does not seem to have greatly interested scholars of the American pioneer period; the bona fide frontier to them is the one that is in forward movement and the point of view is that of the people doing the advancing. It is not often that a frontier is looked at from the other side. Turner never approached his studies from that vantage point. However, it must be remembered that every frontier is actually two: the frontier of those who are advancing and the frontier of those who are being advanced upon. The Irish typify the latter, and their reaction to those who advanced upon them has been an important factor in their subsequent history.

The development of the Mediterranean frontiers can be roughly dated from about the year 1000. At about that time, occasional Normans had begun to make pilgrimages from the English Channel to Rome. Just before this time, the Holy Roman Empire's attempt to annex Southern Italy had failed. There were from three to five small Italian states between Rome and the toe of the boot and some that were dependent on the Byzantine Empire; in Sicily and on the mainland were numerous little colonies of North African Arabs and Berbers. The southern Italian peninsula was a borderland of little states where princelings scrambled for power.

Between the approximate date of 1000, when the first Norman adventurers appeared in the Mediterranean, and the end of the century, when the last Moorish stronghold had been taken, the Norman state of South Italy and Sicily emerged. It was in many respects a frontier operation. Settlers from central and north Italy, with Italian language and culture, were brought in to occupy the land. New centers of settlement were made and old ones, dating back to the Greek and other city-states, were re-established. The Western European church, church law, and other institutions and ways of life were introduced into this alien culture, all at the expense of Greek and Arab civilizations and political organizations. The Normans did not stop in Southern Italy but continued on, forming part of the stream of Germans, Italians, Lorrainers, Frenchmen,

Norwegians, Englishmen, and others who built the European states in the Holy Land between 1100 and 1190.

A segment of history that interests Western Europeans, especially those of English orientation, is that of the Crusades proper— the First Crusade, the Second Crusade, and others. Normally the whole movement is painted in terms of a great rush that finally slows down, a few desperate last efforts, and then nothing after the era of Richard the Lionhearted. However, this is not an accurate picture of the Mediterranean frontier advance, except in the Holy Land proper. By 1190, the states established there by the Crusaders were in decline and, as the standard histories show, the end came between 1290 and 1292, when the last Holy Land settlements were liquidated.

However, the whole Eastern Mediterranean frontier did not collapse at this time. Indeed, the last of the colonies established in the East was lost by the Venetians as late as the time of Napoleon. If one wants to examine the record of a retreating frontier, then the history of the Western Europeans in the time between 1250 and 1280 should be consulted. This is the period when the great victories and conquests of the first three crusades ended in disaster and withdrawal. The large feudal grants held by one part of the Crusaders and the trading concessions held in the cities by others, in an area inhabited by Greeks and Arabs of both Christian and Mohammedan persuasion, came to an end when the European went home.

The third great push of Western colonization in the Mediterranean began about 1190. Richard the Lionhearted, on his way to the holy places in Palestine, was one of the first to open a newer European frontier in eastern lands. En route he seized Cyprus, held for the moment by a Greek despot, and from that time the great island, so strategically located, was a useful hub for the launching of numerous colonization operations.

Beginning in 1190 and then rapidly after 1200, the Westerners, still under the banner of the Crusade but now at the expense of the Greeks, occupied nearly all the sea-washed islands between Cyprus, Crete, and the Aegean Coast. On the mainland, a number of states were established, resembling in most respects those which were just being liquidated in the Holy Land. There was even a special foreign concession established in the Byzantine Empire at

Constantinople, first by the Venetians and later by the Genoese. These frontier outposts, mostly on the islands, flourished as colonies until about 1350.

A century before the fall of Constantinople, the Ottoman Turk became a serious factor in the politics and wars of the Eastern Mediterranean. In that period, these island possessions slowly lost their economic and political importance and, when Constantinople fell in 1453, they were ready to fall from their own lack of internal vitality. The colonies established by the Italians in the Black Sea proved an exception; they remained durable and relatively prosperous though they were cut off by Turkish guns after the fall of Constantinople. They were much more important and indeed far more lucrative than those established earlier in the Holy Land or than those on the Greek islands.

The Black Sea frontier was largely Crimea. That part on the side below the mountains became especially Italianized in politics, language, and, to a considerable degree, in religion. It was the great gem in the crown of the Genoese Republic and its business world. One of the cities there, Kaffa, became another Genoa in size and served as a leader among the colonies. Though the Italians could reach this frontier for administrative and commercial purposes only by land, through Hungary and Poland, after 1453, these colonies lasted until the Tartars and Turks combined in 1475 to liquidate them.

In the development of the Italian frontiers in the Eastern Mediterranean, are there any points of comparison with or contrast to the Western Hemisphere colonization during the last two centuries? Does the experience on this frontier support or negate the over-all thesis that Frederick Jackson Turner brought forward as a key to American history? Let us examine some of the things that Turner himself emphasized as important in the development of the American frontier.

In the first place, he called attention to conditions in his "East," in the old society that encouraged emigration to undeveloped frontier areas, showing that lack of opportunity, population pressure, or other factors influenced the American frontier advance. Similar conditions existed in Europe between 1000 and 1350. In that epoch there was a great increase in population despite famines and plagues. Since population growth is seldom evenly distributed, there appeared areas where food supply and opportunity were limited, and there was a surplus of people for emigration.

This surplus not only supplied settlers in this early period, but also fighting men. Indeed, the excess of fighting men among the Normans, the men who did most of the pushing in Southern Italy and much of the fighting in the Holy Land, was astonishing. In the eleventh century, a young Norman had a difficult time finding his way in a world where families were large and opportunities restricted. A father could pass his holding along to only one of his twelve sons, making it necessary for eleven to take the high road of adventure to find land and perhaps a totally new life in an alien place. There is no doubt but that population pressure had an influence upon the supply of fighting men in the eleventh, twelfth, and thirteenth centuries.

There was also in Europe in the medieval period, as there was in the time of the American expansion, a remarkable advance in technology. Europeans generally improved their ships and machinery and the quality and the quantity of the goods they produced. This gave them a hunger for markets. They supplied traders who went out to sell what was produced, and since these merchants brought home foreign products in return, foreign trade allowed Europeans progressively throughout the medieval age to indulge their appetites for not only spices and sugar, art work and carved ivory objects, but also such practical things as Moorish steel and leather goods. This trade with the distant frontier areas enabled the European standard of living gradually to rise and provided a more ample life to more people during the period of medieval expansion.

In this era, there was also an increase in the number of towns, of population in the towns, and in the amount of trade flowing between cities and between rural areas and cities. The whole pattern of distribution changed as agricultural and manufactured products from rural areas were channeled through the main trade centers for customers in all parts of Europe and overseas, and as foreign products found their way back to rural areas. A large part of the energy expended in establishing colonies in the Holy Land went to obtain outlets where exports could be exchanged for commodities needed in Europe.

Still another chance for profit existed. Though the trade between the Russian frontier (Crimea) and Italy was great, the most profitable trade for the Genoese was between Egypt and Russia. This paralleled the experience of European traders in eastern oceans in later centuries who took over the carrying trade between India and China to their great benefit.

In making comparisons between the world frontiers, it must not be forgotten that it was trading companies that established the first European outposts on the transatlantic frontier. Little settlements such as Quebec, New Amsterdam, and Charleston were intended first to be trading centers where the manufactured goods from Europe could be exchanged for the goods of the natives. As the back country filled in, the frontier moved back from the coastal trading posts. But newer posts grew to perform the same service. However, Western European settlement of the Eastern Mediterranean lands never got into the back country; Acre, Kaffa, and other coastal trading colonies remained throughout what Vera Cruz or Montreal or Fort Orange started out to be.

When the Western Europeans pushed into southern Italy, Sicily, the Greek islands, and the Holy Land, they set up fiefs. Frenchmen, Italians, and others of high position got duchies and counties, while those who followed in the second rank were given viscounties and baronies. We are prone to think of the development of the Western Hemisphere as free of feudalism; yet the granting of large fiefs to the first generation of gentlemen was one of the normal steps in the original projects of the Spanish, Portuguese, French, Dutch, and English. Indeed, it is quite difficult to think of Columbus' facing the hardships of discovery had he not been promised in advance, in writing, a great fief. It is to be noted that his heirs, the Dukes of Veragua, hold to this day a great title in the Spanish world simply on the basis of a fief granted Columbus and his family. Such a great fief was one of the great incentives for important men and a small fief was a motivation for lesser men. The gentlemen who wanted to become barons and the squires who wanted to become knights but could not attain their goal at home, found the New World a way up the class ladder. The seigniories of the French, the patroonships of the Dutch, the captaincies in Brazil, and the encomiendas in Mexico, all were similar to the fiefs, counties, and duchies acquired by gentlemen earlier in the Aegean Islands and along the Palestine Coast.

The operations of the Calvert family, the Lords Baltimore in Ireland, well illustrate this type. They already had one frontier barony (in Ireland) when they were granted another in the New World. When they got Maryland, they had something not hard for an English lawyer to describe. The grant in America simply gave them the rights of the medieval English frontier county palatine of Durham. This grant had first been made in the eleventh century by William I and William II as a frontier post on the Scottish border.

The development of such feudal states on the frontier of Europe in the medieval period was not completely alien to the experience in the Western Hemisphere. However, there was another type of colony that had no counterpart on the American frontier. This was the foreign concession that might be private, semiprivate, or governmental, depending upon the time, the place, and the nature of the relationship with the dominant population.

In the Middle Ages, nearly any group that had a distinctive religious, linguistic, or economic character had an organization. (Nothing is more medieval than the American ability to organize anything and to have practically everything organized.) Governments normally utilized the natural heads of the different groups under them for purposes of government. They did not govern all subjects or citizens equally through universally impartial courts but reached the shoemakers through the Shoemakers Guild, alien groups such as the Flemings in London through their own natural heads, the people of a city or ward through the mayor or alderman, professors and students through university chancellors, and so on.

To illustrate this tendency as it affected the development of the frontier concession, assume that the Genoese would find a good trading center owned and ruled by other people. As soon as there were more than a few Genoese there, one of them or the group would buy or rent a house. Perhaps there would be a little continuity in the personnel of the traders. The local ruler would find it necessary to appoint one of these residents as consul. In time this consul simply expanded his powers. From a private holder of little importance, he might in time become the proprietor of a market, baths, and bakeries. Finally, he or the corporation of Genoese could gain complete autonomy for the Genoese business section within the larger city. Around this city within a city, a wall could be placed. Thus, there rose a Genoa in the heart of Acre, another alongside Constantinople, others on the coasts that belonged to the Tartar Khan of the Crimea. In them, the Genoese archbishop had jurisdiction over the local priest and his flock, and the church would be dedicated to St. Lawrence, St. George, or St. Sirus, leading Genoese saints. These people lived by their own law; that is, the law of Genoa followed the Genoese to these communities and was administered by a judge or consul who either was sent from home or was elected locally. These concessions, rather than the feudal states, were the typical colonies of the Aegean Islands and the Black Sea and were similar to the earliest Western trading settlements along the coasts of India and Africa or the concessions established by the European powers in Chinese cities in the nineteenth century.

However, in some cases these settlements resembled American frontier experience in another respect. Turner calls attention to the various stages of frontier evolution and notes the development of a cattle frontier beyond the line of agricultural settlement. The concessions in the Eastern Mediterranean were the traders' frontier. They were the Fort Oranges, the St. Louises, the Astorias of America, but they were in civilized instead of backward countries and the trade was between those of roughly equal cultures rather than between an iron-age people and a stone-age people, as on the American frontier. There were no cattle frontiers in the Eastern Mediterranean, though there was one in Spain; and it was from Spain's cattle country that the long-horned cow, the Moorish saddle, the big spurs, and the great stirrups migrated to the New World.

To continue the parallels between these two frontiers separated by both geography and time, one could note the existence of a plantation movement across both of them. After the pioneer settlements had been made in the Old South, the cotton plantation moved from Georgia to Texas and tobacco culture spread from Virginia to the Mississippi. Since tobacco grew only in the New World, there were no tobacco plantations in the Eastern Mediterranean. However, there were sugar plantations. Here is the route of sugar through the frontier colonies of the Mediterranean world: the Arabs were raising sugar in Palestine, North Africa, and South-

ern Spain in the ninth and tenth centuries and converting the
cane into syrup and the syrup into sugar. When the Europeans
arrived in these parts, they had their sweet tooth extraordinarily
sharpened, and this new appetite was as important in motivating
European trade as was the appetite for pepper and spices. But
unlike spices that had to be brought from a long way off, sugar
could be produced in the Mediterranean area and they set to work
to produce it.

The first large sugar plantations under European management
of which we have fairly good records existed in Cyprus in the
thirteenth century. There were also others in the dying colonies
along the Palestinian Coast and a few in Sicily. We do not know if
the latter plantations were newly reintroduced from the Eastern
Mediterranean or left over from the time when the Arabs were
there.

Normally, a sugar plantation was the proprietary holding of a
very well-to-do man who had acquired a goodly stretch of native
territory by feudal grant or purchase; or, commonly, plantations
were established by a corporation of men such as the Knights
Templar, who gained control over a large area. The Knights of
Malta (or Rhodes) and other orders, business and church corporations, and partnerships and corporations of financiers entered this
field. To create a plantation out of a land grant took considerable
initial capital and technical knowledge. First, cane had to be imported and a labor force gathered and trained for the handling of
the product. Importing black slaves and depressing the local
Greeks to a point where they were practically gang slaves (though
technically serfs) was a normal first step to the launching of such an
enterprise. After the thirteenth century, both white and black
slaves were associated with the business. Next, there was need for
accumulating the very important pieces of machinery. Hand presses
at first and, later, water and other mechanical power-driven presses
came into general use, and as time went on the larger, more expensive, and more efficient they became. There had to be a supply
of fuel, which often called for transportation to bring it in. For
the purpose of refining there was need for rather high-level technical supervision. The owners were almost exclusively absentees.
Proprietors were large operators, even for our time. One operation
of the Knights Templar in Cyprus seems to have involved forty-

two villages. These plantations are to be equated with the great Hawaiian pineapple and Latin American banana enterprises of today.

Such sugar and indigo operations flourished in Sicily and were financed by Genoese, Venetians, and others from the north. They were also found in the garden spots of the Moors on the southern Spanish and Portuguese frontier, and in the fifteenth century they spread to the overseas colonies in the Atlantic—the Cape Verdes, the Canaries, and the Madeiras. Madeira became one of the great sugar producers. We can trace, without a break, the transmission of the ways of setting up and running a plantation from Sicily and South Spain to the Atlantic islands.

From the Iberian peninsula and these islands, the knowledge moved on to Brazil and was carried from there to the new British islands such as St. Kitts, Barbados, and the rest of the Antilles. It was from these islands that it made the jump to the American colonies. With this migration of technical knowledge and planter practice went the slave trade, which followed a channel from the source of slave supply to the plantation, from South Russia and the Sudan in the early period, from the Berber Coast later, and from the coast of Africa to the Western Hemisphere in the days of the American colonial frontier.

In the Mediterranean, as in America, there was another type of frontier. This was the one of settlement, though a rare one in the period under review, except in Spain, where the blockhouses in Castile became the centers of settlement when conditions became peaceful. There was some bona fide agricultural colonization undertaken elsewhere. For example, we have the written contracts (like indentures) by which settlers were attracted to Sicily from North Italy. These contracts were similar to the American colonization contracts in that a community leader was first put under contract and became the agent for further recruitment. The practice of getting one man interested and then using him to attract his sisters, cousins, aunts, and all the villagers back home is an old device. A Genoese family, trying to do this in the thirteenth century, worked very hard on the colonization of potential great estates in Sicily. The contracts provided for such things as.these: free use for a few years of an acreage that a man with good equipment could handle properly, a house built on the land at no cost, free use of an ox until the renter could buy one for himself, exemption from taxes and from such duties of citizenship as military service for a few years, and a bonus for every recruit brought out by the "indentured" emigrant.

While the settlement frontier was a very rare thing in the Eastern Mediterranean, the mining frontier was more in evidence; it existed in Sardinia, Sicily, and along the coasts of Asia Minor. We know that there were prospectors drifting around at great danger to life and limb in the interior of Sardinia in the twelfth and thirteenth centuries. These men returned to their home towns in Genoa and promoted companies for the exploitation of these mines. Investors were drawn in and engineers and workers sent out, but apparently these companies failed. This was to be the pattern in such operations for a long time. Silver and lead were the lodestones primarily, except in Sardinia, where other metals were sought. Sardinia was always luring unlucky people there to prospect and develop mines.

One of the large mining developments was in Phocaea in Asia Minor, the home town of so many early Greek colonists. From having been a mother of colonies in the era of Greek colonization, it had become a deserted land with some good minerals near by, alum and alum-bearing salts, that attracted the Genoese. In the latter part of the thirteenth century a Genoese got a grant in the Phocaea alum-bearing region. Before he did any mining, he built loading docks, warehouses, and refining equipment, all of which were large, extensive, and certainly very costly. Then he built a company town. His engineers sank the proper shafts and slideways that would bring the material from the mines to the refining center and onto ships. He had previously built a number of ships, and once the mine was in full operation, he chartered quite a number of others. By 1300, this capitalist was pushing his product all over Europe and soon had a cartel that forced his competitors out of business. In a sense, this man was like those who struck it rich in Virginia City, or like the Huntingtons and Stanford, who gained as complete a monopoly as they could in transportation. He was not born on the frontier but was a Genoese of noble birth and great wealth who found his opportunity on the frontier of his time. It might also be said that John Jacob Astor made his part of the frontier what it was and the frontier made John Jacob Astor the rich man he became, though he was born in a German village. To be a frontiersman, it was not necessary to have been made and shaped by the frontier; the Genoese who became the first great cartel operator and mining magnate shaped the frontier rather than being shaped by it.

How about the way these colonies were set up and their relation to the home country? By and large, the feudal settlements were separated organizationally from any home government control. The Norman, French, and other lords in the Holy Land looked back with great awe and respect to the king of France or the Holy Roman emperor, but they were in no way governed by them. Likewise, the Genoese, Venetian, and other proprietors who had great holdings in the Aegean and Black Sea areas tended to cut loose from home control. Their allegiance to the mother country was probably conditioned chiefly by self-interest. By the fourteenth century, Genoa no longer ran its frontier areas strictly from headquarters; it had become in some respects the head of a commonwealth of colonial states and powers. Proprietary holdings and some others tended to go in the direction of autonomy.

Company holdings were common on this frontier, where corporations were formed to develop and exploit overseas grants. This was something the Genoese worked out, and the *Maona* or *Mahona* device which they used resembled in many respects the trading companies of the European powers, although in other respects it differed. A company had the power to go to war, make treaties, manage the established colony, and draw profits from their grant. The smart New Englanders under Winthrop's leadership who formed a company back in England and transferred themselves and the company to Massachusetts were not alone in such operations. A group of Genoese did the same thing in the fourteenth century. They formed a company back in Genoa, moved to the Island of Chios, and there the company was run and there they lived. Incidentally, the people took one name to show that they had become one great family. The Chios settlement largely gained its freedom from the central government by simply moving the whole company, lock, stock, and barrel, including the women and children, out to the colony that they had grabbed by conquest.

In general, the attitude of these colonies toward resident populations was similar to the American relationship to the Indians. However, on the more permanent Crimean frontier, the Genoese adopted the policy of amalgamation and friendly treatment of the Christian natives, creating there something of a melting pot.

It has been shown that the peoples of Europe had long experience in frontier expansion before the opening of the New World. The colonization of the Eastern Mediterranean between 1000 and 1400 was characterized by the extension of European institutions and ways of life into the islands and coastal areas of many parts of the world. Motivated by the lack of opportunity and the pressure of population at home, aided by the great advance in technology and the organization of trade, adventurers either alone or in corporations sought fame and riches in the economic opportunities of that distant land. These frontier settlements usually evolved from trading posts into other types, and speculators and large operators emerged. Several of the same factors that shaped the frontiers of the Mediterranean world, or were shaped by them, also were present in the frontier period of the New World.

READINGS

For further reading in the history of topics discussed in this essay, there is no better guide than the fine bibliography compiled by Professor Robert S. Lopez, in pages 537–556 of the second volume of *The Cambridge Economic History of Europe* (2 vols. Cambridge: Cambridge University Press, 1941–1950). Data bearing on these subjects will be found elsewhere in the same work, particularly in Professor Lopez' "The Trade of Medieval Europe: the South," II, 257–354.

SILVIO ZAVALA

The Frontiers of Hispanic America

The spotlight is turned on the frontier experience of Hispanic America by Professor Zavala, the eminent Mexican historian. The Spaniards were prepared for this conquest of America by the reconquest of Spain and the expulsion of the Moor. Armed with a distinct ideology of expansion, the conquistadors went after riches, glory, and the native's soul. They subdued the Indians, introduced a revolutionary influence in the form of European livestock, intermarried and produced a new racial type, and saw their social institutions adopted throughout the new land.

Was this frontier a safety valve? Did the masses get land in the process? Was this new race of man more liberal than others? Professor Zavala expresses doubt on these questions and asserts that sufficient evidence is not yet at hand to draw any final conclusions. He recommends further study of this part of the world frontier, especially in that segment where the frontiers of Mexico and the United States touch.

This essay has been translated from the Spanish by Clifton B. Kroeber with the aid of Renato I. Rosaldo, Professor of Spanish, University of Arizona.

BACKGROUND

THE advance of Spanish civilization into the New World, considered in its broadest context, seems but a continuation of the struggle between the Christian and Moslem that characterized Iberian history in the days of the Reconquest. For nearly eight centuries, these two peoples had lived together, and though mutual distrust and frontiers existed, cultural borrowing and personal alliances also characterized their relationship. The struggle to drive out the Moor touched all Christendom, causing warriors from beyond the Pyrenees to go forth to stop the Moslem advance and reclaim the peninsula, and inspired historical chronicles and literature, including the twelfth-century poem in the frontier mood *El Cantar de Mío Cid*. The Reconquest was not only a war against the infidel; it was also an experience in colonization of the conquered areas. Considering all the varied circumstances under which the Christian advance took place over the years, it now seems but a "fabric of conquests, of founding of towns, of reorganization of new provinces wrested from Islam, of expansion of the Church into the new domain; the transplanting of a race, a language, and a civilization." [1]

This crusade against the nonbeliever and this experience in colonization gave force to Spanish and Portuguese expansion down the African coast and to the Atlantic islands. It assumed new form in 1492, after the fall of Granada ended the Reconquest.

The conquistadors of the New World in the late fifteenth and early sixteenth centuries believed themselves defenders and propagators of the Christian faith and in their capacity as subjects of the crown extended the royal domain and gained honor and profit for themselves. They were charged with spying out the secrets of those new lands to see if there were mosques and Moslem priests. They became skilled at using interpreters (*farautes*), leading expeditions, and enriching themselves through slave raiding and gaining other booty. They ruled the conquered people in seignorial style, forcing them to work and render tribute. They founded towns and, as their forefathers had done, named some of them for the frontier (e.g., Segura de la Frontera). In their conquests and colonization, these men were armed with an ideology

[1] C. Sánchez Albornoz, *España y el Islam* (Buenos Aires, 1943), 186–187.

that included the medieval theory of the "just war" of Christians against infidels and the thinking of the Renaissance about the relations of "prudent men" with barbarians.

One aspect of the Hispanic frontier is told through the introduction of the horse, the cow, the sword, the iron lance, and the harquebus. Another may be seen in the two types of colonial settlements. First, there was the domination of an area inhabited by sedentary Indians who lived in farming communities like the Aztec *calpulli* and the Peruvian *ayllu;* secondly, there was the expansion of Spanish rule into the hostile Indian country, as happened in northern Mexico, southern Chile, on the Río de la Plata prairies, and elsewhere. The inhabitants of this latter frontier were known, respectively, as Chichimecas, Araucanians, and Pampa Indians; but there was a wide variety of local tribes within each of these, some being hunters, others foraging for a living, some doing a little farming or, as in southern Chile, breeding llamas.

Though both of these frontier types characterize Spanish colonization in the New World, it was the first that produced the hybrid Hispanic-American society based on the acculturation of Indians and Europeans. However, this type remained frontier only in the brief moment of conquest. For example, the conquistadors built arsenals in the city of Mexico, their houses served as forts, and municipal ordinances required all citizens to keep arms and horses ready for use. In time, stability came, the cultures of the Spaniard and Indian blended, and the frontiers moved on, as they had in the Roman Empire, to the fringes of settlement that lay exposed to the attacks of unconquered natives. The Spanish conquerors understood the differences between the two types of lands, calling the Indians of the central region of Mexico "peaceful" or "sensible" (*indios de razón*) and those of the border areas "wild" or "warlike."

The densely populated provinces where the sedentary Indians lived could be won quickly in pitched battles, while the conquest of the lands of the nomads involved long and indecisive war. The former readily supported the conquering hosts in comfortable circumstances, the wealth and property varying with the province; but the latter, lacking permanent Indian settlements, made distribution of the conquered towns as seignorial grants impossible.

Wars of attrition and slave raids continued for many years while efforts at pacification proceeded through the establishment of forts, the making of treaties, and the forging of alliances with principal tribes. These "lands of war" prompted a special body of legislation and, as on the Iberian peninsular frontier, their checkered history inspired various literary and historical works.

In the lands of sedentary native population, the process of acculturation was so complex and the relations between Indians and Spaniards so variegated that their study would offer ample substance for a treatise on the institutions of the Spanish-American empire. The *repartimiento* and the *puebla* of Reconquest days could be the origin of the *encomienda* and the settlers' *villa* of Mexico and Peru. The peninsular Reconquest was a historical preparation for the conquest of America. The manner in which the Christians made war, the principles by which they justified it, the way they established their rule over the conquered, the distribution of booty and land, the founding of settlements—all these were much alike on all Hispanic frontiers on both sides of the Atlantic. However, it was the second type, the expansion into the hostile Indian country, that afforded not only a new experience in the American milieu but also an extension of the warlike history of the medieval Iberian frontier, a distant migration of that frontier from Europe to America as a part of the process of colonization.

The experiences faced by the Spaniards in the peninsular and the American frontiers were similar but, of course, not identical. In one instance the Christian advance confronted an Arabic civilization, while in the other it faced the native cultures of the Canary Islands and the New World. The Moslem enemy possessed a formalized and hostile faith, while the Guanches and American Indians were looked upon simply as heathen. Thus, by the time of the conquest, Christian thinkers had arrived at doctrinal distinctions among the various kinds of infidels, aside from those of anthropological nature which actual contact was revealing. The peculiarities of the New World experience made themselves felt and the frontier continuum changed as much in the conquest of "sensible" Indians as in the struggles with the "wild" ones. Variations in geography and native populations had, in every case, an influence upon the Hispanic-American frontier. Some

traces of pre-Columbian history were still noticeable. The nomadic tribes of northern New Spain knew no Aztec conquest, and
in South America vast territories lay beyond the scope of Inca
domination. Although Chile had been an object of one of these
invasions, the Inca never gained firm control south of the Bío-Bío
River, a region which also proved costly to the Spaniards. There
are a few cases during the colonial era in which Indians moved
from one frontier to another—as in Chile in the eighteenth century, when the Araucanians, already masters of horsemanship,
crossed the Andean ranges and took part in frontier fighting on
the Argentine pampa. In general and for good historical reasons,
however, there was more continuity on the Christian front than on
the Indian side.

The Indian frontiers were still part of the scene in nineteenth-
century Argentina, Chile, and Mexico, and during that period
important changes came about in institutions and in the means
used to expand that frontier. Ideologically, the opposition between
civilization and barbarism prevailed, and this concept was already
understood in terms of the philosophy of progress. National
governments sent out expeditions of experienced troops, trying to
bring an end to the prolonged Indian wars. The "conquest of the
desert" in Argentina by General Julio A. Roca in 1878–79 was
one example of such efforts. The repeating rifle, telegraph, plans
for railroads, and the outlook for European immigration, all
helped to create the atmosphere in which such expeditions developed. These campaigns brought to an end the frontier cycle
begun by the Spanish conquistadors, at about the same time the
North Americans were subduing the Indian west of the Mississippi.[2]

[2] See E. S. Zeballos, *Recuerdos Argentinos. Callvucurá y la dinastía de los Piedra* (2d ed.; Buenos Aires, 1890; orig. pub. Buenos Aires, 1884), 358. The President's message to Congress, August, 1878, explained that the "old system of successive stages of occupation handed down from the Conquest,
obliging us to scatter our national military forces over a very broad area
and to remain vulnerable to all Indian attacks, has shown itself to be
powerless to guarantee the lives and goods of people living in frontier towns
that are under constant threat. We must give up the old system and seek
the Indian in his encampment, to defeat him or drive him out, leaving
him barred not by a large man-made ditch but by the great and impassible
barrier of the Río Negro, deep and navigable in its whole course from the

CHARACTERISTICS

Advances along the Spanish-American frontier were often caused by the discovery of precious metals. By 1550, silver lodes in northern Mexico had been found and *reales* or mining settlements were being founded. In Chile during the same period, some gold deposits both north and south of Santiago were being worked. The southern mines lay in the "lands of war" and suffered much from the attacks of powerful Araucanian Indians. The plains of the Plata region lacked mineral wealth, but they were excellent for grazing, and stock ranching established itself there.

The geographic distribution of the minerals in New Spain determined the direction of the advance taken by the prospectors. Silver was found near the first settlements established by the Spaniards, as at Taxco, Sultepec, and Pachuca, and also to the north in the lands of the nomads, in Zacatecas, Guanajuato, and Parral. These mining strikes brought settlements into the lands of the nomadic tribes. Roads pushed out from the cities and towns in Mexico to these new population centers. Silver was sent on its way to the European metropolis and served as a means of exchange in obtaining the commodities needed from abroad, especially the mercury used in extracting silver from its native ore. The mining settlements were not isolated economies but were necessarily open to trade with Spain and other parts of the realm. Farming and stock raising were essential to these mining communities (*reales de minas*) for the settlers needed hides and tallow, and animals were the principal source of power. Since local Indians rarely were numerous enough to supply the needed manpower, even if enslavement and forced labor were used, the need had to be filled by attracting natives from areas previously colonized or by using Negro slaves. When the lodes continued rich, a permanent settlement grew up, and as the settled areas expanded, roads were extended and regular and seasonal trade brought in the commodities of urban life and artistic development.

Ocean to the Andes." Zeballos' *La conquista de quince mil leguas* (Buenos Aires, 1878), 372, states that "the military power of the barbarians is wholly destroyed, because the Remington has taught them that an army battalion can cross the whole pampa, leaving the land strewn with the bodies of those who dared to oppose it."

The nomadic Indians were always a threat to the youthful mining towns, particularly when they attacked communication lines that linked the mines with the central provinces of the viceroyalty. To protect the pack trains and carts en route with silver or goods, forts were built at strategic points, settlements were established along the roads, and convoys were organized. A map of the *villas* of San Miguel and San Felipe, made about 1580, shows the great, long-shafted, two-wheeled carts, drawn by oxen and surrounded by armed horsemen bearing harquebuses, their horses protected from arrows by long trappings. Indians are shown on foot attacking horsemen and killing cattle with bow and arrow. One native is shown hanging by the roadside and others beheaded, as examples of the punishments meted out by the Spaniards. As the traffic on the roads increased and the settlements along the way grew, the hostile nomadic zone retreated. Still, in Mexico this was a slow and expensive frontier expansion, one fraught with sudden disaster and constant danger. The mines by their northern location gave impetus to expansion, and the military operations that made the roads secure were direct results of the consecutive mining strikes.

The competition for land between farmers and ranchers in central New Spain contributed to the advance of the stockmen into the unsettled regions of the north, and by the middle of the sixteenth century there was a considerable movement of settlers with their cattle, horses, sheep, goats, and hogs into the wild Indian country. With stock from the Iberian Peninsula or the Spanish islands of the Antilles, these ranchers moved into the good pasture lands that had long been held in low regard by earlier frontiersmen.

The Spanish settlers were horsemen. The figure of the *vaquero* appears in several places on the Spanish frontier: the *charro* in Mexico, the *llanero* of the Venezuelan plains, and the gaucho, both Spanish and Portuguese, in the Río de la Plata. The authorities granted permits for roundup and slaughter of cattle that had been running wild and multiplying on the plains. Thus hides were obtained for trade. These customs, as common in Texas as in the Plata region, greatly reduced the number of herds.

Not all settlers were small operators and not all cattle were wild and unclaimed. There were also the *estancias* or ranches,

composed of buildings set amid an extensive range, where the
owner and his cowboys—half-breeds (*mestizos*), creoles, and sometimes mulattoes—cared for branded cattle and other livestock. On
these remote *estancias*, horsemanship, roundups, the use of knives
and guns, and the presence of hostile Indians, all contributed to
the development of boldness and skill in these men. The owners
were jealous of their seignorial prestige. Possession of a vast estate,
the habit of command, and the holding of military titles made
them prominent leaders in the coarse insecure world of the frontier. Upon occasion, the *estancieros* succeeded in gaining political
leadership, particularly during the civil wars of the nineteenth
century.

The range country most hospitable to stock raising was also inhabited by nomadic tribes. From the Pampa Indians of South
America, the gaucho acquired his weapon, the *boleadora*, which
the native used for hunting the guanaco. The coming of horses and
cattle into the Indian country affected the customs of those who
lived there. They learned to eat meat and to use the hides of
these new animals. Mare's meat was a tender morsel to the nomads
of the Plata region. Thus, if the presence of white men was a threat
to the wild Indians, the same white man also brought with him
elements of life that helped satisfy the Indians' needs and that also
provoked their attacks. When these plains tribes learned to ride
and developed their own horseback style, they were fearsome
enemies on both the northern and southern frontiers of the
American continent.

It was the introduction of European animals among the tribes
that revolutionized their way of life. La Pérouse, in his famous
Voyages, remarked that the importation of domestic animals "has
had its most striking effect on all those peoples living between
Santiago and the Straits of Magellan. These folk observe practically none of their former customs, they wear different clothes,
they do not eat the same foods, and today they affect a style much
more like that of the Tatars, or of the people living on the shores
of the Red Sea, than like that of their own ancestors of two centuries ago." [3] No matter how exaggerated this appraisal may be,
there is some truth in it.

[3] Quoted in José Toribio Medina, *Los aboríjenes de Chile* (Santiago, 1882),
xiii.

The smaller animals, sheep, goats, and hogs, as well as cattle and horses, were important on various Latin-American frontiers and contributed much to the settlement of such territories as Nuevo León and New Mexico in northern New Spain. Wool had long been famous as a commodity of export and manufacture in Spain, and by the middle of the sixteenth century wool of good quality was being produced in Mexico. The association of ranchers for moving their livestock from summer to winter range, known as the *Mesta*, was transplanted to New Spain but never evolved as it did in the homeland. Sheep ranching led to the establishment of workshops (*obrajes*) which manufactured both cotton and wool textiles for the mining towns, and this domestic trade forged another link between the central and northern provinces of New Spain.

The northward expansion in New Spain required the development of new farming centers near the mining and ranching settlements. Since parts of the northern lands were arid, farming was necessarily carried on near rivers and springs. The crops were corn, wheat, beans, peppers, fruits, other vegetables, grapes, and cotton. Cacao was brought into these lands from places like Tabasco and Soconusco in the far south.

Propertied holdings were built up by means of grants of land (*mercedes de tierra*) made by the authorities and by lump-sum payments (*composiciones*) the owners made to the crown to obtain clear titles of ownership. Some settlements were composed of Spanish farmers; others were made by sedentary Indians taken from the central parts of Mexico, e.g. the Tlaxcalans at Saltillo. Some of the northern tribes that had a farming tradition, such as the Tarahumaras, grew crops on their own lands and helped supply food to the mining communities. As will be shown later, the missions can also be considered centers of agricultural development.

As the Spanish colonizers spread into the marginal lands, important changes came about in their labor system. The practice of enslaving prisoners of war continued longer on the frontier than in heavily populated areas. Such enslavement had dated from the early days of the conquest but had been abolished by the crown. Nevertheless, the capture of natives for use as slaves continued in the wild Indian country.

The *encomienda* was able to function with no particular difficulty among the farming populations of Middle America and the Andes, but when the tribes that paid tribute and the Indians available for forced labor began to be scarce, the degeneration of the seignorial system soon followed. For example, in Nuevo León the Spanish colonist lived part of each year with his Indians, putting them to work and in return furnishing them the necessities of life. During the rest of the year these Indians were free to roam the country as they pleased. This mobile *encomienda* (*congrega*) was not based on stable, permanent settlements, and confusion resulted when the Spanish owner returned to put his natives to work. Disputes over the ownership and sale of Indians and their children made this social system different from the *encomienda* in permanent settlements. In Nueva Galicia and Nueva Viscaya *repartimientos* were tried, a system that used Indians in relays for forced labor in agriculture and mining. However, the scarcity of native settlements on the frontier was an obstacle to effective use of this system.

The *encomienda* system suffered the same fate elsewhere. Among the Pueblo Indians of New Mexico, who sustained themselves amid hostile nomadic tribes and lived the settled life of farmers, the Spaniards tried with great determination but without complete success to implant seignorial institutions. Reports from the second half of the seventeenth century show that the Indians in Chile lived on their lords' estates rather than in towns. In southern Chile there were hardly any *encomiendas* "with town and native chief," and the few that did exist were inhabited by a servile group who had been captured in war or had been born on Spanish cattle ranches or farms without ever having known village life. All of these *encomiendas* rendered labor service instead of tribute.

Unstable frontier conditions and wars against the tribes were means of providing the Spanish colonists with a captive labor supply. Soldiers frequently went on expeditions into the Indian country (*malocas*) to capture slaves. These men, women, and children were sold for use in Peru, Chile, and elsewhere. The minimum age for enslavements was ten and a half years for boys, nine and a half for girls; young captives were kept in temporary bondage up to the age of twenty. Those of legal age (*de ley*) were valued between two hundred and fifty and three hundred pesos each, and younger ones (*piezas de servidumbre*) from one hundred and fifty to two hundred pesos. This slave trade was opposed by some of the clergy, and royal statutes alternated between prohibiting and permitting it.[4]

The northward expansion in New Spain does not seem to have resulted from population pressure due to a sizable European immigration in the sixteenth century or from the considerable increase in population in the central region. The frontier was not a safety valve, but it was a land of opportunity. The first conquered provinces were under the seignorial tenure of the original conquistadors and settlers, not a numerous group but one that controlled extensive Indian lands. Thus the expeditions into new lands were attractive to Spaniards who had not profited from the first distributions of property and privilege, who had arrived after the original conquest, or who were still eager for the honor and profit to be gained in such conquering expeditions. For these reasons, the Spanish colonization expanded largely in accord with the interests of both the crown and the captains of the conquest and their men, who were hungry for new opportunities. This expansion was part of the spirit of risk and adventure that dominated sixteenth-century Spanish society. It is interesting to observe the mobility of those Spanish expeditions which led to the geographic extension of the Empire in North and South America, an area that contained 160,000 people of European origin or descent before the end of the first century of conquest.[5]

Wherever an embattled frontier developed, as it did in the Chichimec and the Araucanian country, it was not easy to sustain the conquerors' enthusiasm. The demands of these frontiers, particularly of Chile, were met by offering attractive salaries and awards, by sending men there for punishment, and by using soldiers who had learned their trade in the Spanish campaigns in Europe. The frontiers of the Plata region were no more popular than those of the Chichimecs or Araucanians, exposed as they were to all the dangers and privations common to troops stationed in forts in that area.

The nomadic Indians were in many ways admirably suited to

[4] D. Amunátegui y Solar, *Las encomiendas de indíjenas en Chile* (2 vols.; Santiago, 1909–1910), II, 165 and 223.

[5] See Juan López de Velasco, *Geografía y descripción universal de las Indias ...* (Madrid, 1894).

the type of warfare characteristic of the Spanish-American frontier. They had great mobility, the will to resist, and a sense of adaptation that enabled them to become formidable opponents. They knew the terrain and used it advantageously, scattered when they were hard pressed, and chose the most favorable time and place for their attack. They soon understood the importance of horses in war and upon acquiring them in numbers, they neutralized the Spanish advantage of a mounted cavalry. The gauchos of the Argentine pampa learned very early how rapidly the natives took to the saddle. However, the Christians maintained their military advantage down to the end by their possession of steel weapons and firearms, though when factions of white men tried to gain control of the savages, they often furnished their erstwhile enemies with guns and ammunition. Repeating rifles did not come into general use until the last third of the nineteenth century; this fire-power advantage was too great for the natives to overcome despite their use of the horse and their wise adaptation to the terrain.

In colonial times, the nomadic Indian could not be defeated in open battle or dominated by means of seignorial rule. Thus the conquering lord of the central region could maintain himself on that exposed frontier only by use of cavalry, construction of forts (*fortines*) and presidios, and extermination, enslavement, or deportation of the Indian. These tribesmen were not vassals, as were their sedentary brothers who were subject to forced labor and tutelage. Instead, they were enemies of the Empire, thought of as barbarians, and known to be dangerous because of their attacks upon travelers, traders, silver pack trains, muleteers, ranches, and range stock. Still, there were times when churchmen strongly intervened to impose a policy of peace which upon occasion confined military effort to strictly defensive ends. The authorities sometimes made brief alliances with the Indians, giving them the necessities of life as presents in exchange for peace. However, hostilities would soon break out again because of the colonists' greed, the mistreatment of the Indians, or the renewed attacks made by the Indians themselves in times of real need, aggression, or vengeance.

The amalgamation of races on the frontier occurred at random rather than as a general blending of societies. It is interesting to note that many Christian captives and renegades lived among the Indians of the Plata region during the second half of the nine-teenth century.

Along with the miner, rancher, farmer, trader, soldier, and muleteer, the missionary took his place on the Spanish-American frontier. He played an active part in the invasion of the marginal areas of the Empire. He undertook the most arduous expeditions, established centers for the conversion of the barbarians, and at times suffered martyrdom for his labors. Prepared for his work in the religious schools, he found his Christian discipline tempered by the rigor and danger of frontier life. In the missions, his neophytes learned the rudiments of Christian faith and civil life. These missions were not exclusively religious institutions, since in most cases both social and economic affairs were under the controlling hand of the missionary priest. His Indians practiced agriculture, learned the care of livestock, and acquired a few crafts. Iron tools and domesticated animals thus became a part of the native's material life and went hand in hand with the propagation of the faith. Save for the single case of the expulsion of the Jesuits from Spanish America in 1767, the crown gave military and economic protection to the missions. The work of the missionaries was distinguished by their concept of invading the wild Indian country armed with a message of peace and the benefits of civilization. As it turned out, however, they had to adjust to the conditions prevailing on the frontier. Thus from time to time the mission played a military role. It did not significantly increase the mixing of the races (*mestizaje*). Though many missions did not endure, the records clearly indicate the importance of these establishments and show that they were of equal importance with the mining *reales,* the Spanish towns, agricultural estates, and stock ranches as frontier institutions.[6]

[6] For the foregoing see items in the appended list of readings; also W. Jiménez Moreno, "La colonización y evangelización de Guanajuato en el siglo xvi," *Cuadernos Americanos,* XIII, no. 1 (Jan.–Feb., 1944); J. Miranda, "Notas sobre la introducción de la Mesta en la Nueva España," *Revista de Historia de América,* no. 17 (June, 1944); F. Chevalier, *La formation des grands domaines au Mexique: terre et société aux xvi–xviie siècles* (Paris, 1952); M. González Navarro, *Repartimientos de indios en Nueva Galicia* (Mexico, 1953); Silvio A. Zavala, "Los esclavos indios en el norte de México, siglo xvi," *El Norte de México y el Sur de los Estados Unidos* (Mexico,

EVALUATIONS

It has been noted before that during the Middle Ages, writings about the Iberian frontier began to appear. Other such writings resulted from the overseas expansion, and then more appeared in connection with the Spanish-American frontier. Those works of any merit belong equally to two periods—the age of the post-conquest colonization and the period after independence. Some have literary merit and others are informative as to the native society, religion, or politics. In any case, these works permit an examination of the meanings of these historical experiences, their main orientation and evaluation.

Even before the end of the Spanish settlement, it was realized that the society of northern Mexico was different from that of the central region, that the North had taken on a spirit in which the prevailing dangers and hardships could be confronted. Alexander von Humboldt observed in his *Political Essay on the Kingdom of New Spain* that the struggle against Indians and insecurity had stamped the character of the northern people with a certain energy and temper all their own. He noted the lack of docile Indians whom the whites might have exploited so they could live a life of idleness and indolence. The active life, lived for the most part on horseback, helped to develop physical strength, and in that country men had to be strong to deal with hostile Indians and herds of range cattle. Those men were strong in spirit, of unexcitable nature, and possessed of clean and robust bodies. To Humboldt this picture was—and this explains his benevolent point of view: "a state of nature, preserved amid the trappings of

---

Sociedad Mexicana de Antropología, 1944); Vito Alessio Robles, "Las condiciones sociales en el Norte de la Nueva España," *Memorias de la Academia Mexicana de la Historia*, IV (April–June, 1945), and the same author's *Coahuila y Téxas en la época colonial* (Mexico, 1938). See also reports of inspections (*visitas*) as in Alonso de la Mota y Escobar, *Descripción Geográfica de los Reinos de la Nueva Galicia, Nueva Viscaya y Nuevo León* (2d ed., with slightly altered title, Mexico, 1940; orig. pub., Mexico, 1930); and Nicolás de Lafora, *Relación del viaje que hizo a los presidios internos, situados en la frontera de la América Septentrional . . .* (Mexico, 1939). Miguel Ramos de Arizpe's Memorial to the Cortes of Cádiz in 1811 is in Ramos de Arizpe, *Discursos, Memorias, e Informes . . .*, with notes by Vito Alessio Robles (Mexico, 1942).

an ancient civilization." [7] In the same tone, a native son of
Coahuila, Miguel Ramos de Arizpe, explained in his Memorial to
the Cortes of Cádiz in 1811 that agriculture, source of the wealth
of nations, was the common occupation of people in all the eastern
inland provinces of Coahuila, Texas, Nuevo León, New Mexico,
and Nuevo Santander. He said, "it shapes their general character,
and for this reason, busy night and day in honest work on the
land, receiving their living from it rather than from any person,
they are surely immune to intrigue, are virtuously upright in morals, and are enemies of arbitrary conduct and disorder. They are
worshippers of true liberty and, naturally enough, are the best
fitted for all the moral and political virtues. They are much devoted to the liberal and mechanical arts." [8]

Whether because of a naturalistic bent so typical of Enlightened philosophy or whether because of physiocratic leanings or
localism, the fact is that the distinguishing natural and historical
character of the northern provinces was understood by local people and foreigners alike, even though their conceptions and expressions of it were different. The local conditions, the relations
with the Indians, and the kind of activities typical of the region,
all had contributed to making the northern frontier and its people unique in New Spain. With the coming of independence when
the conservatives and radicals, the federalists and centralists were
struggling over the question of the nation's political organization,
the northern provinces were seen by some republicans as bulwarks
of liberal principles. These regions could more easily avoid in-
volvement in the issues of theocracy, militarism, and the hierarchic
lack of equality that was holding the Indian in subjection. When
the central government was in the control of the conservatives, it
could be resisted by those distant provinces. Seen in this light, the
northern frontier seemed to be the guardian of liberty.

Some men of affairs who regarded the northern provinces in
this way and who observed the thin population of these regions
came to reflect on the possibility of foreign immigration. Thinking of the progress made by the first Anglo-American colonies in
Texas, Lorenzo de Zavala wrote that within two or three genera-

[7] Alexander von Humboldt, *Political Essay on the Kingdom of New Spain*,
vol. II, as cited in Ramos de Arizpe, *Discursos, Memorias, e Informes* . . . , xvi.
[8] Ramos de Arizpe, *Discursos, Memorias, e Informes* . . . , xix and 41.

tions that part of Mexico would be richer, more free, and more civilized than all the rest. Because of its immigrants, Mexican Texas would be an example to other states still in a semifeudal stage and ruled by military and clerical influences, fateful inheritances from Spanish rule.[9] Thus the northern frontier was seen not merely as a different society more favorable for the growth of democratic life but also as a hope for the regeneration of all Mexico. Precisely because these frontier regions had come through the colonial period so thinly populated did they seem particularly promising for new immigration projects in the nineteenth century.

The northern frontier had been ruled by military government, particularly after the *Comandancia de Provincias Internas* was organized in 1776. After several reorganizations, this command included the provinces of Nueva Viscaya, Sonora, Sinaloa, California, Coahuila, New Mexico, and Texas. Ramos de Arizpe petitioned the Cortes of Cádiz for the establishment of a civil government, arguing that a military commander, by his education and character, naturally seeks to execute the laws he knows and is accustomed to enforce, "demanding of the peaceful farmer, the quiet cattleman, the hard-working artisan, that blind obedience, that wordless compliance, that his soldiers must render at command—and this, sometimes, without meaning to do so. Finally, he makes himself a despot, with the worst results for the people, who would never suffer so under civil government which would hold more closely to civil and social law." [10] Thus regionalism did not signify an absolute guarantee of liberty since it could become the refuge of bossism (*caciquismo*) and local abuses.

The loyalty of Anglo-American immigrants to Mexico was not as strong as the ties that bound them to their own people, and they did not bring the hoped-for internal development of the northern provinces or the instructive example it was hoped they would offer the other states of the republic. Instead, there followed the revolt and independence of the Texans, their annexation to the United States, and the war between that nation and Mexico. These events were followed in turn by the loss of lands lying north of the Rio Grande.

[9] See his *Ensayo Histórico de las Revoluciones de Méjico, desde 1808 hasta 1830* (2 vols.; Paris and New York, 1831–1832), II (New York, 1832), 171.

[10] Ramos de Arizpe, *Discursos, Memorias, e Informes . . .* , 58.

For a brief moment during the revolution that began in Mexico in 1910, the northern provinces exercised great influence in national politics. The revolt gained impetus in Coahuila, Chihuahua, and Sonora. In this may be seen an extension of those historic liberal impulses already mentioned, but there were also such new factors as the help in arms and other resources obtained from north of the United States border. In any case, the cavalry and cattle of the North helped sustain the troops in their long marches and campaigns. Among these soldiers were creoles, mestizos, and even Yaqui and Mayo Indians, who went on to pitch their tents in the patios of the National Palace of Mexico City. During that long war, the northern fighter gained great fame for courage and endurance and his leaders were at the helm of a number of the revolutionary governments.

It remains to inquire, finally, whether the northern frontier may be considered a source of the Mexican national type. If a balanced mixture of ethnic stocks may be considered the symbol of what is Mexican, it is possible that the people of the old northern frontier meet this standard. On the other hand, there are scholars who hold that the great number of northerners are ethnically creole, i.e., descendants of whites. If Mexican nativism is based on the blending of the ancient civilization of the sedentary Indians and that of the Spaniards, then the central provinces rather than the northern must have originated the distinctive Mexican character. This is true if we accept a national character rather than a plurality of types that may be closer to reality. Certainly, the sedentary Indians were most numerous in the central region and presumably the greatest amalgamation of the races took place there. In accordance with this last interpretation, then, the North can be considered only a source of social peculiarities. It remains apart, however, from that nativism that stems from the pre-conquest culture of Middle America.

A diversity similar to what we have seen in Mexico—between the inland provinces (*tierra adentro*) and those of the central part (*tierra afuera*) of the viceroyalty—also appears in Chile. The division there is between the central region permanently colonized by the Spaniards and those lands to the south that remained in Araucanian hands or lay on the frontier exposed to their attacks. In the late sixteenth and early seventeenth century, Indian warfare had forced abandonment of the settlements of Arauco, Santa

Cruz, Valdivia, Imperial, Angol, Villarica, and Osorno. Chillán and Concepción had been attacked, but the Christians had managed to re-establish their control in the country lying between the Rivers Maule and Bío-Bío. The policy of defensive war, begun late in the seventeenth century, consisted in holding the line of the Bío-Bío so as to protect the central part of the colony. Only missionaries were permitted to cross that line to deal with the natives. This important frontier, on which depended the conservation of Spanish power in the South Pacific, attracted the attention not only of the authorities of Chile but also of those of the Viceroyalty of Peru and of Spain.

Like the war in northern Mexico, this struggle against the Araucanians went through several stages, expending troops and funds which during the seventeenth century came as a subsidy (*situado*) from Peru. This war, like the Mexican, alternated between attack and defense and led to the capture of prisoners on both sides. There was some mixing of blood due to unions between Spanish soldiers and Indian women and of Indians and captured Spanish women. Historians and students of Chilean literature point out that the war along the Araucanian frontier contributed unique features to the national culture. Among the themes brought forth in this literature as it has developed since the sixteenth century have been the glorification of the Araucanian war, begun by Alonso de Ercilla, and the recognition of the Indian's right to defend his land. The selection of these two themes is not meant as derogatory to any of the authors who praise the expansion of the Faith and of Christian rule or who exalt the deeds of Spanish creole soldiers who fought the Indian wars.[11] As late as the nineteenth century, one can still note the dualism between the regard for the Araucanian's merits and for the final campaign that conquered him.

In the complex patterns of ideas about racial mixture, the vigor of the Araucanian is given credit as soon as it is seen to be a part of the racial stock just as European ancestry, particularly the

[11] After Ercilla's *Araucana*, the anonymous poem given in José Toribio Medina, *Historia de la literatura colonial de Chile* (3 vols.; Santiago, 1878), I, 259; Hernando Alvarez de Toledo, *Purén Indómito* (Leipzig, 1861: written after 1597); and Pedro de Oña, *Arauco Domado* (Santiago, 1917; orig. pub., Lima, 1596), among others.

Basque, is a matter for pride and distinction. Authors discuss the question of whether or not there has been an amalgamation of Spanish and Indian in the great oligarchic families. They speak of the balance attained between the various racial strains in the general population. Some believe in a Gothic origin of the pioneer Spaniards who came to Chile, while others prefer to stress the influence of the German migration of the late nineteenth century. They also single out certain forces drawn from ethnic and historical backgrounds to account for traits in the national character. For example, the laziness and improvidence of the people, their stoicism and courage, their martial spirit, inconstancy, and love of adventure are accounted for through the influence of war and their frugal frontier life. These ideas about the intermingling of peoples and the unity of feeling that results from blending a warlike history with qualities imputed to the national character throw into bold relief the influence of the southern frontier on the shaping of the personality of Chile.

Numerous writings about the plains of the Plata region deserve careful literary, social, and political analysis, and a few themes from the work of Domingo Faustino Sarmiento have been selected here [12] to enable us to compare the image of this frontier with that of others in the New World. Driven by his political desire to attack the tyrannical rule of the cattleman Juan Manuel de Rosas, Sarmiento contrasted the barbarism of the pastoral provinces with urban civilization of European origin. The passion of his argument did not blur the clarity of his description of gaucho life and he was well aware of the promise, implicit in the vigorous originality of this historical development in its American setting, for those who would treat it as a literary theme. As with Francis Parkman, the historian, and James Fenimore Cooper, the man of letters, Sarmiento was attracted by the American frontier. In the United States as in Argentina, he saw the dramatic interplay of

[12] For the most part I follow the fine selection in *El pensamiento vivo de Sarmiento*, comp. Ricardo Rojas (Buenos Aires, 1941). Quotations that follow in the text are mostly from *Facundo, ó Civilización i Barbarie* (orig. pub. at Santiago, 1845, in the newspaper El Progreso, as *Facundo*, then separately in the same year as *Civilización i barbarie. Vida de Juan Facundo Qiroga . . .*), and *Conflictos y Armonías de las Razas en América* (Buenos Aires, 1883). For a recent penetrating analysis, see Ezequiel Martínez Estrada, *Muerte y Transfiguración de Martín Fierro* (2 vols.; Mexico, 1948).

civilization and barbarism between the European immigrant and
the nomadic Indian. He saw these analogies clearly and was perhaps the first of New World writers to make the connection between North American and Spanish-American frontiers. However,
there are in his pages some historical differences which make this
parallel more complex. After all, the gauchos who inhabited the
pastoral pampa and who are descendants of Spaniards, Indians,
and sometimes also Negroes, were organized into a society already
Europeanized during the colonial period. That society had conquered large tracts of the back country by use of cattle, horses,
steel weapons, and firearms. It had founded the cities that Sarmiento pictured as oases of civilization in a cultureless plain.

Contrary to Sarmiento's point of view, we can properly speak
of the existence of a historical frontier only where the Christian
gauchos faced Indian enemies. That other frontier, conceived politically by Sarmiento as lying between the civilized and the barbarous, between urban and pastoral people, between European
immigrants and gauchos—in short, between those who were politically disinherited as was Sarmiento and those who governed under the protection of Rosas—cannot be confused with the historical frontier that did lie between the wild Indians and the
fortified line established during the colonial period. Here we see
the dualism of Sarmiento's thought with respect to the urban and
pastoral heritage of Spanish America. On the one hand, he saw
this heritage as the fulcrum of tradition and civilized progress in
Argentina, although he did try to distinguish between the Spanish colonial period with its backward society and the new policies
directed toward economic progress, European immigration, religious tolerance, educational advances, and political democracy.
On the other hand, he confused that older tradition with American barbarism—Indian, mestizo, gaucho, and colonial in origin
—that was to be eliminated by advancing civilization. This dualism as lived and expressed by Sarmiento with dramatic intensity
helps explain the historical position from which he viewed both
the past and the future.

In explaining that the Argentine prairie wagons were drawn
up in a circle for defense against Indian attack, he was well aware
that the gauchos fought from within the defensive circle just as
did the men of the western United States. Both represented to

him the progress of European civilization on the American frontier in the face of the aborigines. The westward movement in the
Argentine and in the United States began, however, in different
centuries and followed different rhythms until a certain paral-
lelism was reached in the nineteenth century. By that time, there
already existed in South America a gaucho civilization, denoting
an intermediate stage between the newly arrived European immigrant and the nomadic Indian.

The similarity between the frontiers of North and South America which Sarmiento saw derived from environmental conditions
and from the tasks necessary to control these influences, that is,
from factors peculiar to invasion of lands inhabited by nomads. His
attention was drawn to the social and political aspects of life on the
pampa, although the essential vigor of his writing stems from his
poetic re-creation of the peculiar aspects of the countryside and
the personality of the gaucho. He emphasized certain characteristics that may have been common to all men who pioneered in
the new lands of America.[13] He was aware of the significance of
the horse for the civilization of the New World, of the diversity
between the mounted *vaqueros* of the pastoral regions and the
peons or foot servants in the agricultural districts; and he knew the
contributions made by the *llaneros* of Venezuela, for example, during the wars of independence. Nonetheless, his statements do not
coincide with the thesis later formulated by Frederick Jackson
Turner—this despite certain external similarities—since Turner
found on the frontier not the cradle of pastoral despotism, as exemplified in the dictator Rosas of Argentina, but rather the seeds
of democracy and social fluidity.[14] Sarmiento understood and ad-

---

[13] *El pensamiento vivo de Sarmiento,* 136: "Individualism was his very essence, the horse his exclusive weapon, and the immense pampa his theater";
on p. 132: "valor, boldness, dexterity, violence, and opposition to established
justice"; and on p. 127: "The gaucho admired above all else physical force,
skill in horsemanship, and courage."

[14] See R. E. Riegel, "Current Ideas of the Significance of the United States
Frontier," *Revista de Historia de América,* No. 33 (June, 1952), 30: "These
men were optimistic, nationalistic, and expansionist. They were individual-
istic and materialistic, with a sprinkling of the lawless, but withal brave, hardy
and ingenious, willing to experiment until they overcame the difficulties of
each new region. They were the primary source of such American traits as
individualism, democracy, inventiveness, and materialism." Merle E. Curti,

mired the civilization of the United States. He knew how it differed from European society which he himself had seen, and he
thought the American superior to the European. To him the frontier was the battleground between barbarism and civilization. The
origin of democracy lay not on the frontier but in the European
tradition transplanted there, the immigration of the Puritans, the
freedom that rose out of the Reformation, and the life of the Atlantic coast and its expansion. He hoped the European immigrants
would bring a reforming spirit to the Argentine and it mattered
little to him that this might be done at the expense of gaucho
customs which, in his general condemnation of barbarism, he inevitably treated as equivalent with the life of native nomads. Thus
Sarmiento could perceive some of the problems which European
immigration created for the United States and for Argentina, and
in time he came to doubt the civilizing influence of these newly
arrived people.[15] To achieve the goal of progressive virtues, he
placed his best and final hopes in popular education.

The only Spanish-American writer I know who has tested Turner's frontier thesis for Spanish America is not Sarmiento, who
died five years before Turner presented his paper of 1893, but the
Peruvian, Víctor Andrés Belaúnde.[16] He is of the opinion that the
frontier appeared only rarely in the Spanish colonies. He points
out the importance of the beginning of colonial occupation but
believes that when that early period had passed, there was no free
land in which a frontier might have been opened for the many.

Historiadores de América, Frederick Jackson Turner (Mexico, 1949), 26, states
that "the westward movement, he [Turner] argued, developed the essentially
American traits of restless energy, self-reliance, voluntary co-operation on the
part of individuals, practical ingenuity and versatility, inventiveness, and a
masterful grasp of material things...." Note that in this listing of personal
qualities there are as many coincidences as discrepancies with those ascribed
to the gaucho.

[15] *El pensamiento vivo de Sarmiento*, 77–78, 208. See Martínez Estrada,
Sarmiento (Buenos Aires, 1946), 99. The nativist reaction as it was in 1870
is reflected in Lucio V. Mansilla, *Una excursión a los indios Ranqueles*
(Buenos Aires, 1870).

For critical opinion of Sarmiento's historical position, see Martínez Estrada,
Sarmiento, 94, and Ricardo Rojas' prologue to *El pensamiento vivo de
Sarmiento*, 24–26.

[16] *The Frontier in Hispanic America* (Rice Institute Pamphlets, No. X
[October, 1923]), 202–213.

This was because of problems created by the Amazon River valley and the Andean range. From the geographical point of view, he sees nothing comparable to the opportunities held forth by the Mississippi Valley.

After examining the landholding situation in Chile, on the plains of the Orinoco, and in Mexico, Belaúnde pauses to consider the prairies of the Plata region and southern Brazil. Here the geography was more like that of the United States. The pampa, however, was occupied during the colonial period; later, the railroads and government land cessions further impeded the development of a frontier in a social sense, since large holdings prevailed. From this lack of a frontier stemmed a rigid social structure and an absence of vitality and youthful spirit. What Belaúnde emphasizes is the diversity of the situation, and he concludes that Turner's thesis does not apply.

In conclusion, I believe that the evidence is not all in, that the thesis may be examined in other regions and from other points of view. One case that deserves such study is the meeting of the Spanish-American frontier in northern Mexico with the westward-moving American frontier, not in its well-known political, military, and diplomatic aspects, but with reference to social exchanges and adjustments that occurred.

SELECTED READINGS

Barlow, R. H. *The Extent of the Empire of the Culhua Mexica* Berkeley: University of California Press, 1949.

Belaúnde, Victor Andrés. *The Frontier in Hispanic America* ("Rice Institute Pamphlets" No. X [October, 1923]), 202–213.

Bolton, H. E. "The Mission as a Frontier Institution in the Spanish-American Colonies," *American Historical Review*, XXIII (1917), 42–61.

Gibson, Charles. *Tlaxcala in the Sixteenth Century*. New Haven: Yale University Press, 1952.

Powell, Philip W. *Soldiers, Indians, and Silver. The Northward Advance of New Spain, 1550–1600*. Berkeley: University of California Press, 1952.

Ramos de Arizpe, Miguel. *Report that Dr. Miguel Ramos de Arizpe. . . presents to the August Congress on the Natural, Political and Civil Condition of the Provinces of Coahuila, Nuevo León, Nuevo Santander, and Texas. . .*, translations, annotations, and introduction by Nettìe Lee Benson ("Latin American Studies," No. XI). Austin: University of Texas, Institute of Latin-American Studies, 1950.

Sauer, Carl O. *Colima of New Spain in the Sixteenth Century.* Berkeley: University of California Press, 1950.

Simpson, Lesley B. *The Encomienda in New Spain: the Beginning of Spanish Mexico.* Berkeley: University of California Press. 2d ed. rev., enl., 1950.

West, Robert C. *The Mining Community in Northern New Spain. The Parral Mining District.* Berkeley: University of California Press, 1949.

Zavala, Silvio A. *New Viewpoints on the Spanish Colonization of America.* Philadelphia: University of Pennsylvania Press, 1943.

A. L. BURT

If Turner Had Looked at Canada, Australia, and New Zealand When He Wrote about the West

The outward form of the French frontier in America seemed to contradict the Turner hypothesis on the democratic influences of the westward expansion. The French brought to the St. Lawrence a feudal system, a royal aristocracy, and a church far removed from democratic control. However, Professor Burt, whose writings on Canada are both numerous and well-known, believes that the French frontier was democratizing and leveling in its influence. Here where the seigniors competed for tenants and the wilderness beckoned all men, the feudal system was modified. Even the church bent to popular demands and the powers of the autocracy were "hamstrung," says this essayist. Land hunger led the Canadians westward to the prairies and southward into the United States. The desire to control the expansion into the Hudson's Bay lands led to the establishment of the Confederation of Canada. Over on the other side of the world, Australia and New Zealand found their political development influenced by their frontiersmen.

Professor Burt sees significant parallels between the frontier expansion of the United States and the British Commonwealth. He also makes note of the interlocking nature of the American and Canadian westward extension, an insight that nationalist historians have seldom had.

IF Turner had looked north when he wrote about the West, he might have discovered in New France a surprising confirmation of the thesis he was propounding. I say "surprising" because the outward form of the society on the St. Lawrence contradicted his general thesis. This superficial contradiction caught the eye of a critic twenty-six years ago, and in an article attacking the frontier theory he wrote:

When France undertook the planting of colonies in the New World, feudalism was still a prominent feature of French social and economic life, although the political power of the feudal lords had been subordinated to the rise of centralized monarchy. In both theory and fact, France was a despotism; there was almost no self-government, local or national. The essentials of this system were transferred to Canada and remained there during the entire period of French control. In fact, as Professor [W. B.] Munro has shown, the seignorial system in Canada was, if anything, more like the French feudalism of an earlier period than that of contemporary France, and this paternalistic, undemocratic scheme of economic and social relationships outlived its parent stem in France. The religious system which the colonists brought with them retarded rather than promoted the development of a broader distribution of power and privilege.[1]

Seeing feudalism, theocracy, and autocracy in the French colony right beside the English colonies, the author of the article leaped to the conclusion that they demonstrated the impotence of the frontier to emancipate the individual. Turner did not take up the challenge. He was then an old man and he had never investigated conditions in New France. Nor did any of his disciples reply. They could not plead infirmity of age, and they might be charged with infirmity of mind. Apparently, not one of them had thought of checking Turner's thesis by an examination of this neighboring society, or had observed the seeming inconsistency.

The critic who cited New France, of which he likewise possessed no understanding, could hardly have hit upon a more convincing illustration to support the validity of the very proposition that he was trying to disprove. When the sons of France migrated to this continent, they actually developed the same sturdy inde-

[1] Benjamin F. Wright, Jr., "American Democracy and the Frontier," *Yale Review*, XX (Winter, 1931), 350.

pendence of the individual as did the English colonists, and this despite the wide difference between these two peoples in their social and institutional inheritance. It is easy to see why and how this development occurred in New France if we look in turn at each of the three controls mentioned above—feudal, ecclesiastical, and governmental—and examine the effect of the North American environment upon them.

That the seignioral system of New France bore little resemblance to the parent system in old France, except in outward form, was thoroughly established by Professor Munro nearly half a century ago. The royal autocracy, he pointed out, could not tolerate in New France a reproduction of feudalism as it had evolved in old France, and therefore consciously sought to reform it in the new country where no old local traditions stood in the way. This explanation of the divergence between the social and economic system in the homeland and its namesake in the colony is excellent as far as it goes, but it does not go far enough. If Munro had pondered the teaching of the man who became his colleague at Harvard, it would have revealed to him that a mightier power than the mightiest ruler in Europe wrought a complete transformation of the old institution in the new land.

It was physically impossible for anything like the feudalism of France to exist in this French colony, and the reason is really quite simple. A basic competition of the Old World was turned upside down in the New World. Here it was a competition between seigniors for tenants, whereas there it was between peasants for land owned by seigniors. This inversion emptied feudalism of its substance, leaving only a hollow shell. North American conditions of life emancipated the French peasants who migrated to the St. Lawrence, where they cleared and occupied only a narrow ribbon of land running along the banks of the great river and its tributaries. With liberty forever beckoning to them through the trees of the forest just behind their cottages, and up the water that flowed past their doors, how could they be ridden by feudal lords? If anyone found life in the colony too cramping, nothing—not even his wedded wife—could hold him from running away into the woods to live a wilder life with the Indians, among whom he could always find, if he wished, a wife *à la mode*.

The earliest years of French settlement on this continent saw the emergence of this *coureur de bois* type. It was the same, except in name, as that which appeared on the fringe of the English settlement and attracted Turner's attention. That the *coureurs de bois* were relatively more numerous than their English cousins is suggested by a perusal of the official correspondence between Quebec and Paris, which contains numerous references to these outlaws. Certainly no English colonial government was ever so worried as was that of New France over its men who slipped beyond the pale of civilization. If, as seems probable, the proportion of French colonists who thus deserted a sedentary existence was greater than that of the English, does this indicate that life in New France was less free than in the English colonies? There are good reasons for doubting it. One is that nature made it much easier to penetrate the interior of the continent from the lower St. Lawrence than from the Atlantic seaboard. Instead of being hemmed in on the west by a forbidding mountain barrier, the French were invited into the heart of North America by a magnificent network of water highways that was focused in the midst of their settlement. Moreover, the harvest of furs within reach of any English colony could not compare with what could be gathered from Canada. As for the concern of the government in Quebec, it had fewer settlers to spare, and it was losing valuable furs to the English through the *coureurs de bois*.

To extinguish this daring breed of men who seemed to be sapping the life of Canada, the government issued a long series of decrees. The prescribed penalties varied from time to time, being death, confiscation of goods, heavy fines, and the lash. But all were of no avail, and even the enticement of an amnesty was tried in vain. The drain that could not be stopped prevented the colony from growing as fast as it might otherwise have done. Canadian historians have often recorded the fact, sometimes with heavy regret because they have been prone to neglect what Turner so often observed, that the West repaid with interest what it drew from the East. In return for the men whom the wilderness stole from New France, it gave back a priceless boon—the spirit of liberty.

The mere fact that the Canadian settler could depart at will enabled him to remain in freedom. He could not be tied to the soil. He could get, and he did get, much more land than he could ever use, and this at a trifling rent, such was the disparity between supply and demand. As Munro has so ably shown, the habitant's tenure resembled that of most English colonists more than that of French peasants, except in outward form; and even in this there was less difference than has often been supposed, for the majority of the English colonies were settled on the semimanorial system still prevalent in their mother country. The annual seignioral dues that the habitant paid in kind, in money, and in labor were altogether very small and may be equated with the obligations of quitrents and leaseholds in the English colonies; and his possession of his farm was just as secure, unless he thought so little of it that he abandoned it.

No other feudal obligation imposed any burden upon the habitant during the French regime. True, there was a mutation fine known as *lods et ventes,* payable to the seignior on the transfer of tenants' holdings otherwise than by direct inheritance. But how often could a seignior collect it in a country where parents were so prolific and the competition of virgin land was so strong? There were also *banalités,* which in old France were legion and oppressive; but only two of them were ever claimed in New France, and there they amounted to nothing. One was that of the oven, which was practically frozen out. The other was that of the mill, which occasioned more grief to the seignior than to his tenants. Under pain of forfeiting by nonexercise a right that might become profitable to his heirs, he was forced by the government to build the mill and to operate it substantially at cost. The toll was one fourteenth of the grain brought to the mill. Finally, there was the seignorial right to administer justice. It was one of the sorest afflictions of the peasants in old France, where it was jealously guarded by its possessors as a source of revenue. That was because the mother country had a thick population. New France, on the other hand, was so thinly populated that this right had no fiscal value, and therefore it survived only in so far as it was a convenience to all concerned in the settlement of petty cases.

The difference between society in the mother country and in this French colony was as wide as the ocean between them. In caste-ridden old France, a huge, impassable gulf separated peasants from their lords; but in New France habitants sometimes became seigniors, and this change of status made little or no change in their manner of living. Many other Canadian seigniors, including some of the few titled ones, had to live and work like habitants. It was not uncommon for the lord of the manor, his lady, and his daughters to toil together in the fields of the French colony. Such was the leveling influence of frontier life.

According to the Jesuit historian Charlevoix, a contemporary witness who would never tell a lie, the habitant "breathed from his birth the air of liberty" and showed it in his bearing. According to Baron La Hontan, who sometimes told the truth and did on this occasion, the habitant lived in greater comfort than an infinity of gentlemen in France. According to Hocquart, one of the best intendants of New France, the habitant was not a coarse and boorish rustic like the peasant at home, but a well-dressed fellow with good manners. The very name by which he was called reflects his independent spirit. Technically he was a *censitaire* or *roturier*, but his scorn for such labels of servility led to the substitution, even in official correspondence, of the classless appellation of *habitant*. North American conditions had emancipated him from feudal bondage.

Such a man could not be a hewer of wood and drawer of water for his church, no matter how much he might be devoted to it. That he was not a slave of the clergy is sufficiently illustrated by a glance at the history of the tithe in New France. When this ancient institution was introduced at the behest of Bishop Laval, the father of the Canadian church, by a royal decree of April, 1663, ordering the payment of one thirteenth of all the fruits of human labor as well as of the soil, exactly as in old France, the people with one accord refused to pay. In Three Rivers they would not allow the decree to be read or posted, and from Beaupré, hard by Quebec, they chased out the priest. The decree raised such a popular storm that the bishop had to bow before it, and a sort of Dutch auction followed.

Commencing with the parishioners of Quebec, who had contributed to the building of their own church edifice, Laval exempted them from the first year's payment. Next he reduced their obligation to one twentieth for six years, and he soon extended this concession to the whole colony. Still the general opposition was menacing, and he continued his retreat by issuing a *mandement* which explained that the words of the royal decree did not mean what they plainly said. What was to be taxed, he now declared, was not all the fruits of human labor as well as of the soil, but only the produce of labor applied to the tilling of the soil. In old France the clergy collected the tithe on wood, hay, fish, eggs, fleece, and livestock; but they could not do it in New France. The bishop also announced that the lower rate of one twentieth, instead of holding for only six years, was to last through his lifetime, without prejudice to his successor. As the people were not yet appeased, he put off all payments until the vessels of 1665 arrived, when it might be possible to get a royal reply to the popular objections.

But payment did not begin in 1665. The question was referred to the Marquis de Tracy, viceroy of all French dominions in the New World, who arrived at Quebec in that year to install a new governor and the first intendant and to spend a couple of years in the colony while he set it on its feet. Laval appealed to him to put the law in operation, only to find that this high functionary hesitated before the popular resistance. He withheld his decision until after he had convoked the "notables" of the country and got their advice on what the habitants would bear. Then, in concert with the governor and the intendant, and with the consent of the bishop, he issued an ordinance in September, 1667, establishing the tithe at a still lower rate and with a further exemption. Nothing was to be paid from newly cultivated land for five years after it was broken, and only one twenty-sixth was to be taken from any land during the next twenty years. At last, four years after the first demand, the burden was scaled down to suit the people and they shouldered it. Light as it was, however, it occasioned many local disputes with the clergy to the end of the French regime and afterward. It is therefore not surprising that all clerical attempts to raise the rate and to broaden the base of the tithe were defeated.

In 1678, Laval sought a revision of the law to restore the original rate, but in the following year a royal edict confirmed the ordinance of 1667. As this confirmation did not extend the period of twenty years during which only one twenty-sixth was to be collected, the bishop who succeeded Laval in 1688 could maintain—and he did—that the full payment should be exacted. Yet even he shrank from ordering it himself. He wanted the government to command it; and in the autumn of 1705, when he was over in France, there was some fear in Quebec that he might succeed, and the intendant sent a warning to the home government. "The Bishop of Quebec," he wrote, "does not understand the interests of his clergy in demanding that the tithe be fixed at one-thirteenth as in France." At this very time, also, the base of the tax came under official review. Two rural parishes near Quebec were startled by sermons in which their *curés* announced that the tithe, hitherto levied only on grain, would thenceforth be collected on everything produced from the soil, whether by cultivation or not, on cattle, hay, fruit, flax, hemp, sheep, and other things. According to the record, there was *"un grand murmure"* among the habitants as soon as Mass was over. Straightway the matter was brought before the Council in Quebec, which summoned the offending *curés* to appear in person to present their authority for this announcement. Then the Council not only prohibited them and all other clergy from making any innovation in the tithe but also forbade the people to pay any more than was customary. From this decision, an appeal was carried to the king. When the appeal was heard, the question of the rate was also urged, and both were finally dismissed by the royal Council of State in the summer of 1707.

By far the best of Laval's biographers commends him for accepting the compromise of 1667. If the father of the Canadian church had not made this concession to public opinion, he would have jeopardized the existence of the tithe in Canada. So says the scholarly Abbé Gosselin, and in this he is probably right. But the explanations offered by him and others of the cloth invite serious criticism. They place the responsibility upon the bad disposition of the civil authorities and upon the poverty of the people. They completely ignore the fact that it was to the interest of the home government to increase the yield of the tithe and thus reduce the royal obligation to make up the perennial deficit of the Canadian church. For this very reason, three successive governors were instructed to restore the original rate. Only when the experience of forty years seemed to prove that this was impossible, did the Council of State reject the bishop's demand for it. The repeated accusation that the laymen who ruled in Quebec suborned the people against the tithe is not in accord with the known facts.

These officials reflected the spontaneous resistance of the people to the payment of more than what was required by the ordinance of 1667, but the people found no favor whatsoever when they disputed the payment established by law and custom. The other allegation—that the habitants were too poor to give any more—is positively ridiculous. They were much better fed, better clothed, better housed than the peasants of France, who had to render to their clergy more than twice as much in proportion. Here a word might be added to guard against possible misunderstanding. In the habitants' resistance to the tithe, long Protestant noses might smell anticlericalism, but they would be on the wrong scent; that resistance, which was so effective, was as far removed from a challenge to the spiritual authority of the church as is earth from heaven.

The spirit of freedom that permeated the society of New France also hamstrung the royal autocracy, as we have seen in the many futile decrees to stop people from wandering in the woods. The weight of the government fell heavily upon the masses at home, but the population of the colony would not support it. The arbitrary imposition of the royal *corvée* bent the backs and crushed the spirits of the peasantry in old France, but this too was impossible in New France. Here the service was required for the benefit of those who performed it, chiefly in the building and the maintenance of their own roads. As Munro has observed, it was essentially the same, even in the provision for commutation, as the statute labor of the English colonies. The taxes that ground the common people so mercilessly in France were unknown in this colony. Indeed, the habitants paid no taxes at all. Their economy was so self-sufficient that they paid nothing by way of customs duties, and they were never subjected to a direct levy. In 1704, the king proposed the introduction of the *capitation* or the *taille* to help defray the expenses of the Canadian administration, which always exceeded the revenue, and thenceforth ministers repeatedly urged it on governors and intendants; but the officials in Quebec, knowing full well how stubbornly the habitants were opposed to any imposition, were always afraid to undertake it. Government meant relatively little to these independent frontier people. In so far as it touched them, it had to accommodate itself to them.

This accommodation was sought in various ways by governors

and intendants, and they found it most completely in a new institution born of the frontier—the militia captain of every parish. He was never a seignior, and except in the three little towns, he was always a habitant. Originally a musketry instructor in days when hostile Iroquois prowled about, he grew to be the general factotum of the government. He was its mouth, its eyes, its ears, and its hands. Every Sunday after Mass the parishioners gathered outside the church door, where he read and posted all public notices; and it was his duty, like that of the *curé*, to see that the commands he uttered on Sunday were observed on weekdays. Legally he was the agent of autocracy, for he was a commissioned officer of the government, but practically he was the elected representative of the people. The seignior usually recommended to the governor the person he thought the fittest for this employment, or, in other words, the natural leader of the community. The governor then ordered the appointment to be proposed to the parish at the regular Sunday assembly, and he gave or withheld the commission according as the people approved or disapproved. It is doubtful if our more formal and artificial elections produce as true a representation.

Here was real democracy, faithfully conforming to the familiar North American type. Unlike that of the Old World, the product of a proletarian struggle to gain freedom which existing conditions of life denied, it was rooted in the freedom that very different conditions of life conferred upon the individual and that he would not surrender.

If Turner had looked north, he could not have failed to see that the frontier movement crossed and recrossed the international border, a fact which gives a broader significance to that movement. The Revolution, which stopped the migration of New Englanders to Nova Scotia that had been going on for two decades, presented that province, which still included New Brunswick, with a very different kind of population as soon as the war was over. Some thirty thousand American Loyalists then poured in. Unlike those who had gone before, these people were not impelled by the pioneering urge. They were political refugees with a cultivated and propertied background—that of the "upper crust" of society in the old northern colonies. The government gave them land and subsistence until they could make a living out of it, and their lot was now a hard one. Men who had earned a comfortable living in professions or business were ill fitted for the rough task of cutting farms out of forests, yet they had to do it to support themselves and their families; and women who had found life easy with the aid of servants were out of place in the backwoods, where they too had to toil like beasts of burden. The grinding struggle killed some and drove others away, but the great majority survived by conforming to the frontier type of life that their political principles had forced upon them.

Much happier is the story of the Loyalists, numbering scarcely six thousand, who laid the foundations of Upper Canada, the later Ontario. They were not city-bred folk. They were backwoods farmers from the interior of the old colonies, chiefly New York. When the fighting ceased and their military units were disbanded, they simply resumed their old manner of life in the new country under more favorable auspices; for the government gave them more land than they had lost and material assistance such as they had never known to establish themselves upon it. But they experienced a spell of uneasiness that is rather illuminating. As they could not get the promised freehold titles before the erection of Upper Canada as a separate province in 1791, until which time their townships were technically seigniories, the behavior of some ex-officer magistrates inspired a false local rumor that these gentlemen were conspiring to perpetuate the feudal system, with themselves in the saddle. The atmosphere on the Upper St. Lawrence grew dangerously warm before a special commission of investigation went up from Quebec in the summer of 1787 to open the windows and let in fresh air. The commission's report diagnosed the trouble as "premature puberty." We would call it frontier democracy.

The Upper Canadian Loyalists pulled the American frontier north into British territory. Having improved their lot by settling there, they drew after them relatives and friends, pioneers like themselves, whom they had left behind. Then these friends and relatives did the same. Thus began a process that gathered momentum through the years, for there were no difficulties with Indians in Upper Canada, the land was good, and the government practically gave it away. The oath of allegiance, prescribed for even the original Loyalists, was easy to take along with two hun-

dred acres, while the government rejoiced over the more rapid
development of the country and the prodigals' return to their old
allegiance.

The War of 1812 effectively dammed this flood of land seekers,
and here we may note that, according to some of Turner's disciples, the frontier movement precipitated that war. Many years
ago I swallowed this thesis, but later and more careful examination forced me to reject it as untenable for reasons that I have
already explained elsewhere.[2] With the pacification of the Indians after the Treaty of Ghent, the American frontier movement
resumed its full westward course in this country, while Upper
Canada had to wait a few years before the tide of immigrants from
the British Isles revived the dynamic character of the frontier in
that province. There many an English gentleman got broad lands
which he hoped to develop as a typical English estate, only to find
that the facts of life in a frontier community made it impossible.
Land was too cheap, labor too dear, and individuals too independent.

A cloud of contemporary witnesses testify to the leveling, or,
as one of them termed it, the emulsifying influence that prevailed
in Upper Canadian society.

Such conditions also defeated a more ambitious and important
plan conceived by those in high places who would preserve the
remaining colonies from going the way of the lost ones. Interpret-
ing what had happened as a tragic example of democracy running
wild in the old colonies, they sought to impose an aristocratic
bridle upon it in the infant Upper Canada. The constitution enacted by Parliament for the new province authorized the con-
ferring of hereditary titles upon members of the legislative council, who were all to be appointed, and with these titles a hereditary
right to sit in that chamber, which was thus to be modeled after
the venerable House of Lords. It was understood, as the official
correspondence of the time reveals, that the desired aristocracy
would be built upon a firm foundation by endowing it with liberal grants of Crown lands. The military country gentleman who
was sent out to organize Upper Canada and govern it during the
early years of its existence was consumed with zeal to make it

[2] A. L. Burt, *The United States, Great Britain, and British North America* (New Haven, 1940), Ch. XIII.

"the image and transcript" of England. It was all too absurd for a new country where the only production was agricultural and the soil had to be cleared of timber before it could be cultivated, where virgin land was so plentiful that any man could own and work his own farm, and where even the wealthiest merchants dined with their servants.

In the middle of the nineteenth century, the expansion of Canadian settlement ran up against the rocky pre-Cambrian Shield, with the result that the Canadian frontier movement crossed the border, where it became merged in the greater movement to the northern Middle Western states. The consequent drain of population to the United States, and its attendant contribution through the American West to the prosperity of the American East, inspired Canada with a mounting determination to get a West of her own so that she might keep all her own sons and daughters and the immigrants who were still coming from across the sea. The Dominion was formed in 1867 with an eager eye to acquiring the huge empty lands of the Hudson's Bay Company, and when the federal government took them over, it did everything in its power to people them. But this power could not match that of the American frontier for many a long year. Ottawa could not divert to this more distant Canadian West the human stream that was pouring from Canada into the American West so long as the latter offered free land that was good for ordinary farming.

When this offer petered out in the last decade of the century, the frontier leaped across the border again; and Western Canada came into its own as settlers from the United States, Eastern Canada, the British Isles, and the continent of Europe crowded in to build a new society of agrarian democracy in the great open space of the Canadian prairie. Of the million Americans who moved into it before the outbreak of war in 1914, it has been calculated that approximately half were of Canadian families that had tarried a generation or two in the United States, and it is well known that many others were the children or grandchildren of American immigrants from the British Isles.

In writing on the subject of the frontier, Americans have too commonly failed to see that the movement was North American, not just American in the narrow national sense of the word. About twenty-five years ago, the most distinguished historian of the frontier wrote a little book, *When the West Is Gone,* based on the supposition that the frontier had disappeared. Because he wore a blinker on his north eye, it had simply disappeared from his view when it passed beyond the national boundary, where it was still operating vigorously, as Professor Paul Sharp has since shown.

If Turner had looked north, he might have been tempted to peek around to the other side of the globe in order to check the effect of physical environment on British colonists in North America by a comparison with the effect in Australia and New Zealand, whose white population was drawn almost entirely from the British Isles. There he would have found a striking contrast that throws a flood of light upon his thesis.

Shortly after the gold rush to Australia, which began in 1851, society on that continent became set in a pattern very different from that which was familiar in North America. By a purely fortuitous coincidence, the rush occurred at the very time when the Australian colonies had just received from the British Parliament the power to make their own constitutions; and the pastoral oligarchy, there commonly known as squatters, were using this authority to perpetuate their own political control. It was a crucial turning point in the history of Australia. There might have been a very different tale to tell if the constitutions that emerged from the squatter mold had had time to harden before the lure of gold swamped the country with a population that was strongly imbued with Chartist principles. Indeed, what was left of Chartism in England after the fiasco of 1848 seems to have migrated to Australia. One may wonder why it did not turn up in British North America too, but the reason is quite simple. It had nothing to feed upon in British North American society, which was already democratic, whereas in Australia it encountered a repeated challenge. Although gold did not give Australia responsible government, for that was bound to come soon anyway, it introduced a strong democratic force that quickly altered the shape of the new constitutions. By the end of the decade, the three most populous colonies had adopted manhood suffrage, and by 1890 all the Australian colonies had enacted most of the Chartist program. Meanwhile, another democratic battle was fought and lost.

The swollen population of the gold fields shrank in the late 1850's because the surface deposits were being worked out. The

diggers' day was done, and that of the mining company had come.
How could the stranded diggers make a living? The question was
urgent and the answer seemed easy. It was by tilling the soil, an
occupation that was little developed in that country. On the eve
of the gold discoveries, there were almost as many people in
Australia as there were acres under crop. The gold rush drew
labor from the farms, causing a temporary shrinkage of the cultivated area. Then the new demand for food made it expand. But
at the end of the decade, the balance was much the same as in
1850—scarcely more than one cultivated acre per head of population—and the imports of grain had mounted with the number of
mouths demanding bread. Why could not the country feed itself
with bread as well as meat? The failure of the diggings made
people look around for land on which they might support themselves, and what they found was that most of it was locked up by
the squatters, who had leased it from the Crown for their large
sheep runs. Then began a powerful political drive to unlock the
land and throw it open for agricultural settlement on such easy
terms that any man might there establish his own independence—
as in North America. The squatters lost the initial round of the
battle over the land because they had already lost the political battle
over the franchise. Democratic legislation overrode their leases and
gave anyone who wanted to farm the right to select his own land
and to possess it outright when he had resided on it for three years
and paid the government £1 per acre in easy installments.

This legislation precipitated a conflict similar to that which was
fought between cattlemen and dirt farmers of the semiarid
American West. There seems to have been less violence but more
fraud in the Australian struggle. The fraud was a notorious
scandal, and the government did little or nothing to stop it. Too
many people were too interested in the lax administration of the
new law. Strangers wandered at will over the squatters' holdings
to find choice patches which they "selected" for their strategic
rather than their agricultural value. Such rascals could ruin flock
masters by depriving sheep of access to water, which was scarce;
and in many other ways they could be an intolerable nuisance.
Consequently, the squatters bought them out. To checkmate this
racket of dishonest land selection, which was known as "pea-
cocking," and also to defeat honest selectors, the squatters de-

veloped a racket of their own called "dummying." Using hired "dummies" as well as members of their own families—the law of New South Wales, where the main battle raged, allowed anyone over two years of age to select land—the squatters "picked the eyes" of their own sheep runs and thus acquired ownership of the vital parts of their holdings. The impetus of the struggle also carried many squatters on to take advantage of an earlier law that permitted them to purchase what they were renting. So it came to pass that the land was locked up more securely than ever.

The pastoral industry not only consolidated its position but also extended its geographical domain at this time. Following on the heels of explorers, it invaded the interior of Queensland, where drought was common. As cattle could travel farther for water than could sheep, and since the pastures of the north were more suitable for cattle, Queensland then became the chief cattle area of the continent. It was not until the eighties that the tapping of artesian wells made Queensland also a sheep country. For a while, also, danger lurked in the northern scrub. The aborigines fought the intrusion more strenuously than they had done elsewhere. They murdered isolated white people and even besieged large station households. But the pest declined with "the natural progress of the original race towards extinction," to quote the callous euphemism of a contemporary official.

The price of the ultimate squatter victory was heavy. As the contest dragged on through the 1860's and 1870's, the pastoral industry had to pay out a great deal of cash in order to buy security, which meant that it had to find much additional capital. This the banks supplied and, as a result, the industry emerged with a debt that has burdened it to our own day. Another legacy of those unhappy years was the practical exclusion from public life of the squatters, the most substantial class of men in the country.

Australia has missed the balancing influence that the small independent farmer gave to society on this continent. The population of Australia, unlike that of North America, has been predominantly urban since the early 1860's. The failure to spread the people over the land forced the development of native manufactures for domestic consumption, a development that had begun

in New South Wales before the gold rush and derived some benefit from it. Though the market was small, the distance from England was enormous, and this added so much to the prime cost of
many manufactured goods imported from the mother country
that it was as cheap to produce them in Australia. Thus the cleav-
age between labor and capital was much more pronounced than in
North America. Even farming was more capitalist, while the
grazing, mining, and manufacturing industries were wholly capitalist. The average Australian was not his own economic boss. He
was a wage earner, like the average native of Britain, whence he
had recently come. It was therefore doubly natural that the labor
movement in the mother country should project itself bodily into
Australian society. Before the gold rush, there was very little
trade unionism in Australia. When the rush subsided, there was
much of it; and it spread from the mines and the urban industries
to include the migratory army of shearers on the sheep runs until,
in the late 1880's, it embraced a higher percentage of the population than in any other country in the world. Then it plunged
into politics, forming a Labor party in each of the colonies and
devising a system of party discipline more rigid and more effective
than can be found almost anywhere else in the democratic world.

In form and in spirit, Australian democracy belongs to the Old
World type, and the primary reason for this similarity lies deeper
than any squatter villainy or governmental laxity. Even the strict-
est enforcement of the conditions that the selection laws prescribed
could not have made Australia a nation of small independent
farmers such as grew in this country and in Canada. Heaven had
decreed otherwise, by withholding the necessary rainfall. Nature
made the heart of North America the largest and richest and
solidest agricultural region in the world, but it made the heart of
Australia a desert. What the squatters defeated was really an
attempt to break up their great pastoral estates for the sake of
planting a few small farmers on the occasional pieces that could
grow crops, which would have been more wasteful than the extravagant slaughter of the buffalo on our plains for the sake of their
tongues, then counted a delicacy. It was not for lack of trying that
Australians failed to build a society like that which our forebears
built almost unconsciously on this continent.

To drive home the point of this contrast between Australia and

North America, one has only to glance at what happened in New Zealand, where a struggle similar to that of Australia had a very different outcome. Half a century after the founding of New Zealand in 1840, that colony was in the doldrums. Immigration had fallen off until it was exceeded by emigration. In the South Island, where most of the population then lived because of troubles with the Maoris in the North Island, the land was largely monopolized by a pastoral oligarchy whose influence had long dominated the government.

Then came a political upheaval born of desperation and released by a reform of the electoral system in 1889. The reform was the abolition of plural voting, which had enabled property owners to stultify manhood suffrage from the time of its adoption some years before. The political upheaval, which occurred when the people went to the polls in 1890, soon wrought a veritable revolution in the life of New Zealand. The first important measure of the new regime reversed the principle of taxation that had prevailed in the colony. In place of a property tax that was regressive in character and inelastic in yield, it substituted a land and income tax that was progressive in incidence and produced an expanding revenue. This act of 1891 also provided for self-assessment and, as a check upon it, gave the government the right to purchase at the assessed value. The owners of one huge estate tried to bluff the administration into accepting a reduced assessment, and they paid for it by the enforced sale of the whole property, which was then broken up and settled with land-hungry people who had been collected in the towns.

This was the beginning of a rural transformation that was speeded by further enabling legislation in the early 1890's and by the opening of an abundance of Crown lands in the North Island, which Maori hostility had preserved from falling into the clutches of big sheep owners. New Zealand then became a nation of small independent farmers who formed the backbone of society as they did here. This achievement of the New Zealanders, coming on top of the failure of their cousins in Australia, is rather striking. But it is not at all surprising because New Zealand had what Australia lacked—a combination of soil and climate that was ideal for close agricultural settlement over most of the country.

A little knowledge of contrasting Australian experience thus brings out the fact that the pattern of life which we inherited, and which has been a source of no little pride, was shaped more by nature and less by man than we have been wont to admit. Even if Turner had looked no farther than Canada, he might have taught his disciples this wholesome lesson in humility, though not so forcefully; for north of the international border he would have found abundant evidence that the frontier of which he wrote was not peculiar to the United States.

Here we touch upon what is perhaps the most serious criticism that can be leveled at the Turner school. It is that they have studied and written as national historians without realizing that the besetting sin of national history, in this as in every other country, is too exclusive a concern with what has happened within its own borders. To avoid this insidious snare is not easy, for nationalism by its very nature is introspective and given to self-glorification. If Frederick Jackson Turner and his followers fell into this sin, they are not alone. They have plenty of company.

SELECTED READINGS

Adair, E. R. "The French Canadian Seigneury," *Canadian Historical Review*, XXXV (September, 1954), 187–207.

Burt, A. L. *The Old Province of Quebec*. Minneapolis: University of Minnesota Press, 1933.

———. *The United States, Great Britain, and British North America*. New Haven: Yale University Press, 1940.

———. *A Short History of Canada for Americans*. 2d ed. Minneapolis: University of Minnesota Press, 1944.

———. *The Evolution of the British Empire and Commonwealth from the American Revolution*. Boston: D. C. Heath, 1956.

Hansen, M. L. and Brebner, J. B. *The Mingling of the Canadian and American Peoples*. New Haven: Yale University Press, 1940.

Langton, W. A. (ed.). *Early Days in Upper Canada: Letters of John Langton*. Toronto: Macmillan, 1926.

Munro, W. B. *The Seignorial System in Canada*. Cambridge, Mass.: Harvard University Press, 1907.

Paxson, F. L. *When the West Is Gone*. New York: H. Holt, 1930.

Pratt, J. W. *The Expansionists of 1812*. New York: Macmillan, 1925.

Rose, J. Holland, *et al.* (eds.). *The Cambridge History of the British Empire*, Vol. VII. Cambridge: Cambridge University Press, 1933.

Sharp, P. F. *The Agrarian Revolt in Western Canada*. Minneapolis: University of Minnesota Press, 1948.

Wright, B. F., Jr. "American Democracy and the Frontier," *Yale Review*, XX (Winter, 1931), 349–365.

A. LOBANOV-ROSTOVSKY

Russian Expansion in the Far East in the Light of the Turner Hypothesis

The history of Russia, says Professor Lobanov-Rostovsky, is the history of expansion toward the Pacific by a Caucasian people. In this eastward movement he notes the similarities between the American and the Russian frontier experiences. Both peoples moved in diverse directions toward the Pacific. Both had a jumping-off-place: the Ural and the Mississippi-Missouri Rivers. Both moved into an area inhabited by natives. The Russian pioneers were Cossacks interested in furs and silver and in trading with the backward peoples. These soldier-traders built posts and upon occasion fought the natives. They were followed by an organized emigration of prisoners and peasants who settled first around the forts and, much later, along the Trans-Siberian Railway. Promoters and wealthy adventurers followed these waves of settlers. Both individual initiative and government policy played significant parts in this process.

While Professor Lobanov-Rostovsky describes a frontier that has many similarities to the American, he also sees significant differences. The Russians spent six hundred years getting to the Urals and one hundred moving from there to the Pacific, a much longer period of conquest than the United States required. The Russian frontier ran into the expansion movement in northern and western China, which deeply influenced its character and direction; and *conflict long characterized the relationship between the Chinese and Russian frontiers.*

"SCRATCH a Russian and you will find a Tartar" was the saying coined by Polish *émigrés* in Paris after the Polish Revolution in 1831 to win sympathy for their cause against the Russians. Earlier, in 1799, Nougaret, the French historian, wrote of "a catastrophe which seems to be preparing before our eyes and which may make the second Rome fall into the power of the Tartars who are now called Russians." [1] In both cases, the propaganda implication of horror and danger by associating the Russians with the ruthless Asiatic conquerors was obvious and could be explained in the first case by the failure of the Polish insurrection, in the second by the Russian army's conquering Italy under Suvorov and menacing France. But the question of whether Russia belongs to East or West, whether she may be regarded as the vanguard of Asia menacing European civilization or as the bulwark of Europe against Asia, was hotly debated in Russia itself at the time.

To answer this question, one must turn to the impartial verdict of geography and the role of the frontier in Russian history. The pertinent fact is that the history of Russia is a history of the colonization of the vast expanse stretching from the Baltic to the Pacific by a Caucasian people, the Slavs, whose original home was in east-central Europe, approximately eastern Germany, Poland, and western Russia. Hence this colonization moved west-east, towards Asia, and not from Asia. Furthermore, by obtaining their religion, their written script, and the basis of their culture from Byzantium, these Slavs had definitely associated themselves with the cultural stream of Christian Greco-Roman civilization and not with the great competing Asiatic civilizations such as the Persian, Arabic, or even Chinese.

But nature abhors a vacuum and the Great Russian or Eurasian plain was just such a vacuum. Hemmed in to the south and to the east by great Asiatic empires, this vast expanse sucked into it the restless barbarian tribes from the fringe areas, and they spread as a thin layer over it and became dissolved in it. Thus came the

[1] A. A. Vasiliev, *History of the Byzantine Empire, 324–1453* (2d English ed., rev., Madison, Wis., 1952), 12.

Sarmatians, Scythians, and other Indo-European or Iranian tribes and the subsequent waves of Turco-Mongol peoples ranging from the Huns, the Avars, the Khazars, the Bulgars, and the Magyars to the Pechenegs and Cumans—roughly fifteen hundred years of continuous invasions from Asia, limited, however, to the broad belt of the steppes north of the Black Sea. Further to the north stretched the limitless forest, across which veins were cut by slow, meandering rivers. There the Slavs settled amidst peaceful Finnish folk; here along its western fringe passed the Goths on their trek south from Sweden, down the rivers. Had there not been the lure of trade down these same rivers to the great markets of Byzantium and of the Arabic East as far as Bagdad, it is possible that the Asiatic invaders, nomads preferring the wide expanse of the steppe, would never have clashed with the Russians.

But the Russians trespassed upon the nomad by coming out into the steppe. Kiev, the capital of the first Russian state, was boldly set in the plain outside of the forest zone, and the war was on—a war of attrition which lasted four centuries, roughly from the ninth to the thirteenth century, a war between Europe and Asia fought not west-east, but north-south. In this war, the Russian state, with a more intricate political organization and a highly promising and rapidly rising Christian civilization, had the advantage over the nomadic tribes, but it was drained of its strength by this everlasting task of keeping the nomad at bay. Then in the thirteenth century, the pattern reversed itself. Kiev and the whole of the forest zone of Russia fell prey to the Chinese-trained Mongol armies led by a conqueror of genius, who had overnight created the greatest empire the world was to see. For the next two and a half centuries, the Russian principalities were to be integrated into the vast Mongol dominion stretching from Korea to Bagdad, and Western Europe forgot Russia since Russia had become a part of Great Tartary. But the Mongols themselves looked upon Russia as a European colony that could be ruled by remote control from their capital, Sarai, on the lower reaches of the Volga. Hence Russia's national consciousness was not lost, and it rallied around a new center—Moscow. Moscow reunited Russia under the Tartars and then threw off the Mongol yoke in 1480.

The weakened Mongol state could not oppose this resurgence of Russia. The Mongols had ruled a Russia divided into many prin-

cipalities, but now the roles were reversed. Moscow had reunited
these states into one powerful state, while the Mongol Khanate
was breaking up into three weak states. These could not any
longer oppose the Russian drive into Asia.

It is well to stop here and draw a parallel between the westward
movement in America and the eastward movement of the
Russians, both aimed at the same goal, i.e., the Pacific, but in
reverse directions, the great difference being the time lag, the
Russian movement being infinitely slower. It took the Russians
some six centuries to reach the Ural mountains and then a century more to reach the Pacific. The reason for this was the
onrush of counterinvasions from Asia, which like breakers sub-
merged the Russians or blocked their advance, while in the westward drive in America the greatest resistance came from local
Indian tribes.

Thus the pivotal point in Russian history was attained when the
course of the Volga was reached and incorporated into Russia by
the middle of the sixteenth century. Indeed, in 1552 and 1556,
Ivan the Terrible conquered the two fragments of the Mongol
Empire which had survived to the east of Moscow, the Khanates
of Kazan and Astrakhan, both situated on the Volga. This ended
the centuries-old duel for the possession of the Eurasian plain
between Russia and Asia, and fate decreed that henceforth the
Russians were to be its masters. The logic of history and geography
seemed also to prove that states of various races could not cohabit
peacefully on this plain and that the domination of the whole
plain from one center, i.e., Moscow, was to become unavoidable
through the very nature of the plain.

The Volga thus enters Russian history much as the Mississippi
with the Louisiana Purchase enters United States history. It becomes the economic backbone of Russia, the river of legend, song,
and tradition, and more important, the jumping-off-place for the
great drive to the Pacific Ocean, much like the Mississippi three
centuries later, for the westward drive. Thus, the axis of Russian
colonization and advance, after having been northeast in the
preceding centuries, changes to due east. The drive east beyond
the Volga opened immediately, and thirty years after the fall of
Kazan, in 1581, a band of Cossacks under Yermak crosses the
Ural mountains and conquers Western Siberia up to the Irtish

River. Once the drive had started, it could not be stopped, and by the 1640's both the Pacific Ocean and the Amur River, the boundary with China, had been reached. In 1697, Kamchatka was annexed, and throughout the second half of the eighteenth century Russian pioneers crossed the Bering Straits and settled in Alaska.

The technique of this expansion originally resembled the conquest of the overseas empire by Spain but later came to resemble more and more the American westward drive. At first, bands of adventurers led by conquistadors were driven into the wilderness by the urge for finding wealth in the nature of silver and furs. That these adventurers were Cossacks and that their leaders were known as *Atamans,* be they a Yermak, a Vlassiev, or an Atlassov, did not change the picture. They fought their way with firearms against bows and arrows. Yermak with eight hundred men broke the resistance of some thirty thousand men defending the capital of Khan Kuchum, Sibir. Vlassiev with one hundred and thirty men conducted a fierce war against many thousand Buriats in the region of Lake Baikal, while Atlassov all but exterminated the peaceful Kamchadals. On occasion, these bands were accompanied by priests who baptized the natives but were unable or unwilling to restrain the Cossacks from committing terrible atrocities. The territory once conquered, the Cossacks would erect a fort (an *Ostrog*), and its garrison, perhaps fifty men, would patrol hundreds of miles of adjacent territory. Behind these screens the peasant-colonist would settle, government administration would be established, a *Voevoda* or governor responsible to the Siberian Department in Moscow would be appointed. Little by little, cities grew out of the forts and Siberia became more and more the extension of Russia proper, with the natives either dying out or assuming the position of the American Indians.

Two striking idiosyncrasies of Russian colonization, however, must be mentioned. The first was the systematic use made by the government of the Cossacks from about the middle of the eighteenth century for the purpose of colonization. Prior to that, the Cossacks were bands of adventurers acting pretty much on their own. Now they were formed into "hosts" or irregular cavalry and were used for the purpose of advance colonization and as a protective screen. Thus a chain of Cossack hosts came into existence and were planted as "hedges" along the advancing frontier: first came the Ural (or Yaik) Cossack host, then the Seven River host, then the Transbaikal host, then finally the Amur and Maritime hosts at the turn of the twentieth century along the borders of Manchuria and Korea. The second feature to be noticed is that the Russian is not racially minded and shows no discrimination toward the natives. Though the Siberian colonist would often cruelly exploit them and take advantage of their ignorance and credulity, he treated them as equals and made no attempts to change their way of life or religion. If the natives became Christian and orthodox, the Russian would consider them members of his own family and would intermarry freely with them. If there was any distinction, it would be more along religious than racial lines.

The question arises at this point whether it is possible to apply the Turner theory to the Siberian frontier and what similarities or dissimilarities can be found in comparing the westward movement in America and the eastward movement in Russia. If we compare the Cossacks with the pioneers—which can be done without straining the point if we limit ourselves to the earlier days before the Cossacks were organized into a semiregular military force, we will find that the starting point and the goal of both movements are the same. Furthermore, the Cossack turns from warrior and conqueror to trader, or, as the expansion proceeds, the trader joins him. The demand for the furs, silver, and other wealth of Siberia led to the supplying of the native with arms, liquor, and primitive manufactures, thus creating what Turner calls the "trading frontier." In both western America and in Siberia the resistance was sporadic. After the opposition of Mahmetkul's forces was broken by Yermak, the Khirgiz tried to block the southern expansion and the Buriats fought desperately to preserve their independence in the region of Lake Baikal. After their resistance was broken, it was not till the Russians reached the Amur River that they again met determined warlike foes. These were the Daurians, bolstered up by Chinese regulars. Thus the fighting did not have the unifying and consolidating effect of bringing the whites together which the Indian wars did in the United States. Moreover, by the turn of the eighteenth century all fighting had ceased in Siberia, which was henceforth strongly governed by a centralized administration directed from the capital. Peaceful colonization replaced what might be termed the "heroic age" of conquest. The nineteenth century did see an organized military drive, but only in Central Asia.

Turner describes the colonization of the frontier as proceeding in three waves. Quoting Peck's *Guide to the West,* published in 1837, he mentions first the pioneers who occupy and start exploiting the land; then the emigrants who purchase the land and open it up by building roads, bridges, etc.; and finally, capital enterprise which builds the cities and industries. The first and third waves are found in Siberia in a fairly clear-cut fashion; the second wave differs considerably owing to special conditions in Russia.

Cossacks went in their boats along northern rivers, sent bands out in every direction, brought the natives under subjection, built ostrogs. After them came the fur traders. Hunters scattered in the forests far across the subjugated territory and built themselves huts and small blockhouses. They formed *artels*—co-operatives—for hunting and fishing, they prospected ores. . . .[2]

and again

the Cossacks saw that men can live in this country. There was plenty of freedom there, an abundant nature, and a scarcity of authorities. They determined to settle there.[3]

So much for the first phase. The second wave was composed of prisoners and peasant colonists evading the hardships of serfdom in Russia proper. Both have to be examined in more detail, since Siberia owes its development to these two elements.

The idea of using Siberia as a penal settlement seems to have appeared in Moscow shortly after the conquest. The great jail in Nerchinsk in eastern Siberia was erected in the 1730's, while in the same period many leading statesmen of the day who had fallen out of favor were sent in exile to Beriozov, a city far north in western Siberia. These included such men as Princes Menshikov and Dolgoruky, General Münnich, and others. Thus from the outset, a distinction was made between *katorga* (hard labor) and *ssylka* (exile). When in the 1750's Empress Elizabeth abolished

[2] Yuri Semyonov [Iurii Nikolaevich Semenov], *The Conquest of Siberia . . .* (London, 1944), 102.

[3] *Ibid.,* 105.

the death penalty for ordinary nonpolitical crimes, Siberia received a further influx of life termers. This forced colonization brought into Siberia two elements—on one side the hardened criminal, on the other the most enlightened, cultured, and advanced strata of society. To the latter belonged the so-called Decembrists (the later Nihilists), the cream of Russian aristocracy, involved in the revolutionary outbreak of 1825. A great many of these, after having served their terms, remained permanently in Siberia and contributed powerfully to the development of the country. In the main, however, the criminal element far outnumbered the political exiles. It has been calculated that during the nineteenth century somewhere between eight hundred thousand and a million prisoners were sent to Siberia, of which the political cases represented some 10 to 15 per cent. As the revolutionary movement grew in virulence after 1860, the number of political cases increased. But on the other hand, toward the end of the century most of the *katorga* cases were transferred from eastern Siberia to the island of Sakhalin.

The free peasant colonization of Siberia, which by the very nature of the case caused that land to become a haven for runaway serfs, was strenuously fought by the government. After the liberation of the serfs in 1861, this colonization was still frowned upon by the government and remained limited, though schemes of organized settlement were very occasionally put into effect without too much success. A natural hindrance was the problem of transportation. In the 1880's, for instance, an attempt was made to bring settlers to coastal regions near Vladivostok by the sea route around Asia.

The situation changed completely after the building of the Trans-Siberian Railway and the Russo-Japanese war. Under the energetic sponsorship of Stolypin, the last great statesman of the Tsarist regime, a special department of internal immigration was created which earmarked the land available for colonization in Siberia, provided free transportation, monetary aid, and agricultural implements for volunteer settlers. This policy resulted in the settling of some four million peasants in western Siberia in the great agricultural belt along the Trans-Siberian Railway. Under the Soviet regime, as already noticed, the colonization of Siberia has become one of the main concerns of the government and all methods have been used from "slave labor" camps to rendering free settlement more enticing by grant of special privileges, coupled with widespread industrial development of the area.

The coming to life of Siberia in the nineteenth century produced the appearance of the third type mentioned by Turner, namely, the capitalist and industrial promoter. A special type of the Siberian millionaire came into existence. Like his American counterpart of the sixties and seventies, he was a rugged individualist, adventurous, energetic, often ruthless. He loved ostentation and was proud to show off his acquired wealth. There is a story about such a millionaire hiring all the droshkies (horse-drawn taxis) in one of the larger cities of Siberia and forming a procession of empty droshkies through the city streets, led by himself in the first droshky, to impress the citizens with his power and wealth. However, again like his American counterpart, he generously donated his money for philanthropic or civic purposes, and many Siberian cities boasted fine school and hospital buildings bearing the name of the donor. It is curious to note that this type is to be found as far back as the seventeenth century. Indeed, Khabarov, the great explorer of the Amur region in the 1650's, was a peasant from Veliki-Ustug in Russia, who had made a fortune in Siberia in salt and real estate and who equipped his expedition down the Amur at his own cost.

The importance of Siberia as a colony to Russia may be seen by the growth of the population. By 1662, the population of Siberia was around seventy thousand. Fifty years later it was two hundred and fifty thousand, and a post road with regular mail service had reached Yakutsk on the Lena. In 1822, the growth of Siberia necessitated an administrative split into two governor-generalships, one for western Siberia and one for eastern Siberia. By 1914, the population had risen to nine million, and at present it is around forty million.

This drift of the population, though far from filling the empty spaces of eastern Siberia, produced the inevitable result of overflowing into neighboring areas beyond its borders. It must be remembered that Siberia is encompassed on the north by the Arctic Ocean and on the east by the Pacific. The only overflow possible was east into Alaska and only a handful of the hardened pioneers

went across the Bering Straits. The greater mass drifted across the
land frontier to the south and thus the first contact with China
was established. It started as early as the beginning of the sixteenth
century, when the early conquerors of western Siberia made their
way up the Irtish and penetrated into Dzungaria (west of Mongolia), the home of nomads owing a loose allegiance to the emperors of China. It was through this contact that tea was received
in Russia and became the national drink. Also, since this territory
was inhabited by the Kara Kitans, Kitai remained the name given
to China in the Russian language. Half a century later, the
Russians sailed down the Amur River and began to infiltrate into
Manchuria, along its tributaries. This led to a thirty-year undeclared war with emperors of the newly established Manchu dynasty, who were particularly sensitive to this Russian colonization
of their homeland. The war was concluded by the treaty of Nerchinsk in 1689, which forced the Russians to evacuate not only
Manchuria but the valley of the Amur River as well. But the
Russians gained the inestimable advantage of the right to trade
freely in China a century and a half before the other powers of
Europe. It is interesting to note that this is the first of the three
times in history when the Russians made an attempt to settle in
Manchuria; the second time was in the 1890's and the third
during the final months of World War II. They were never able
to stay. The logic of history and geography seems to have drawn a
line to their colonization, saying thus far and no farther—and this
line is the Amur River.

The Treaty of Nerchinsk supplemented by a treaty in 1727
established peaceful and friendly relations between Russia and
China for well-nigh two centuries. Russian diplomacy was occupied elsewhere, and the Far East faded out of the picture. Perhaps
we may call this period, which lasts up to the middle of the nineteenth century, a time of sporadic accidental exploration and
expansion. Certainly the movement of Cossacks into Manchuria
and of pioneers into Alaska was spontaneous, while the Russian
Academy of Sciences in coöperation with the navy had initiated
in the eighteenth century a vast scheme of exploration and geo-
detic survey of the coasts of Siberia, and owing to this Russian
vessels found themselves in Japanese waters. The second and much
more important phase opens in the 1850's.

This chapter starts as a result of the double impact of England and the United States on the Far East. The treaty of Nanking signed by the Chinese after the loss of the Opium War in 1842 had opened the China Coast to British trade and had resulted in the cession of Hongkong to Britain. Eleven years later, Perry carried out his successful venture to open Japan. These two events changed the balance of power in the Far East and deeply affected Russia's interests, particularly since the Anglo-Russian rivalry in western and central Asia was reaching a culminating point. Worried that the coast of Siberia on the Pacific was completely undefended and that the British, having established themselves in the treaty ports along the coast of China, had merely to push a little northwards to reach the mouth of the Amur, Czar Nicholas I appointed an energetic young governor-general, Muraviev, to eastern Siberia with the task of making Russia's coastline secure.

Muraviev lost no time. He founded a naval base at Petropavlovsk, Kamchatka, and ordered a naval explorer, Captain Nevelskoy, to sail around the Sea of Okhotsk to find a better base. The latter, sailing up the River Amur in a sloop, annexed the territory north of the river (which nominally belonged to China) and on August 6, 1850, established a base a few miles upstream. The resulting diplomatic conflict with China ended with the signing of treaties in 1858 and 1860 in which China ceded not only the territory north of the Amur but also the coast of the Pacific from the mouth of the Amur to the Korean border. Here in a fine bay was founded the city of Vladivostok, which became the definitive Russian naval base on the Pacific and later the terminal of the Trans-Siberian Railway. The border between China and Russia drawn in 1860 has remained the same to the present day. This completed the expansion of Russia on the mainland of Asia. But opposite the newly acquired coast stretched the island of Sakhalin, populated by Ainus. Japan claimed the island as an extension of the Japanese Archipelago, north of Hokkaido. The energetic Nevelskoy sent his lieutenant Boshniak on dog sleigh across the frozen straits of Tartary and the Russians took possession of Sakhalin as well in 1852.

The very next year and exactly at the same time that Perry was in Japanese waters, a Russian squadron composed of three vessels under Admiral Putiatin sailed into Nagasaki Bay with the mission of obtaining for Russia what Admiral Perry was demanding for the United States, namely, the opening of Japan to Russian trade and navigation. Putiatin was instructed not to use force but to achieve his ends through patience and diplomacy. Though Putiatin lost his flagship, which was sunk in a tidal wave following an earthquake, he was able to achieve his goal by the signing of the treaty of Shimoda in February, 1855. There remained, however, friction with Japan over the seizure of Sakhalin. Still too weak to face Russia, Japan came to terms with Russia by accepting an exchange of Sakhalin for the Kurile Islands in 1873. Thus came to an end the second wave of Russian expansion, which, in contrast to the earlier unorganized, glacierlike advance, was carried out by diplomatic and naval means.

The third phase, which opens in the 1890's, introduces a new factor into the picture. As a result of the industrial revolution gaining momentum in Russia, we now enter the period of economic imperialism and the scramble for foreign markets. Not being able as yet to compete successfully with the more highly developed industrial nations, Russian industry profited by the geographical advantage of having an undeveloped area along the Siberian border, which was relatively remote from the ports of entry for western manufactured goods. Thus a belt of territory running from northern Persia through Sinkiang to Manchuria came within the economic orbit of Russia, and here all the earmarks of economic imperialism were displayed, from obtaining concessions for the development of these areas to the establishment of banks to carry out the required transactions. Thus Russian financiers founded the Discount Bank of Persia to be followed with the aid of French capital by the Russo-Chinese Bank and the Bank of Mongolia. Railway building kept pace, so far on Russian territory. In the 1880's, the Russians built the Transcaspian Railway from Krasnovodsk on the Caspian to the gates of Sinkiang. This railway skirted the northern border of Persia, and a branch line led to the border of Afghanistan. After the revolution, the Transcaspian was extended through the Turk-Sib to link up with the Trans-Siberian, encompassing western and northern Sinkiang. The Trans-Siberian, built a decade later, reached the Pacific at Vladivostok and encircled China from the north. Next came the phase of building on foreign soil.

The spectacular defeat of China at the hands of Japan in 1895, revealing the weakness of the decadent Manchu Empire, initiated this phase. The Li-Lobanov treaty of 1896 gave Russia the right to build across northern Manchuria a railway which was named the Chinese Eastern Railway. A branch line cut southward from Harbin to the Yellow Sea at Port Arthur. In the twentieth century, the Russians built a railway to Tabriz in Persia, and in our own days a branch line of the Trans-Siberian was extended to Ulan Bator, the capital of Mongolia, and now has been extended across the Gobi to Peiping.

The next phase following the signing of the Li-Lobanov treaty of 1896 resulted in the nearly complete absorption of Manchuria by the seizure of the Liaotung Peninsula with two ice-free ports, Port Arthur and Talienwan, the first of these converted by Russia into a naval base and the second, renamed Dalny, into a commercial port. Strengthened by the Anglo-Japanese alliance of 1902, Japan struck back and the Russo-Japanese war put an end to what may be termed the period of runaway Russian imperialism.

Considering the gravity of the defeat inflicted upon Russia by Japan, the destruction of Russian naval power at Tsushima, and the revolution breaking out in Russia, the treaty of Portsmouth, which ended the war, was most favorable to Russia. She retained northern Manchuria and the Chinese Eastern Railway, ceding to Japan half of Sakhalin, Port Arthur, and Dalny and approximately half of the branch line leading from the main trunk of the Chinese Eastern Railway to these ports. She also acknowledged Japan's right to a free hand in Korea. Russian diplomacy took a realistic view after this disastrous war and let bygones be bygones. By the agreement with Japan in 1907, a division of spheres of influence in the Far East eliminated all points of conflict between the two countries. Manchuria was divided by a line passing through Changchun (Hsinking), and Russian influence was consolidated over northern Manchuria, through which passed the Chinese Eastern Railway. Japan similarly was given control over southern Korea, which she annexed in 1910, while in compensation Japan acknowledged Russia's interests in Mongolia. Thus Mongolia, which after the Chinese Revolution had proclaimed its independence from China, became the next field for Russian economic and political penetration.

The subsequent World War, the Russian Revolution, and the

collapse of Russia invalidated the whole picture and it looked for a moment as if the Russian factor had been eliminated from eastern Asia. Between 1919 and 1922, all frontiers disappeared in anarchy, and the contending White and Red Russian armies swept freely over the Manchurian and Mongolian borders, Japan occupied eastern Siberia up to Lake Baikal, and the Chinese Eastern Railway passed under Allied control. But when the new order, i.e., the Soviet regime, finally emerged out of the chaos and brought Russian Asia under its control again, a remarkable and significant thing happened. The border was once more restored as of 1914, or more exactly as of 1860, proving that the logic of geography and history demanded the restoration of this line. The next milestone in this long procession of history was the Sino-Soviet agreement of 1924 which brought Russian influence back into Manchuria, and the administration of the Chinese Eastern Railway was placed on a joint fifty-fifty basis between Russia and China. Concomitantly, the same year saw the proclamation of a Soviet republic in Mongolia, thereby eliminating the weak theocratic regime of the Khutukhtu which had precariously ruled independent Mongolia. The Chinese were perturbed, and in 1929 Chang Hsueh Liang, the Manchurian war lord, attempted to drive the Russians out of Manchuria. This brought swift Soviet retaliation, and in an undeclared war the Soviets reasserted their hold over northern Manchuria and the railway by a lightning invasion by the Red Army. Thus the pendulum swung in favor of the Soviets, who were rapidly regaining their strength in Asia. But just as dramatically the pendulum swung to the other extreme, when Japan in 1931 embarked on her great conquest of Asia, partly because of the great fear of Russian resurgence.

Once more the stage seemed to be set in the Far East for a headlong clash between Russian and Japanese imperialism, with a weak and divided China paying the costs; only the roles were now reversed, with Japan aggressively pushing forward in Manchuria and the Soviets on the defensive, particularly in view of the Hitler menace on their European border. Notwithstanding hundreds of armed clashes along the Amur and Ussuri borders, war was avoided. But the inner workings of obscure historical forces were actually favoring China. Millions of Chinese were settling in Manchuria under Japanese occupation, making it more

Chinese than it ever was. The evanescent hold of Japan on the conquered territories in Asia was revealed by World War II, and on the surface Russia seemed to have garnered the fruits of Allied victory in Asia. Indeed, the all-time high watermark of Russian expansion was achieved by Russia in 1945 with the return of Sakhalin and the Kurile Islands.

But the postwar years revealed a different outline, gradually shaping itself, of the real balance of forces in Asia. For one thing, the collapse of Japan, coupled with the expansion of Russian influence, produced the appearance of the United States as a balancing factor in Asia as revealed by the Korean War. For another, whatever be the temporary ideological alignment between Russia and China, the factor determining the future is the rapid transformation of China into a first-class military and, possibly later, industrial power. China is usurping the position previously held by Japan. In the past, when China was strong, she tended to overflow into the neighboring belt of states, be it Mongolia, Sinkiang, Tibet, or Annam. A similar trend is visible at present under Communist rule and may form an automatic barrier to further Russian expansion. Thus the belt of territories lying between the Siberian border and the Great Wall of China, nominally Chinese but in reality the field for Russian economic and political penetration, will inevitably become more and more the bone of contention between the two great Communist powers of Asia, and the Chinese are showing an active interest in countering Russian economic development by their own. For example, the Russian railway network reaches the gates of Sinkiang, while the Chinese are constructing a line from Lanchow to Urumchi (Tihwa) and thus linking up with the Russian railheads. It must be remembered that if Siberia is the land of the future for Russia and is being colonized and industrialized by Russia, the territories stretching from Sinkiang to Manchuria play the same role for China. Thus demographically and economically, both countries are coming nearer to each other, and their borders, previously separated by vast desert regions, are now becoming contiguous in reality, not only on maps. Though it must be granted that China has a long way to go to become economically developed, it must not be forgotten that Russia changed herself in two generations from a weak economy to a leading industrial nation. This seems to be the main problem and the main trend in the balance of power of Asia. Whatever the present alignment or ideological conformities, the day may not be so far off when Russia will be on the defensive on her Siberian border, as this border once more proves to be the real frontier between Slav and Chinese.

Thus if the Turner hypothesis is in the main applicable to the Siberian frontier, as we have seen, it is equally applicable to China's far western and northern frontiers, and to understand the real balance of forces in Asia we have to consider a situation which Turner did not have to face, namely, the existence of two parallel, expanding, and competing frontiers. It is this aspect of the frontier problem that makes the greatest difference in the development of the American and Russian frontiers.

SELECTED READINGS

Dallin, D. J. *The Rise of Russia in Asia.* New Haven: Yale University Press, 1949.

Golder, F. A. *Russian Expansion on the Pacific, 1681–1850.* Cleveland: Arthur H. Clark, 1914.

Lobanov-Rostovsky, A. *Russia and Asia.* New York: Macmillan, 1933. Rev. ed., Ann Arbor: Wahr's, 1951.

Semyonov, Yuri [Iurii Nikolaevich Semenov]. *The Conquest of Siberia, an Epic of Human Passions.* London: G. Routledge & Sons, 1944. Orig. pub. at Berlin, 1937.

Vladimir. *Russia on the Pacific and the Siberian Railway.* London: Sampson Low & Co., 1899.

EUGENE P. BOARDMAN

Chinese Mandarins and Western Traders: The Effect of the Frontier in Chinese History

The role of the frontier in Chinese history has been significant, writes Professor Boardman, but its contribution was much different from that which has been attributed to the American frontier. The Turner hypothesis does not apply to China, though its implications do: the environment and developments of a borderland can deeply influence a nation.

This penetrating essay deals with the northern frontier of China over many centuries. It shows how the absence of rainfall made that borderland a grazing area inhabited by herdsmen. South of that region was a farming society that built walls around its villages and even the Great Wall to protect itself from these barbarian frontiersmen. The threat of invasion was ever present, and this real danger conditioned the attitudes and habits of thought of Chinese leaders toward all foreigners. Even when the English traders came by sea, they too were barbarians and should pay tribute. The Chinese were a superior people and to them all barbarians must kowtow. This frontier influence was a disservice to China, for it gave the nation an inadequate set of attitudes to meet the demands of the nineteenth and twentieth centuries when the West entered aggressively into Eastern commercial affairs.

The Chinese frontier was much different from the moving

*frontiers of Russia and the United States. It was generally fixed. It
was the direction from which the invader came. It provided no
land of opportunity for the masses. In this sense, the Chinese frontier was unique among those surveyed in this volume.*

SO far as this writer has been able to discover, Frederick Jackson
Turner never wrote about China. His thinking was directed
mainly to the North American frontier. This was not by his own
account "a fortified boundary line running through dense populations," but a line of settlement marked by the presence on its
farther side of a vast amount of unoccupied land. To the existence
of this kind of frontier, Turner ascribed the nationalization of the
American government and the formation of a composite nation-
ality for the American people. The presence of free land conferred opportunity on all for a competency. That possibility amid
universal hardships and necessity for hard work bred individualism and democratic institutions—institutions that elevated the
position of the individual. Resourcefulness, optimism, exuberance, largeness of design were the traits which the frontier experience brought out in the American make-up. In Turner's
words, "For a moment, at the frontier, the bonds of custom are
broken and unrestraint is triumphant." [1] Frontiersmen brought to
the rim of settlement their differences of culture and Old World
backgrounds, but the struggle with the unoccupied land, he said,
furnished an element that was unique in the creation of American
institutions.

Critics of the Turner thesis deny that the frontier created
democratic institutions; instead, the pioneers brought their distinctive institutions to the frontier from farther east. Till 1890,
the city was far more of a safety valve for the discontented than
was free land at the frontier. In contrast to Turner's conception,
the frontier was simply the growing edge of Western European
civilization. Turner is too preoccupied with environment, too
narrowly sectional, and too materialistic. "In what it [the Turner
thesis] proposes," George Wilson Pierson concludes, "the frontier
hypothesis needs painstaking revision. By what it fails to mention,

[1] Frederick Jackson Turner, *The Frontier in American History* (New York,
1920), 38.

the theory today disqualifies itself as an adequate guide to American development." [2]

It is certainly improper—even if it were possible—for me to determine the applicability of the Turner thesis to what has happened along the borders of settlement in North America. I can express, however, my gratitude for two of Turner's implications. First, what happens along borders is important and should be watched for its influence on attitudes and institutions. Second, the factor of environment at the frontier may be especially important. These seem particularly applicable to Chinese history.

I now propose to explore the role which China's historic northern frontier has had, especially its influence upon the development of attitudes and institutions which the Chinese used in dealing with Western traders in the nineteenth century. What I have to say is based upon the researches of a Far Eastern counterpart of the Turner school, whose writings are subsequently listed.

We begin with the great northern frontier of China indicated roughly by the line of the Great Wall. This stretches from the plains of southern Manchuria past the arid wastes of Inner Mongolia and across the old silk road, soon to be the roadbed of a Chinese Communist railroad, to the mountains of Tibet. China has had another frontier, corresponding more nearly to the West in North America. For South China was originally peopled by non-Chinese whom the early bearers of Chinese civilization, proceeding from North China, overcame and civilized. Remnants of the native population survive today in southern and southwestern China. But by far the more important in its effect upon Chinese life has been the northern border I am describing.

There was no limitless supply of free land here. Instead, the absence of rainfall rather than the presence of unoccupied land determined the border. It divided the south, the land that could be farmed, from the north, which was not tillable. Peoples that lived on either side were farther apart in their modes of life than the American Indian and the frontiersman. The northern frontier was likewise a dividing line between two sets of institutions. To the south, life depended on success in growing grain under

[2] G. R. Taylor (ed.), *The Turner Thesis Concerning the Role of the Frontier in American History* (Boston, 1949), 83.

conditions of scanty rainfall; to the north, it was sustained by skill in finding pasturage for animals. Manchu, Mongol, or Turkic-speaking nomads to the north depended on animals for dairy products, meat, clothing, and the coverings for their portable dwellings. If one excepts the oases of Chinese Turkestan, there were few settled communities. The nomads were organized into clans and tribes living in temporary encampments. Their religion, originally a type of shamanism, became after the thirteenth century A.D. the Tibetan form of Buddhism called Lamaism. Warfare depended upon skill at riding and upon the discharge of arrows from horseback.

Chinese settlers to the south cultivated grain and vegetables and lived in settled communities. These Chinese developed irrigation, water transport, and systems of administration. Local affairs were managed through the family and heads of local communities, but there was also the central administration of the Chinese Empire, established when China came under unified rule in the latter part of the third century B.C. To a system of belief in local deities and in the spirits of their ancestors, the Chinese added the moral teachings of their philosophers. Chinese of the tillable area had developed and were using writing by the first millennium B.C., whereas writing came to the nomads very much later. For example, the Mongol written language was first taken from the script of a neighboring people, the Uigurs, in the thirteenth century A.D. There may have been a greater need for written records, hence for a system of writing, among the settled peoples than among the nomads. For defense purposes, the settled peoples developed the walled city and built the Great Wall itself. The use of the mounted archer and of cavalry to supersede the chariot came to them from the nomads.

There was a more even balance of power on either side of this northern Chinese frontier than existed between the American frontiersman and the American Indian. When nomad tribes became unified and gathered strength, they could invade northern China, engage in extensive plunder, and establish barbarian dynasties that ruled China sometimes for long periods. Between 220 and 589 A.D., China north of the Yangtze River was under control of a succession of such non-Chinese peoples. For two periods of its history, the Mongol era between 1279 and 1368 and the era of Manchu rule between 1644 and 1912, all of China was under such barbarian control. On the other hand, periods of Chinese unity and strength such as from 202 B.C. to 220 A.D. or from 589 to 907 A.D. would see Chinese troops in control of southern Manchuria, the Gobi Desert, and the trade routes of Sinkiang. Indeed, the measure of a Chinese dynasty's strength was its ability to control the nomads of the borderlands. For perhaps three thousand years the northern frontier has been a factor to be reckoned with.

In their contact with each other, it was necessary for both the nomads and the settled Chinese to create procedures of accommodation. The frontier was responsible for these procedures to the extent that it provided the usual place of contact.

Chinese rulers discovered that the capital of a dynasty, to facilitate defense against the nomad invader, must be situated so as to control the frontier as well as to administer the broad lands of the lower Yellow River valley. Two such favored locations were the Sianfu area, in the Wei River valley, and the site of Peking. A sure sign of dynastic decadence was the removal of the capital from such locations near the border to a city such as Loyang on the North China plain.

Further, the necessity to provide tens of thousands of mounts for cavalry made imperative the control of large grazing and breeding areas for horses. A dynasty that lost control of such areas on China's borders cut down its capacity for defense. The strong Chinese dynasties maintained their borderland sources for the supply of horses. *160838*

To provision the large population of a capital away from the centers of grain supply made necessary the creation and upkeep of a system of waterways devoted to the transport of tribute grain. The T'ang capital of Ch'ang-an (in the vicinity of Sianfu), for example, was served by a combination of man-made and natural waterways that brought grain from the Lower Yangtze to Ch'ang-an via the Wei River at the last great bend of the Yellow River. The famous Grand Canal, completed by the Mongols in the thirteenth century, was such a waterway, enabling the delivery of rice from Hangchow, south of Shanghai, to Peking. This functioned until 1852, a route secure from pirates and other hazards of the sea.

As time passed, the settled Chinese came to possess a set of attitudes created by their experience with the nomad peoples of the northern frontier. For one thing, their leaders developed an orientation toward the land rather than the sea, both as a matter of defense and of contacts with outsiders. If one excepts the Southern Sung period (1127–1279 A.D.), when Chinese rulers were driven out of North China and controlled only the area south of the Yangtze, and the first sixty years of the Ming dynasty (1368 ca.–1430), Chinese neglect of naval power is the rule. For example, instead of meeting Japanese pirates with suitable naval forces, later Ming rulers set up a coastal warning system and ordered the evacuation of coastal areas. The Manchu rulers of China responded to the outbreak of the first Anglo-Chinese war in South China in 1839 by first ordering the northern passes manned and the northern borders defended, an automatic and traditional response to the threat of danger from outside. Dangerous invaders were expected as a matter of course from the land frontier. Had they not always come from that quarter?

Partly because of the circumstances of their environment, the nomads north of the border failed to form a rich civilization comparable to that which Chinese of the settled lands were able to create. The rich material civilization of the Chinese was matched by a development of philosophical ideas, administrative theory, and educational practice far above the achievements of the nomads. In the process, the doctrines of Confucius were modified and made to serve the uses of administering a large empire. On lower levels of activity, Confucian norms of behavior were used by informal social groups for purposes of local government. The creation of such a complex of civilization, combined with the fact that China before the advent of modern modes of transportation was cut off by formidable land barriers and hazardous seas from contact with other major centers of civilization, fostered among the settled Chinese a natural sense of pride in their accomplishment. The only peoples they knew were of inferior culture and were accordingly termed, in Chinese, *barbarians.* Barbarians were then differentiated according to the direction from which they came. The Koreans and Annamese, who looked to China for patterns of life and behavior, were rated as cultural younger brothers, higher than barbarians but still inferior. The English and other Europeans were commonly called "Barbarians of the Western Ocean." Hence the disparity between cultures on either side of China's frontier, much greater than that between the American Indian and the American frontiersman, fostered an ethnocentric sense of superiority that conditioned the Chinese view of foreign relations.

The Chinese view of relations with barbarians, indeed, crystallized around notions of cultural superiority. China was the Middle Kingdom, as the Chinese term denotes, the center of the world and the source of civilization. Semienlightened barbarians like the Koreans and the Annamese, or even the Japanese during the T'ang period, were to be dealt with as the older brother treats the younger through processes of reasoning and admonition. Other barbarians, rude and unruly, with whom reason might not prevail, would have to be pacified. The use of physical force was sanctioned as though permitted for the correction of a misbehaving child.

The Chinese superiority complex expressed itself in due course in what became known as the tribute system. All barbarian countries were expected to comply with a procedure that emphasized the superior position of the Chinese. The accession of a new barbarian monarch or of a new Chinese emperor was an occasion for the sending of a tribute mission from the barbarian nation. In addition, regular and even annual missions (in the case of Korea) were expected of near-by barbarians. The barbarians brought presents, usually specified samples of native products, and presented themselves in audience before the Chinese emperor in the ceremony of the *kowtow*. The *kowtow*, a procedure involving three kneelings and nine prostrations, three for each kneeling, done at the command of imperial ushers, must have left little doubt as to which of the parties involved was supposed to be superior. The *kowtow* was expected of all barbarians, whether representatives of the English king or of the Loochoo Islands. At its conclusion, the Chinese emperor would confer presents upon the tribute envoys and send them home with seals or scrolls recognizing the authority of their rulers. The tribute system became an inexpensive and, to Chinese, a gratifying system of foreign relations. It could and did become, as with later Ming emperors, a protective device for avoiding trouble.

Trade with the barbarian was provided for in connection with the tribute mission, first at the capital, and then, to save expense, at specified places of entry where traders accompanying a mission would be dropped off to rejoin their party on its homeward journey. The official Chinese view was that China, a self-satisfied economy, needed nothing but would deign to trade with the barbarian solely as a benevolent accommodation. In theory, the tribute system was probably meant to control trade, but the practice fell far short of the theory. In any event, the tribute system, built upon presuppositions of cultural superiority, was far removed from western notions of diplomatic equality.

Chinese attitudes and devices of accommodation were thus created by contact with peoples of lesser cultures in the course of dealings mainly across a land frontier. By the same token, the barbarian developed his own attitudes and devices of accommodation as a result of his dealings with Chinese, with certain additions.

In times when barbarian strength was inferior to that of Chinese, the tribute system governed, but occasions arose in Chinese history when strong dynasties declined. Then barbarian warriors, more successful than the American Indians against western settlers, stormed the passes, sacked the Chinese capital, and set up dynasties themselves. One such period of barbarian kingdoms in the north has been mentioned, from 220 to 589 A.D. Another was the era from 907 to 960 A.D. At such times, the non-Chinese groups in control discovered in their new position of political superiority that previous experiences north of the frontier did not fit them for ruling settled areas. To be successful, the natural tendency was to adopt prevailing Chinese modes. This could be accompanied by intermarriage and alteration of old ways of life so that the barbarian became Chinese in culture and perhaps as a consequence also became militarily unfit for action against other barbarian nomads or against resurgent Chinese. In time, the barbarian problem of ruling Chinese clarified itself into two subproblems, how to administer the affairs of Chinese in settled areas and how to maintain identity and military efficiency.

It may be stated as a general proposition that with one possible exception during the Northern Wei dynasty, barbarian peoples were not conspicuously successful with either problem until the tenth century. Then three peoples established rule over the Chinese and apparently did better than their predecessors. These are the Ch'i-t'ans (907–1125), the Ju-chen Tatars from Manchuria (1115–1234), and the Mongols (1279–1368). The first two established dynasties that ruled Northeast China only, while the Mongols were the first barbarian group to rule all of China. Kublai Khan, whom Marco Polo served as an official, was the first barbarian emperor of the whole of China. Not much study has yet been made of the Ju-chen accomplishment, but the Mongols and particularly the Ch'i-t'an peoples did not seek refuge with Chinese; the latter split into two groups, one retiring to Manchuria and the other migrating to Chinese Turkestan to found a refugee state.

Once their long conquest of China was over, the Mongols showed an ability to learn quickly, to improvise, and to use the talents of gifted foreigners in ruling China. Foreign administrators of diverse origin dominated the higher echelons of government; Chinese were relegated to the lower posts. Moslem Arabs were conspicuous in positions of financial responsibility. The Mongols became sufficiently naval-minded to organize respectable amphibious operations against Japan. Under their guidance, trade by sea boomed and the port cities of South China contributed largely to their tax revenues. The Mongols failed to use the Chinese in the upper echelons of their government, however, and this in the long run cut down the length of their rule. Measures for preserving identity were not as carefully worked out, apparently, as were those of the Ch'i-t'ans. In the end, a native Chinese uprising drove them from China back to the area of present-day Outer Mongolia.

It is instructive that all three—Ch'i-t'an, Ju-chen, and Mongol —used Peking as a capital. All three, also, preserved their experiences in a Chinese-style dynastic history.

The barbarians who finally mastered the two problems of ruling Chinese were the Manchus, originally obscure peoples from Northern Manchuria. The dynasty which they installed began its rule over China in 1644, maintaining itself until Sun Yat-sen's Chinese Revolution of 1912. The Manchu rule of 268 years, a respectable term of power for a strong Chinese dynasty, is the longest any outside group has been able to rule the Chinese. To accomplish this, Manchu leaders took particular pains to examine the record of the Ch'i-t'ans, the Ju-chens, and the Mongols for help with their two major problems. In addition, they were able in earlier stages of their conquests after occupying South Manchuria to employ Chinese and Chinese methods in governing agricultural areas. Manchus served in Ming frontier garrisons. They learned Chinese and became attached to Confucian modes of thought—all before their installation in China itself.

As a result, when the opportunity came for their installation in China proper, Manchu leaders could tell the Chinese that the change in masters involved no change in ideas or institutions for administration. The Manchu emperors subsidized the production of great works of Chinese scholarship—encyclopediae, bibliographies, editions of the classics. The emperor caused to be written a history of the preceding dynasty just as though he were a Chinese. The traditional Chinese civil service examinations and the traditional Confucian material for these examinations were continued. Intelligent, trained Chinese who passed the proper examinations were appointed to the highest administrative posts in the government. The Manchus embraced Chinese culture and Confucian orthodoxy. In some respects, they were as Chinese as the Chinese. In effect, the educated upper ruling classes of Chinese, which can be designated as landed gentry, scholars, and officials, were taken into partnership, forming what John King Fairbank calls the Manchu-Chinese dyarchy. In the nineteenth century when serious rebellion threatened the dynasty and the traditional Confucian culture, these upper-class Chinese remained loyal to the Manchus and the Chinese culture which the Manchus had adopted. The emperor's position was universalized to make him monarch of all under heaven. The Manchu leaders thus succeeded in enlisting the services and loyalty of educated Chinese. No other barbarian rulers of China had been able to do as much. It did not matter that in the process the Chinese scholar-gentry were rendered incapable of popular leadership when conceptions of nationalism, industrialization, and social reform were introduced into China.

While busy with the enlistment of Chinese assistance, Manchu leaders were still mindful of the dangers of engulfment at the hands of the numerically superior Chinese. Unlike many American fur traders who adopted the dress and customs of the Indians, the Manchu adopted measures that maintained their cultural identity. They put into practice a series of carefully considered, protective measures. All Chinese were compelled to wear their hair in the pigtail or queue as a sign of the original subjection to Manchu rule. Manchuria, the cultural homeland, was closed to Chinese immigration and deliberately kept empty. A Manchu form of social organization known as the *banner* was perpetuated as a means of keeping Manchus together and channeling their activities. Intermarriage between top-level Manchus and Chinese was forbidden. Unlike Chinese women, Manchu women did not bind their feet. Each large Chinese administrative city had its Manchu or Tatar section and its garrison of Manchu bannermen, under a Manchu general. The walled city of Peking, containing the imperial palaces, was reserved for Manchu residence. Peking was thus divided into a walled Tatar City and a Chinese City outside the walls. The imperial clan controlled succession to the throne and the court. The tombs of the Manchu rulers of China were outside China, in Jehol in Eastern Mongolia. Manchu officials did not take the same examinations as Chinese but were subject to different requirements for skill at archery and military horsemanship. Manchus were associated with Chinese in the highest governmental posts in the proportion of at least one to one. The command of native Chinese forces in the provinces was so spread as to guard against possibilities of organized revolt. Local Chinese forces were consequently seldom good for more than keeping order. State documents were written in Manchu as well as Chinese; separate state files were kept in Mukden, which continued to be the Manchu capital of Manchuria. These measures seemed successful as long as the barbarian Manchus were able to preserve their military proficiency and political ability—in short, until the end of the eighteenth century. Though ruling all of China, these aliens apparently did as well in maintaining identity as did the Ch'i-t'ans, who had had only China northeast of the Yellow River to control.

Now our story turns to the nineteenth century, when the Industrial Revolution was bringing European traders to the coast of South China in greater numbers and with greater insistence than ever before. What amounted to a maritime frontier situation

had been handled previously through the application of traditional Chinese attitudes and methods. Foreign merchants—Portuguese, Dutch, English, Scandinavians, and also Americans—
were restricted to trade at the one port of Canton, part of the
year, in a foreign factory quarter outside the walls, as befitted the
low status of people who were both merchants and foreigners. All
transactions, including communications with government officials,
took place through special merchants. Tariff requirements could
never be predicted, being dependent on a condoned system of
"squeeze." If foreign sailors got into trouble with Chinese, the
Chinese notions of criminal justice, far different from Anglo-
Saxon concepts, prevailed. Diplomatic relations on the basis of
equality were impossible. When Portuguese, Dutch, or British
embassies were received at Peking, they were received by the
emperor as barbarian tribute envoys. With almost no exceptions,
they were asked to perform the *kowtow*. Until the 1830's, this system of dealing with inland barbarians worked when applied to
barbarians who came to China by sea from the regions of the
Western Ocean. But the factory system broke down finally in
1839, because of its inability to handle the desire of Chinese for a
comparatively new article in their trade with the outside—opium.

The conflict of interests between, on one side, the British government and British traders who wanted conditions of equality
and free access to the China market and, on the other, Chinese
government officials who could see no reason for change, could
not be resolved without resort to arms. The first Anglo-Chinese
war, in 1839–42, resulted in a complete victory for the British
with a series of four treaties designed to make Western rather
than Chinese ideas prevail. A second Anglo-Chinese war, during
the years 1858–60, in which the French coöperated, completed the
work of the first war and enlarged the treaties. All foreigners including Russians and Americans shared in the results of these wars
through an economical device called the most-favored-nation provision. If one nation obtained a concession, all the others auto-
matically and without the need for separate negotiation shared
in its enjoyment. Thus was established what the Chinese called
the unequal treaty system.

To meet the emergencies of the period 1839–60 the Manchu-
Chinese dyarchy possessed only those attitudes and practices developed along China's northern frontier and the Manchu adapta-

tions to problems of ruling China. These proved shockingly inadequate in warfare and had to be steadily modified to suit the periods of fulfillment of the treaties that succeeded both wars.

One is impressed by the depth of intellectual unpreparedness shown by the Chinese officials who made the first treaties. China had no such informed cosmopolitan diplomats as Franklin and John Quincy Adams. Chinese ignorance of elementary facts of Western geography, even of the identity of separate peoples such as the Dutch and the Portuguese, is very evident. The results of an almost complete absence of prior curiosity are plain. Ch'i Ying, the Chinese plenipotentiary at Nanking in 1842, endeavors to control the barbarian envoy Sir Henry Pottinger by a display of sheer personal friendship. The most-favored-nation clause is agreed to on the theory that the emperor from on high wishes to treat all barbarian nations with equality. The Chinese at the making of the Treaty of Nanking, the first treaty, are chiefly concerned about getting the English out of the Yangtze River and keeping down the size of the indemnity payment demanded. They seem not to know the meaning of what is conceded by the other clauses of the treaties. Further, the belief that barbarian matters are not worth learning about persists through the second Anglo-Chinese war. At this point, it becomes modified by the thought, held as yet by only a few enlightened ones, that it is permissible for Chinese to borrow Western arms and learn the tricks of making them so as to keep the barbarian away. Any inkling of what features of Western society contributed to make the arms completely escapes the Chinese.

The bankruptcy of Chinese ideas of defense against naval attack and the effect of neglect of a navy were, of course, completely revealed when British war steamers with their swivel guns could move at will in Chinese waters and dispose of the fire-junks sent to intercept them. The vaunted Manchu military strength, thought to be so carefully preserved, was exposed as useless, as were the forces of local Chinese, before the attacks of determined foreign landing parties. Manchu military prestige never recovered from the experiences of the Anglo-Chinese wars. It was to take a hundred years before an entirely new style of Chinese army would be ready to meet Western armies on equal terms.

The first treaties stipulated that Western consuls might deal directly with Chinese officials in certain designated open ports, but that negotiations with Peking must proceed through a commissioner at Canton. One of these commissioners acted successfully for a time on the theory that he could prevent this style of barbarian relations by refusing to see foreign representatives. His attitude was remedied after the second round of treaties by the creation of a Chinese Foreign Office, where slowly the Chinese learned about Western nations and how to deal with Western ambassadors. Western diplomats thereafter could reside in Peking, where access to the emperor could not be denied. Chinese missions abroad were established very slowly, however. On one pretext or another, foreign ambassadors were not received by the imperial court in satisfactory audience until the 1890's. The attitudes of the tribute system died a slow death.

The first round of treaties had stipulated the creation of a fixed tariff for foreign goods entering certain ports designated for trade. Chinese attitudes now showed the effect of long official neglect of foreign-trade matters. Hence, Chinese port officials used every opportunity to extract additional duties on foreign goods. This in practice made regular assessment and collection of a fixed treaty tariff hopeless. At length, in the 1850's, an arrangement was worked out whereby a foreign staff under a foreign inspector-general fixed the customs duties, which were then collected by Chinese officials. This scheme was so successful that it was continued at Chinese request in the 1930's after the treaty tariff which gave it birth had been abolished.

The first series of treaties granted Westerners privileges of residence in the treaty ports. Foreigners were allowed to purchase land and erect buildings. In time this grew into an institution known as the foreign settlement or concession, with its own governing body and police. The most famous of these was the fabulous International Settlement in Shanghai. Rights of extraterritoriality, acquired at the time of the first treaties, placed the foreigner under his own consular establishment. Such rights also covered the activities of foreign Christian missionaries, who after 1860 were allowed to carry on their work in the interior.

In these various ways—the treaty tariff, the right of direct access to the emperor, the China Maritime Customs, the foreign settlement, extraterritoriality—did the Western trader accommodate himself to doing business in China and did China accommodate its attitudes and practices to the new barbarian, the Westerner, with his odd obsession for trade. The Manchu-Chinese dyarchy came to include the Western trader in its scheme of special privilege. A host of Chinese helpers, cultural half-breeds, today called the comprador class, arose to serve the Westerner and facilitate his business. Shanghai, with its unrivaled command of the water communications of central China, became a center for the development first of Western-style trade and then of Western-style manufacturing. But the old ethnocentric notions of superiority lingered, delaying urgent changes and condoning superficial reforms. The notion of an eminent viceroy that traditional Chinese culture could form the base and Western material civilization the superstructure for a Chinese adjustment to the West, current in the 1890's, was a reflection of this attitude. It took major shocks—a Japanese defeat in 1894–95, the subsequent partitioning of China into spheres of Western control, and the total defeat of the antiforeign Boxer Uprising in 1900—to make Chinese leaders consider thoroughgoing reform.

What might Turner have said if he had studied the effect of the northern Chinese frontier upon Chinese history? What is the significance of this frontier in Chinese history?

The answer is that the frontier did a signal disservice to the Chinese. Attitudes and institutions developed along a land frontier, however well they might enable nomads and settled Chinese to get on, were of no use when it came to dealing with an insistent seafaring Western barbarian bent on trade.

To both China and America, then, the frontier has been important. For American frontiersmen, the frontier was the perpetuator if not the creator of progressive institutions. For the Chinese, it proved an impediment, delaying necessary change and handicapping their twentieth-century search for adequacy.

SELECTED READINGS

Fairbank, John K. *Trade and Diplomacy on the China Coast. The Opening of the Treaty Ports, 1842–1854.* 2 vols. Cambridge, Mass.: Harvard University Press, 1953.

Lattimore, Owen. *Inner Asian Frontiers of China.* New York: American Geographical Society, 1940.

Taylor, G. R. (ed.). *The Turner Thesis Concerning the Role of the Frontier in American History.* Boston: D. C. Heath, 1949.

Teng Ssu-yü and Fairbank, John K. *China's Response to the West,* a *Documentary Survey, 1839–1923.* Cambridge, Mass.: Harvard University Press, 1954.

Wittfogel, Karl A. and Feng Chia-sheng. *History of Chinese Society—Liao.* Philadelphia: American Philosophical Society, 1949.

WALTER PRESCOTT WEBB

The Western World Frontier

In this essay Professor Webb takes the reader on a philosophic excursion over the world frontiers since 1500. He calls attention to the many frontier settlements founded by the European nations as they expanded into Africa, Australia, New Zealand, North and South America, and calls these "Wests" the World Frontier. In the interaction between this frontier and Europe lies one of the important keys to modern civilization, for the European "Metropolis" stamped the frontier and the frontier influenced Metropolis. Capitalism, democracy, laissez faire, slavery, international law, and the use of precious metals found their seedbed in the milieu of the World Frontier.

Instead of modifying the Turner hypothesis on the influence of the American frontier, Professor Webb has taken it out of its national encasement and applied it to the world. His hypothesis may well be called the "Webb thesis." It poses a distressing question to the modern world: What happens to democracy, capitalism, and the other ways of life now that the World Frontier has closed?

WHEN Frederick Jackson Turner launched his frontier thesis, he must at times have wondered what the effect would be on his future reputation. Would it be more sensible to follow the tradition of his elders and glean the fields they had harvested, either substantiating their views or modifying them so little as not to dis-

turb their sacred principles? His other choice was to strike out
for himself and have a look at the country from a vantage point
which others had not used. Though I am not an authority on
Turner's life, I dare say he made his important decision not from
considerations of policy, but because of an inner compulsion
which drove him to make it regardless of the effect it might have
on his career. A statesman has been described as a man who perceives a single truth of tomorrow. Occasionally there comes a
historian who perceives an important truth of yesterday, discovers
a set of relationships which throws a light on the past, and, if he
sets it forth, and it is eventually accepted by a reasonable number
of people, finds a place as an interpreter. No interpretation of
history based on a general idea is ever universally accepted, and no
interpreter escapes the tonic of criticism.

It would be bad taste for me to elaborate the basic idea that the
frontier exerted a profound influence on American life, culture,
and institutions. That idea is accepted and has by now pervaded
all the fields of thought about this country. That idea is permeat-
ing other lands similar to this, such as Canada, Australia, South
Africa, and New Zealand. It is also being considered in the
Latin-American countries to the south, and it will in the future
be examined elsewhere.

I am submitting here what seems to me to be a truth of yesterday, an extension of the idea that the frontier exerted a far-reach-
ing influence, not only on American life and institutions, but on
all of Western civilization, and therefore on world history. The
idea I am advancing is as simple as the one Turner announced
and that others have elaborated. The American argument runs
that there was for a long period a settled East and an unsettled
West, a civilized region and a frontier region, that people were
moving from the settled region into the unsettled one, that the
process of moving and occupying raw land had its effects on those
who moved, and that the whole long process had a reflex effect on
the older region whence the people came. We may differ as to the
extent of the influence, but it would require a strangely perverse
mind to deny that there was some effect.

Here we have a principle of history demonstrated to be applicable in this country. It is gradually dawning on thinkers about
other frontier countries that it is applicable in other countries

too. If this principle of frontier influence is applicable in all the separate parts of the frontier, in Canada, Australia, South Africa, and New Zealand, in the twenty republics of Latin America, then this influence was exerted wherever the people of Western Europe took over frontier lands. In each of these countries there was in the beginning a little "East" and a greater "West." In each of them the little "East" ate into the greater "West," gradually reducing the West until in each country we can say there is no longer raw frontier. Also in each country, as in the United States, the process of eating up the frontier exerted influence on those who did the eating and had some reflex effect on those who did not participate. Thus, in each of the frontier countries, the scholars who have considered the frontier principle have followed the American lead and examined their own frontier as if it were an isolated example confined to their own country.

This limited procedure has been necessary and is invaluable. It was the method of Bacon, who believed that we should examine many details before inducing a general conclusion. This minute examination of the many little frontiers, little "Easts" and little "Wests," has resulted in the accumulation of a wealth of data about the processes that went on and has revealed a small central core of uniformity. The invasion of the little "West," the area of free land, has always had some effect on the little "East," on the civilization of that particular fragment.

The next step is to assemble all the little "Wests," all the fragments of the frontier, into the whole frontier, the greater "West," and when we have done this, we have a greater frontier than we have previously been examining; we have the whole instead of a parcel of parts of which the United States is only one. This whole Great Frontier originally would have comprised the three and one half continents and the thousands of islands opened up by Columbus and his associates. This is a synthesis that was inevitable and is logical, once the idea of frontier has been accepted as a force in history.

But once we perform this act of synthesis and visualize all the scattered parts of the frontier brought together into a Great Frontier, we ask ourselves what of the little "Easts" and the little "Wests" with which we have been so concerned in such fragments as the United States and other dominions. We are for the moment looking at the whole frontier as analogous to the American West, thus merging the little "Easts" and the little "Wests" into one big "East." We have only lost—and that temporarily—the fragmentary "Easts," replicas of a greater "East," the existence of which has almost escaped notice. What we need look for now is the Mother East that gave birth to the little "Easts" tucked away on the fringes of the distant new lands. Our chief difficulty is psychological in that we have been concerned hitherto with the struggles and activities of the children and have lost sight of the home where the mother of all the little "Easts" resides. By an act of resolution, and at the expense perhaps of some preconceptions, we need to focus attention on the Mother East, which we can see by now is none other than Western Europe. Western Europe is *the* "East" in the American sense, bearing the same relation to the Great Frontier that the Atlantic Coast settlements long bore to the traditional American West. The name I have applied to Western Europe to set it off from the Great Frontier is the Metropolis. Since all of the frontier did not lie to the west of Europe, we must get away from our figurative use of East and West and substitute respectively the Metropolis and the Great Frontier. When we do this, we are in position to view the interaction and relation between the whole things rather than the relation between two parts—the civilized part and the frontier part—of a fragment of one of them only.

It is necessary for us to back away from the detail, the fragment, and have a fresh look at the *whole* Frontier and the *whole* Metropolis as they interacted on each other after 1500. There are advantages and disadvantages in shifting to this longer perspective and to this larger geographical canvas.

The disadvantages are: Since the whole frontier is greater than any of its parts, so the task of thinking about it is of greater scope and magnitude. The whole frontier is a complex thing, varying with the varied geography and dissimilar people, whereas a single frontier has both geographic unity and a measure of cultural unity. It is difficult for one person to know all the lands and the languages and literatures, but he who shrinks from difficulties should not elect to be a historian.

It would seem that the advantages of taking the long perspective and looking at the whole frontier instead of a part of it overbalance the difficulties. The fundamental gain derived from the long perspective and the world view is this: It enables us to see the whole, the Great Frontier on the one hand and the whole of Metropolis on the other. We see the extent of the forest, its relation to what is around it, and we see over the centuries the people of the Metropolis moving out on it, nibbling tentatively at its edges along the Atlantic seaboard, upward from the Cape, inward from Sydney and Melbourne, and inward from the South American shore. From all these points, the migrating hordes from the Metropolis move in rough unison on the forest and the plain, and eventually they claim a simultaneous victory on a broad intercontinental field because they have destroyed that which so challenged and lured them.

When we view this interaction from this high vantage point, things seem to fall into place. What in closer perspective appeared as separate and disconnected historical phenomena now appear as scattered manifestations of a single action. For example, I mentioned the little "Easts" and the little "Wests" with which we have been so busy. We now see that they are cut of the same two cloths. The little "Easts" are but extended fingers of the Metropolis; the little "Wests" are what is left in various places of the original Great Frontier.

When from this same vantage point we observe the interaction between the Metropolis and the Great Frontier over a period of four and one-half centuries, we feel that we have perhaps found one of the important keys to modern Western civilization. In this interaction, we see a prime example of Toynbee's challenge and response; we see a backdrop of Spengler's philosophy of rise and decay, which he probably did not see. This interaction between these two gigantic forces developed so much power that, like a diesel engine, it picked up all the other historical movements, such as the price revolution, the commercial revolution, the industrial revolution, and the democratic revolutions, and moved them like a long train down the track. Whatever got in the way of this interaction was altered or destroyed; whatever harmonized with it or served it, prospered. In the long perspective, both capitalism and democracy appear as by-products of the interaction, the use of the precious metals as a medium of exchange appears as an episode now ended, and the rise of modern Negro slavery appears as a device adopted by the Metropolitans in order that they might have cheap and permanent labor with which to hew their fortunes out of the raw materials of the Great Frontier. Before this interaction, the old ideas about economics, based on scarcity, were wrecked because they were not applicable to the new age of plenty. Mercantilism gave way to laissez faire, which lasted only as long as the frontier lasted. These are some of the vistas that open up when we view the whole Frontier and its relation to the whole Metropolis, vistas which cannot ordinarily be reached by the most minute examination of a single frontier fragment.

What has been said above applies to the period of the open frontier, say from 1500 to about 1900. By 1900 or thereabout, the first phase was over because the Metropolis had in effect eaten up the Frontier. The challenge to the Metropolis prior to that date was the challenge of the open frontier; the challenge since that date is that of a closed frontier. The Metropolis has destroyed the Frontier and now for the first time in several centuries must stew in its own juice. There is no longer the dramatic interaction to which I have attributed such power and influence. There is no longer the dynamism to which we were accustomed, no longer the free migration of people or the return cargoes of windfall wealth. Many practices, ideas, and institutions which arose and served well when the interaction was going on have been discarded, and all—even democracy and capitalism—are being modified. The precious metals no longer serve as a medium of exchange; laissez faire has been discarded and slavery abolished; the free-wheeling individual, the pampered pet of the frontier era, is being brought under control and required to reassume some responsibility to the society in which he lives. To put the same fact in another form, the state is reasserting its sovereignty. The vaunted freedoms of which we boast, both economic and political, appear as incidental to a temporary situation which enabled the sovereign to release the individual from accustomed obligations and duties to the state. The sovereign could release the individual because he was reaping such harvests from the new lands that he could dispense with services he had formerly needed and required.

With the windfall prizes of the Great Frontier all appropriated, the nations realigned—the "haves" on one side and the "have-nots" on the other. An important difference between them was that members of the first group had frontier possessions, or were of the frontier, while those of the second group had none. The two groups have fought two wars which may in retrospect appear as an attempted adjustment to the closed world frontier. These wars resulted in the two groups' approaching nearer to each other, not because the "have-nots" have more but because the "haves" now have less. Another such war could very well bring them to stand on common ground where neither has anything. With the Frontier swallowed up, there is no escape to a new frontier by the enlarged Metropolis, which must now face a condition comparable to that which obtained when the society was released by the opening of the Great Frontier in 1500.

These are some vistas—not too pleasant—that appear when we take the long perspective and view the *end* of the interaction between the Metropolis and the Great Frontier. What we view now is a condition created by the cessation of the interaction. There is no interaction because one of the leading characters is dead. The Metropolis has destroyed the Frontier and stands triumphant in the midst of the magnificent ruins. We may recall Byron's description of Rome:

> The Niobe of nations! There she stands
> Childless and crownless, in her voiceless woe;
> An empty urn within her withered hand,
> Whose holy dust was scattered long ago.

Perhaps the historian should never be moved by compassion for his subject, however deeply he may feel it. My business here is to present a single idea, elaborate it, and illustrate it. I have presented the idea and elaborated it briefly, and now I would like to illustrate the effect of the Great Frontier on two important segments of Western civilization. The first illustration has to do with the management of land and the second with modification of law.

THE MANAGEMENT OF LAND

It is often said that land is the basis of wealth, and here land may be taken as wealth's synonym. The acquisition of the Great Frontier by the Metropolis was the biggest land deal in the history of the world. In a relatively short period of time, in almost an instant, the Europeans increased their land holdings from three and three-quarters million sections to some twenty-four million sections, more than a six-fold increase. The sovereigns of Europe acquired this land almost without cost, by finding it, claiming it, and ignoring the rights of any natives. It was to them a windfall of gigantic proportions and the sudden possession of it soon involved them in one of the most bizarre land transactions known to man.

By 1600 the sovereigns of Europe held in their hands eighty million quarter sections of land which from their point of view had never had an owner; they began to alienate it to their needy subjects on practically a free basis. This is what William Graham Sumner had in mind when he said, "The very greatest, but . . . least noticed significance of the discovery of America was the winning of a new continent for the laboring class." [1] I would amend Sumner by saying that it was three and a half continents that were made available, rather than one. This land dispersion got under way in the sixteenth century and went on little abated until the first decades of the twentieth. If it were possible to compile the dates appearing on the first page of some eighty million abstracts where alienation from the sovereign is recorded, we would have a curve beginning near zero in 1500, rising through the centuries, reaching its apogee probably in the second half of the nineteenth century, and falling to near zero by 1910. That curve would tell the story of the opening and ending of the Great Frontier. This transfer of land from sovereign to subject, from state to citizen on practically a free basis, was an economic transaction of such magnitude as to affect everything in the society. It warped history out of its course. It set up the framework in which politics operated and it provided the economic climate into which capitalism was born. Keeping in mind this long-continuing dispersion of land and wealth on a free basis, let us note some illuminating patterns of land management that emerged.

When we ponder over the phenomenon just described, namely, the sovereign states' dispersing eighty million quarter sections of land on a free basis from 1600 to 1900, and put with that what the states have been compelled to do since the dispersion ended—here

[1] William Graham Sumner, "Earth-Hunger or the Philosophy of Land Grabbing," in Sumner's *Earth-Hunger and Other Essays,* ed. by Albert G. Keller (New Haven, 1913), 41.

reference is made to the imposition of heavy income taxes and a general reassertion of state authority in all the democracies—we see emerge a new economic principle which is best described as the Vertical Pulsation of Wealth. If this theory of the Vertical Pulsation of Wealth in society proves valid, the economists and historians will need to re-examine some of their previous assumptions.

Up to now the economists have been primarily concerned with what they call the circulation of wealth, the movement of wealth from hand to hand among the citizens or subjects. This I have called the *horizontal* motion of wealth in the society. Practically all the thinking in economics has been done on the assumption that this horizontal motion was the *only* motion that wealth has had. This is, for modern times at least, a fatal error.

The truth is that wealth has in modern times had two motions, one horizontal and one vertical. In the horizontal motion, which we know as circulation, wealth moves from one person to another; but in the *vertical motion it moves between the sovereign and the people, either upward from the people to the sovereign or downward from the sovereign to the people.* Ordinarily it moves in both directions and we have a *vertical circulation* of wealth.

This vertical circulation between sovereign and people is normal in any organized state. But we are dealing with states in an abnormal period of three hundred years. In those three centuries the balance was disturbed; there was no balance because wealth moved predominantly in one direction—*downward* from the sovereign to the people. This predominant flow downward became possible because the sovereigns of the Western world acquired the windfall of the Great Frontier. For once they got wealth—land and all it contained—without taking it from their own people. They could now give without taking, and from 1600 to 1900 we can observe a singular spectacle: the sovereign casting down on his subjects or citizens a never-ending shower of wealth, free land, free gold, free grass, free water, free minerals and timber.

This process of free giving by the sovereign created the climate in which modern Western economic and political practices and institutions developed. Let us look first at some economic features, such as competition, monopoly, and the theory of laissez faire.

The competition which characterized this age was carried on

largely for the wealth that the sovereign was sifting down. It was carried on horizontally, moving the prizes about from hand to hand. This competition could not result in extreme monopoly because the sovereign was always staking the losers so that they could get back in the game. The competition was not cruel, as it later became, because it was easier and more rewarding to take wealth from the willing sovereign than it was to take it from a reluctant fellow individual. Under these conditions laissez faire was a tenable theory because the wealth was so abundant, so easily obtained, that men could be turned loose to do as they pleased with it. It was as renewable as annual rainfall.

Let us now look at the political climate. The rise of liberalism is probably the dominant political feature of modern times. We are wont to attribute its growth to the efforts of men. But let us bear in mind that liberalism arose in the climate of tolerance fostered by the general free land dispersion just described. It is our custom to think that such benefits as we enjoy we got by taking them away from an unwilling sovereign. It may be permitted at this late date to point out that the sovereigns, in dispersing the Great Frontier, were performing an act of liberalism that dwarfs all the others. The sovereign was making men wealthy from the bounty which he did not take from them, making them independent and free, whether or not he was willing to recognize what he had done after he had done it. Because he had this bounty, he could excuse the people from taxes and other obligations which a sovereign ordinarily requires of subjects or citizens. By his unconscious generosity, the sovereign was also relaxing his authority and laying the groundwork for the emancipation of the individual and the setting up of a democratic government. The revolutions simply confirmed by law what had already occurred in fact. This means that as long as the frontier lasted—as long as wealth was flowing predominantly from the sovereign to the people—the Western world became progressively liberal, free, and democratic.

By 1900 or 1910, the vertical flow of wealth from the sovereign to the people virtually ceased, for the simple reason that the sovereign had pretty well cleaned out the frontier cupboard. He could no longer stake the losers. The means of his generosity were exhausted. Competition became cruel, resulting in a dangerous threat of monopoly. The inevitable crisis came in 1929, affecting all the Western world. The sovereign wanted to resume the old process of giving, but he had nothing to give. He solved the problem by the simple expedient of *reversing the vertical flow of wealth. He began taking from the people instead of giving.* In the democracies, what he took from some he gave to others, thus setting up the *vertical circulation* of wealth, thus signaling the end of an abnormal period when wealth flowed predominantly in one direction, the abnormal period in which most of our current economic principles originated and our cherished political institutions were born. The citizens are now being required to reassume many of the normal obligations and duties from which the sovereign so long excused them when he was making them both free and rich.

The view advanced here is that the free dispersion of frontier wealth, the vertical flow primarily downward, formed a frame and backdrop for modern practices, economic and political. This prevailing downward flow of wealth from the sovereign fostered competition, prevented monopoly, made laissez faire tenable, and put the sovereign in the van of the liberal movement out of which political democracy came.[2] Let us now look at the law.

MODIFICATIONS IN THE LAW

It is obvious that with the opening up of the Great Frontier, lands and people beyond Christendom, new and unusual demands were made upon the law, lay and clerical. Since the sovereign and not the Church held title to all the Great Frontier, there was a distinct gain by the secular power, and a corresponding loss by the ecclesiastical. Consequently the Church played a minor role in the evolution of law in the New World.

The law grew and changed because it was required to answer practical questions that rose immediately and for which there were no precedents. Francisco Vittorio, better known to us as Vitoria, was a professor of sacred theology at the University of Salamanca. Spain was in a quandary as to what rights she had over the Indians and what rights the Church had. The controversy was

[2] For a fuller discussion of the vertical pulsation of wealth, see Walter Prescott Webb, *The Great Frontier* (Boston, 1952), 150ff.

referred to Vitoria, who in 1532 delivered a lecture, "On the Indians Lately Discovered." Vitoria said:

> The whole of this controversy and discussion was started on account of the aborigines of the New World, commonly called Indians, who came forty years ago into the power of the Spaniards, not having been previously known to our world. This present disputation about them will fall into three parts. In the first part we shall inquire by what right these Indian natives came under Spanish sway. In the second part, what rights the Spanish sovereigns obtained over them in temporal and civil matters. In the third part, what rights these sovereigns of the Church obtained over them in matters spiritual and touching religion.[3]

In seeking to answer these practical questions, Vitoria evolved the principles of modern international law. He was the first of the Spanish School of International Law and preceded Hugo Grotius, the last member of that school, by a century. In consideration of the plight of the strange people found overseas, Vitoria dealt with the following subjects, which sound quite contemporary: title by discovery, ambassadors, compulsory acceptance of pacific settlement, conscientious objectors, intervention, letters of marque and reprisal, booty and prize, neutrals, and *temperamenta*. "These *temperamenta*," says James Brown Scott, "were designed to mitigate the harshness of war . . . in the absence of a court between the nations. The creation of such a court is not the least contribution of the successors of those first Americans [Indians] to whom Vitoria extended the law of nations " [4]

Hugo Grotius, the reputed founder of international law, made his notable contribution under circumstances which demanded an immediate answer to a practical problem. As a young attorney for the Dutch East India Company, Grotius was given the task of defending one Captain Heemskirk, who had captured a Portuguese galleon in what was considered a *mare clausum*, or closed sea. In preparing the defense, Grotius evolved his theory of the free seas and published it under the title *Mare Liberum* in 1609. His conclusion is found in one sentence: "Every nation is free to travel to every other nation, and to trade with it." His considera-

[3] James Brown Scott (ed.), *The Spanish Origin of International Law: Francisco de Vitoria and His Law of Nations* (Washington, D.C., 1934), 3.
[4] *Ibid.*, 286.

tion of the alternative of a free sea led him into a study of war, and in 1625 he published his classic *The Law of War and Peace*.[5] The sea was the only road to the Great Frontier, and the rules made for the road were international. And since the Great Frontier lay beyond Christendom, the rules were made by the states and not by the Church, a good example of the secularizing influence of the frontier.

As a final illustration of how the law changed under the impact of the frontier, let us see what happened to the law governing land tenure. (In all this study, it is hard to get away from land, the essence of the frontier.) In the Metropolis prior to 1500, land was so valuable, so scarce, that the law dealt with it in a highly protective manner, and without much regard for what we now think of as individual rights. The individual was not important, but the land was. It was usually handed down by primogeniture to the eldest son, and its unity was preserved intact through entail. In both cases, it was the land and not the individual that the law was determined to preserve.

With the advent of the Great Frontier, the relationship between man and land was radically altered. Whereas land had been the scarce factor and men the abundant one, land suddenly became abundant and men relatively scarce. Therefore, the law slowly, tardily, and reluctantly turned from an attitude of protecting the land to one of protecting or rewarding the individual. There was enough land now for every child to have a portion, and the result was that both primogeniture and entail were swept away in all frontier countries. In the United States, these laws passed out in many of the states prior to the Revolution, and in all states after it. In its place have come the law of equal inheritance and a prohibition of entail. The abolition of primogeniture and entail extended with modifications and revisions throughout the Western world, even back in Europe. Thus we see equality among the children of one family emerge from an abundance of land.

This line of reasoning leads us to an unpleasant question, unpleasant because we resent the answer. If the abundance of land caused the law to act on behalf of the individual, to give each one equal rights, will an approaching scarcity of land in relation to people cause the law to turn again to protecting the land and ig-

[5] *Ibid.*, 159.

noring equality, the supposed right of individuals? Will the law
always act in favor of the scarcer of two commodities, the commodities being in this case land and human beings? Now that
the population of the Metropolis and the Great Frontier is
greater per square mile than it was in 1500, will we return to
the equivalent of primogeniture and entail? Will we abandon our
ideal of human equality?

The date when the law should logically turn from the individual and begin to act on behalf of the land can be determined
rather accurately by simple mathematics. What we are concerned
with is the land-man ratio. Prior to the advent of the Great
Frontier, there was for each individual in the Metropolis about
24 acres of land, good and bad. The ratio can be expressed as

$$X = \frac{L}{M} = 24$$

When the frontier lands were added, L increased faster than M,
hence X was greater than 24. It was after the census of 1930—the
year of the world depression—that the *character* of the equation
changed. By that time, population per square mile was greater
than it had been in 1500; M increased faster than L, and hence
X became and remained less than 24 acres per person.

Theoretically the law should have shifted its attention from
human rights to land protection in 1930; but the law is a tardy
servant, and it never closes the gate until the best horses are gone.
Eventually, however, the law will close this gate when human need
and welfare require it. There is no country where a return to
primogeniture and entail will meet with more resistance than in
America, because we are so deeply committed to equality for all.
The idea of giving the estate to the eldest son is repugnant to
judge, jury, and populace. Therefore, it may surprise all of
us to find that an agricultural seminar at Columbia University
has published a book recommending a return to the equivalent of
primogeniture and entail. The editor-author is Leonard Hastings
Schoff, and the title is *A National Agriculture Policy: For All the
People of the United States*.[6] Of course, Professor Schoff does not
use the objectionable words *primogeniture* and *entail,* but the
wolf is poorly concealed under the fleecy verbiage.

[6] This book was published by Harper & Bros. in 1950.

The Schoff argument runs as follows: There is a minimum land unit for one family, and to divide that unit for any reason is to destroy its value and contribute to human woe. Therefore, such a unit should go to one heir, the one who remains on the land and uses it. He never pays his brothers and sisters any principal for their share but does pay them 4 per cent interest as long as they live. If one dies, there is no further payment. If all die, the farm is his.

There is a long lag between a professor's theory and a nation's law, but Schoff's book may well become a landmark, an early contribution in a great body of future legal literature justifying legislation on behalf of land, the scarce commodity, rather than on behalf of people who are too abundant to take care of it.

I have attempted here to stand on a high peak and point out a few features of the Great Frontier as I see it. In detail, I have tried to point out that in the long perspective we may see things in a new relationship, things we cannot see nearly so well when we restrict ourselves to viewing a fragment such as the one we have in this country. I have tried to illustrate what I believe—that the whole is simpler than any of its parts, and greater than all of them considered separately. If we know the whole, we understand better where the parts belong. Illustrations of the impact of the Great Frontier have been drawn from two fields, that of land (or wealth) and of law. These are but two of the avenues that open to the inquiring mind. I have not touched on the impact the Great Frontier had on the human imagination as expressed in a literature of romance and adventure, or its impact on science when it flooded Europe with so many new life specimens as to lead Linnaeus and Lyell to make their classifications. This same frontier furnished Darwin the specimens on which he founded his theory of evolution. If we are disturbed because the American frontier has been too well tilled, then we may move out into the Great Frontier, using the techniques learned here, and have a go at a broad land which lies fallow before us.

SELECTED READINGS

Alexander, Franz. *Our Age of Unreason, a Study of the Irrational Forces in Social Life.* New York: J. B. Lippincott, 1942.

Alexander, Frederick. *Moving Frontiers, an American Theme and its Application to Australian History.* Victoria: Melbourne University Press, 1947.

Dennis, Lawrence. *The Dynamics of War and Revolution.* New York: The Weekly Foreign Letter, 1940.

Gillespie, James E. *The Influence of Overseas Expansion on England to 1700.* New York: Columbia University Press, 1920.

Hamilton, Earl J. *American Treasure and the Price Revolution in Spain, 1500–1650.* Cambridge, Mass.: Harvard University Press, 1934.

Hancock, W. K. *Survey of British Commonwealth Affairs.* London: Oxford University Press, 1937–1942.

Keynes, John Maynard. *A Treatise on Money.* 2 vols. New York: Harcourt, Brace & Co., 1930.

Smith, Adam. *An Inquiry into the Nature and Causes of the Wealth of Nations.* 2 vols. London, 1776.

Sumner, William Graham. "Earth-Hunger or the Philosophy of Land Grabbing," in his *Earth-Hunger and Other Essays,* ed. by Albert G. Keller. New Haven: Yale University Press, 1913.

Walker, Eric A. *The Frontier Tradition in South Africa.* London: Oxford University Press, 1930.

Webb, Walter Prescott. *The Great Frontier.* Boston: Houghton, Mifflin, 1952.

———. "Ended: 400 Year Boom," *Harper's Magazine,* CCIII (October, 1951), 25–33.

———. "Windfalls of the Frontier," *Harper's Magazine,* CCIII (November, 1951), 71–77.

PART II

THE AMERICAN FRONTIER

THOMAS PERKINS ABERNETHY

The Southern Frontier,
an Interpretation

The southern frontier was in some respects unique among the frontiers of the world. It moved from the Atlantic to the dry plains in a century and drew westward both the aristocracy and the masses of the South. The lodestone was a rich land in a temperate clime. In this essay, Professor Abernethy, who has written extensively of the southern frontier development, points out that the process of settlement there was considerably different than what has been attributed to the American frontier. He casts serious doubt on the presumed contribution of this frontier to social and political democracy and states that it takes more than a forest to break a tradition of aristocracy.

There were three frontiers in the South: the Atlantic seacoast was once a part of an aristocratic English frontier; the Appalachian highland and its valleys through which filtered the Scotch-Irish and German immigrants softened the old-world traditions and encouraged democracy; and the settling of the Lower and Upper South by the masses, the middle classes, and the planter aristocracy produced a blend of the old and the new, the tradition of government by the few for both the few and the many. The failure of the Turner hypothesis to understand that democracy was not the inevitable evolution of frontiers seems to Professor Abernethy a significant omission. This borderland gave opportunity to the few as to the many, and the resultant society was a compromise between the two.

THERE are several ways in which the southern frontier differed from any other, and within the South there was of course a series of frontiers. The first of these lay along the Atlantic Coast and was settled by Englishmen during the seventeenth century. Abundant land, primitive conditions, and the Indian menace gave this region the characteristics which we associate with pioneer settlements; yet since none of the first colonists had had previous experience with such conditions, it was, in a sense, a frontier without frontiersmen.

One of the important features of frontier development is that an element of natural selection is always involved. Only men of certain types and conditions are inclined to pull up stakes and live for a generation on the outskirts of civilization. Back-breaking toil and exposure to manifold dangers were involved in most cases, and there were many who shrank from such harsh conditions. In general, it was only the hardy, the brave, the ambitious, and the unfortunate who voluntarily chose to become frontiersmen, and this natural selection was reflected in the human characteristics which colored the life of pioneer communities.

As for the Atlantic seaboard, the nature of this selection was unique. In the case of later settlements, the adventurers normally migrated of their own free will, under their own power, and at their own expense. In the case of the first colonists, on the other hand, the freemen came voluntarily and usually at their own expense, but the indentured servants—who made up a large part of the population—had their passage paid for them, and some did not come voluntarily. Therefore in the southern colonies where indentured servants were most numerous, the population lacked some of the hardihood that is characteristic of the frontiersman and cautiously hugged the coast for a hundred years. This, along with their lack of experience, was responsible for many of the disasters that befell the early colonists. If the men who settled at Jamestown had possessed the same qualities and training as those who later settled Kentucky, the story would have been a very different one; but the pioneer John Martin who stepped from the

Susan Constant to the sands of Jamestown in 1607 was markedly different from the pioneer Daniel Boone who traveled the Wilderness Trail to the Kentucky country in 1775.

But this was only one of the peculiarities of the tidewater frontier of the seventeenth century. It is typical of most—though not of all—frontiers that they should be almost completely self-sustaining. Having little contact with the outside world, the pioneer farmer produces his own food and clothing and develops an independence and resourcefulness in action that are commonly referred to as "rugged individualism." He is fairly innocent of the amenities of cultured society and is likely to be restive of restraint, but he recognizes the need of leadership and accepts it readily, especially when there are Indians to be fought. He is proud of his independence but is no equalitarian.

The second peculiarity of the Atlantic frontier was that it was never self-sufficient. After the first few years the colonists were able to produce their own food, but during the seventeenth century they were never able to clothe themselves or to produce even the simplest manufactures. Constant communication with the mother country was necessary in order to supply many of the necessities of life, and much besides commodities came over in the ships which sailed from London and Liverpool. Few American communities have had the freedom or the originality to shape anew their own basic institutions, but none has been more closely bound by law and precedent than those of the South Atlantic seaboard. Though there were local differences and a degree of colonial self-government, all political institutions were based upon English precedent and the mother country always had the final authority. Even in religious affairs, Anglicanism exerted the prevailing influence.

The social life of the southern colonies, too, was shaped, in the main, according to English ideas. But there was some difference in the make-up of the population on the opposite sides of the Atlantic. Though many indentured servants were brought by force to America, there was yet no pauper element on this side of the ocean. Nor were there, in the seventeenth century, any nobles who made America their home. Thus, the top and the bottom strata of English society were eliminated. And because of the abundance and cheapness of land, there was greater fluidity

within the strata which existed. Yet class distinctions were maintained, and we cannot say that colonial society was truly democratic.

The colonists were accustomed to a stratified society and had
never heard of the doctrine of human equality. They did not rebel
at the thralldom of class just because they had arrived on a frontier. The simple farmer doffed his hat to his wealthier neighbor
and looked to him for leadership. The larger landowners were
often justices of the peace or vestrymen who served without compensation and usually performed their duties conscientiously. This
sense of public responsibility on the part of the gentry was
inherited from the English squirearchy, and it produced a remarkably stable society.

The tradition of hospitality was another contribution of the colonial South. England was a tight little island where the world
was likely to be too much at hand and the aristocrat valued his
privacy and resented intrusion. The southern colonies were
sprawling domains and the population was thinly spread over the
face of the earth. Solitude was often oppressive and human associations were welcomed. The planter, who often was lord of all he
surveyed, welcomed the sight of a new face and invited the
stranger to tarry and talk. Consequently, the respectable traveler
rarely had to spend a night at a tavern, and his host knew how to
put him at his ease.

In general, it can be said that the southern colonies carried on
the English tradition more nearly intact than did the others. New
England represented a dissent from the English tradition in
ecclesiastical, political, and social matters. The Middle colonies
had large foreign elements in their populations, and there was
much diversity in religion. In the South, there were modifications
produced by local conditions but the forms and ideals of English
life continued to be recognizable. As settlement extended westward, these traditions were not altogether lost.

The first westward movement in the South occurred during the
first third of the eighteenth century, and it carried civilization
into the northern and central Piedmont regions of Virginia, that
is, into the area lying between the fall line of the rivers and the
Blue Ridge Mountains. Frederick Jackson Turner speaks of this
region as "the uplands," but there are few mountains until one

reaches the foothills of the Blue Ridge, and it is mostly a gently rolling terrain. The soil consists largely of red clay and it is moderately fertile. In Tidewater, the large plantations lay along the river fronts, and there was room for only a limited number of them, but in the Piedmont there was enough good land for both rich and poor. Furthermore, tobacco could be grown just as profitably on a small farm as on a large one. A democratic society should have been the logical result of these conditions, but actually Tidewater institutions were transferred with little change.

Since it required no great effort to get above the fall line, it would seem natural that many poor men, ex-indentured servants and others, would have penetrated the backwoods of the Piedmont and squatted on the public lands. But careful search has revealed few traces of such a population. The landless poor apparently clung to navigable water and migrated to the sounds and inlets of North Carolina, leaving the Virginia Piedmont to be first settled by more substantial citizens. Many of the earliest grants in this region were for thousands of acres, and their owners were either abandoning their depleted Tidewater acres or providing for their numerous progeny. Of course the majority of the newcomers took up the standard four-hundred-acre tracts, but they accepted the leadership of their wealthier neighbors, just as they had always done, and Peter and Thomas Jefferson were among these squires.

There was no Indian menace on this frontier and it was never self-sufficing. Tobacco was the money crop and there were boatable waters to take the hogsheads down to Richmond or some other port. Luxuries from England could be brought back in return, but transportation was more expensive than in Tidewater, and more of the necessities of life were produced at home. The leadership was not so well entrenched and the larger number of middle-class farmers produced a more democratic spirit, but institutions did not appreciably change. Thomas Jefferson's democracy came from European philosophers, not from his contact with the wilderness.

The next frontier was settled during the second third of the eighteenth century, and it was of a very different character. About 1730, Scotch-Irish and German settlers began to pour into the Shenandoah Valley, just beyond the Blue Ridge. They came from

Pennsylvania and were seeking fertile fields for cultivation. Virginia offered them religious toleration and cheaper lands than those of the Quaker colony, and they migrated in considerable numbers. Settlers from eastern Virginia joined them and the population came to consist of about one-third Germans, one-third Scotch-Irish, and one-third Virginians. Most of the tracts on which they settled had been granted to speculators, as was the case throughout the Valley of Virginia all the way to the Carolina line, but the terms of sale were reasonable, and the soil was rich. There was little room for squatters and the land was occupied from the very beginning by substantial small-scale farmers.

This region is often spoken of as an extension of Pennsylvania, but that is hardly a correct interpretation. The immigrants did not begin coming to Pennsylvania in appreciable numbers until the second decade of the eighteenth century and most of them tarried in that province only long enough to work out an indenture. Thus, they had hardly had time to acquire local characteristics; they were really Europeans who presently became Virginians. For some generations they kept up their ancestral customs and their ancestral speech, but the Virginians who lived among them exerted a strong influence and they gradually lost their local peculiarities.

The Germans were the best farmers that the colonies ever had, but they took little interest in politics and were not inclined to leave the farms which they had established. Harrisonburg was a German community, but the German settlers did not usually penetrate much farther south, and Staunton, the next town just below Harrisonburg, was distinctly Scotch-Irish. By mid-century, these hardy and adventurous people had gone down the Great Valley of Virginia as far south as the North Carolina line, and they had been joined by many native Virginians.

When they reached the neighborhood of present-day Roanoke, they had the choice of two routes to follow. Some continued down the Valley, crossed into North Carolina, and by 1786 reached the site of Knoxville, Tennessee. Others crossed the Blue Ridge where the Roanoke River cuts through it and, leaving some settlers in the foothills of that mountain chain, passed on into the piedmont region of the Carolinas. Some made their homes on the headwaters of the Yadkin River, where Daniel Boone and Christopher

Gist settled in the early 1750's and the Moravians from Bethlehem, Pennsylvania, founded their Wachovia colony at about the same time.

Those who went to the Piedmont of South Carolina found that they had been preceded by Scotch-Irish and Germans whom Governor Johnson of that province had encouraged to migrate and settle on the frontier. Lands were made available to them on easy terms, and, fed by the two streams of immigrants, the population increased rapidly during the middle decades of the eighteenth century. Thus there was established, along the whole line of the Southern frontier, a chain of settlements that furnished a barrier against the Indians and a source of food for the staple-growing inhabitants of the tidewater communities.

In contrast to the eastern communities, this entire region was inhabited by men who lived simply, practiced a self-sustaining economy, and had little regard for the aristocratic English way of life. In the Carolinas, there were graziers whose herds, numbering hundreds or even thousands of head, roamed the woods and sustained themselves both summer and winter on the natural forage. During the calving season, the animals were penned and branded, some being driven to market and others slaughtered for their hides. There were also farmers who squatted on the public lands, cultivated a few newly cleared acres, and lived on a diet of hog and hominy. Still others bought lands and established grain-growing farms.

This is the frontier which Turner describes in his essay on "The Old West," but it does not appear that the three types of economy followed each other in regular succession. The land that was good for grazing was usually not good for farming, and though the land-owning farmer sometimes bought up the improvements of the squatter, this was not commonly the case. The herdsman, the squatter, and the land-owning farmer often lived in the same region at the same time, each selecting the land that best suited his requirements.

In the Valley of Virginia, the herdsman never existed. Since the land had to be bought from speculators, the settlers could not afford the large acreage required, and there was no precedent for such an economy in the Old Dominion. Farmers usually kept herds of between twenty-five and fifty head of cattle. The calves were penned so that the milk cows would be available, and occasionally an animal was slaughtered for beef, but Jefferson never killed a cow before it was ten years old. No barns and little feed were provided for the herds during the winter, and there are many witnesses to the fact that the quality of beef was very poor.

Life on the Scotch-Irish and German frontier was simple. It was here that the log cabin first became a standard habitation, and it ordinarily had but one or two rooms. The squirrel rifle had only recently been perfected in Pennsylvania, and it became the usual weapon of the frontier, both for hunting and for war. The hunting shirt and the moccasin were adopted as the costume of the woodsman. These of course were made of deerskin, but as deer became scarce, the leather furnished by the herdsmen—this being their principal product—came to be much used. The early southern frontier as we usually picture it—the frontier of Daniel Boone and George Rogers Clark—was the Scotch-Irish and German frontier.

Life here was quite different from that of the landed aristocrats of Tidewater. The poorest man had his horse, and the richest had few luxuries. The English tradition of a stratified society was not strong among the Scotch-Irish, but they nevertheless had their leaders. Being good Presbyterians, they respected their clergy, and they also respected official position. In both Virginia and the Carolinas they had to accept the political and legal institutions which had been established on the seaboard, and these were not democratic. In the Valley of Virginia, certain leading Scotch-Irish families tended to pre-empt the county offices and pass them on from one generation to another. Thus a certain community of interests was established between the East and the West which prevented sharp regional conflicts. In the Carolinas, where the pine barrens separated the Piedmont from the Tidewater, there was a greater contrast between the regions, and rivalries were keener.

Since there were few slaves and few great estates among these people, they favored democratic institutions. They opposed established churches and royal prerogatives, and during the Revolution they were staunch patriots. At the battle of King's Mountain, their rifles spoke out for freedom. As far as this frontier is concerned, Turner is certainly right in saying that it promoted the development of democracy.

The next frontier was settled during the last quarter of the eighteenth century, and it again differed from the one which preceded it.

The first settlements in Kentucky were planted in 1775, and Nashville, Tennessee, was founded four years later. Judge Richard Henderson of North Carolina claimed the land and the jurisdiction in both areas and was the leading promoter of settlement. Though he soon lost his claims, other speculators and men of means took up the best lands, and consequently this was never a poor man's frontier.

The reasons for this are obvious. The Bluegrass region of Kentucky and the Nashville Basin in Tennessee possessed unusually fertile soil, and both areas were separated from the older settlements by several hundred miles of Indian-infested wilderness. Poor men seeking a subsistence rarely possessed the means, the courage, or the initiative to seek out such distant and dangerous locations. They tended to drift to the nearest vacant lands, and they left their more fortunate and enterprising contemporaries to look far afield for their fortunes. After these leaders had opened the trail and broken the ground, then the humbler citizens followed, but they found the best lands already pre-empted and had to content themselves with less desirable tracts.

The early settlers of the Bluegrass region of Kentucky and the Nashville Basin of Tennessee were neither Tidewater aristocrats nor poor whites. Just as the Tidewater colonies did not attract nobles or paupers, so this new frontier, being even more difficult of access, did not get its settlers from either the top or the bottom rung of the older society. It offered considerable rewards to the enterprising members of the middle classes who were anxious to rise in the world, and the spirit of speculation was strong among them.

But they carried with them something more than ambition. Most of them came from the piedmont and valley regions of Virginia and the Carolinas and were able in this rich country to buy slaves and establish prosperous plantations. Through their contacts with the older settlements, they had become familiar with Tidewater traditions, and their object was to live as the southern planter lived. Tobacco and cattle furnished them with marketable products, and presently they learned to make bourbon whisky and to produce a number of manufactures on a small scale. Though it was Presbyterian and democratic to a degree, the Kentucky Bluegrass came to be more like the Tidewater of Virginia than the Valley.

But many poorer people, especially from Pennsylvania and New Jersey, moved into the less fertile areas of Kentucky, and even the Bluegrass people had something of the spirit of the frontier. When Kentucky became a state in 1792, her first constitution provided for manhood suffrage, but this concession to democracy was somewhat limited by the provision that the governor and senate were to be chosen by an electoral college. Seven years later this provision was abolished, but loud demands made by a minority for a more radical democracy were turned down.

Tennessee, admitted to the Union in 1796, was the first state to have passed through the territorial status and was without precedent to guide its transition. In its eastern valleys it included the first organized transmontane settlements. The frontiersmen who planted them had, therefore, been shackled neither by powerful precedent, crystallized opinion, nor petrified institutions. How then did Tennessee respond to this unique opportunity? She adopted almost *in toto* the constitution of North Carolina, with some interesting modifications in which democratic advance was more apparent than real. As in North Carolina, the Tennessee constitution required officeholders to believe in God and a future state of rewards and punishments. It provided also that justices of the peace should be elected for life by the Assembly and that they in turn should choose most of the other county officials. The experience of the Tennessee frontier makes it clear that it takes more than the forest to produce democracy.

The next southern frontier was that which was established along the Gulf Coast during the first third of the nineteenth century. There were earlier Spanish and French settlements here, but the purchase of Louisiana opened up a vast region to American immigration, and Jackson's victories during the War of 1812 and the purchase of Florida in 1819 made much of the Gulf region available for settlement.

Unlike the situation in Kentucky and Tennessee, this land belonged to the Federal government and was sold under its system of regular surveys and public auctions. The best tracts, of course, were surveyed first and were offered for sale at a minimum price of $2 per acre. Most of the purchasers came from the South Atlantic states and had to make long and arduous journeys in order to reach their new homes. Such conditions did not attract men without property. The result was that the best lands were sold to men of means, sometimes to speculators, and the poorer people became squatters on the less desirable tracts which had not yet been surveyed. Thus, instead of a rotation as between squatter and substantial farmer, there was a degree of segregation from the beginning. And the herdsman was also present; his cattle roamed the more isolated regions which were not desired by the planters.

It was the development of the culture of upland cotton that furnished the stimulus for migration into the Gulf states, and it dominated the economy and the way of life there. Large plantations with many slaves came into existence, and the planter, looking nostalgically back to the traditions of his earlier home, wished to live as the eastern planters lived. He was not really a frontiersman but only a settler upon the frontier; and yet his life was in many ways governed by the primitive conditions under which he existed. His first home was often a log cabin; for a time, to all outward appearances, he lived much as the squatters and the poor whites. But he was vastly different in caliber, and presently the profits from his crops enabled him to build a pillared mansion in the Jeffersonian style and to indulge in the lavish hospitality which was characteristic of the South Atlantic seaboard. Thus the Gulf states came to be an extension of the Old South.

These cotton planters were not so well entrenched as were their counterparts on the Atlantic Coast; and they were, of course, outnumbered by the humbler folk who settled among them. If they wished to be elected to office, they had to cultivate the favor of the people, and thus democracy made some headway in the region. The first Alabama constitution, adopted in 1819, provided for manhood suffrage, but Mississippi and Louisiana required the payment of taxes in lieu of other qualifications. These states in their social and political life represented a compromise between frontier democracy and plantation aristocracy. There was no sharp conflict between the two because the one deferred to the other, and there was no economic rivalry between them. The self-sustaining farmer did not require the best lands; he did not raise much cotton, and he could supply the cotton planter with necessary produce. In politics, he accepted as a matter of course the leadership of his more prosperous and better-educated fellow citizens.

There was still another southern frontier which is easy to understand but difficult to define. It was divided into two parts, of which the most distinctive was the great Appalachian chain of mountains extending all the way from the Pennsylvania border to central Alabama, in some parts at least a hundred miles wide. The valleys and coves of this region were settled largely by the Scotch-Irish who came down from Pennsylvania; and, being isolated from the world, they maintained their traditional customs and practiced a self-sustaining economy. Though they were primitive in their habits, they were self-respecting and courageous, and they had little in common with a society which was dominated by slave-owning planters. Since they constituted only a small minority in the states in which they lived, they exerted no great influence in politics until the Confederate War came on. In that crisis, most of them adhered to the Union and one group established the state of West Virginia.

The other part of this frontier existed in the lowlands. The poorer and more isolated lands in all the southern states were gradually occupied by men of the simpler sort, most of them squatters during the early years. They had little or no capital, and their only object was to live an independent life. Some were herdsmen whose numerous cattle grazed on the public lands and furnished a meager subsistence through the sale of hides. Some were farmers who did not own the land on which they lived, but whose swine flourished on the abundant mast and whose corn patches furnished bread and sometimes drink as well. In time, an occasional squatter bought his land, or it was bought by a more substantial farmer, and thus we have a frontier which closely approximated the Turnerian pattern. This frontier still exists in isolated regions; it was and is the home of the Southern "poor white." It was never a constructive force in Southern society but it has always had considerable weight on election days, and it accounts for some of the peculiarities of Southern politics.

What, then, is the significance of the southern frontier? Some regions failed to experience all the phases which Turner envisioned as the typical evolution of a frontier community. By the use of indentured servants or slaves, plantations were established at an early date, a loosely stratified society developed, and the more prosperous landlords undertook to live as nearly as possible like their English prototypes had lived before them. Slavery made their manner of life possible, but it did not furnish their ideas. The South produced the only well-established landed aristocracy that this country has known, and its principal merit was that it furnished competent leadership in a rural society. Much has been made in recent years of the conflict between the small farmer and the planter, but in fact they usually coöperated for the reason that their economic interests did not seem to conflict. Many small farmers hoped to become planters, and their traditions were such that they readily accepted the leadership of their "betters."

On his isolated estate the planter practiced a hospitality that was unknown in England. He had accepted the Revolutionary doctrine that all white men were equal before the law and were equally entitled to respect. His private life was his own, but he was a democrat in public, partly from conviction and partly because he was often a candidate for office. It was not altogether an accident that both Thomas Jefferson and Andrew Jackson were Southerners.

The colonial tradition of gentility permeated all the more prosperous areas of the South, and the upper classes shaped their lives according to its tenets. Since the simpler folk tended to imitate those who ranked above them, there was a general tendency to conform to a single pattern. But the frontier persisted in the back country and continued to exert a powerful influence in politics. Thus southern life presented its own peculiar compromise between sophistication and simplicity, between the old world and the new.

SELECTED READINGS

Abernethy, Thomas P. *The Formative Period in Alabama, 1815–1828.* ("Historical and Patriotic Series") Montgomery, Alabama: Alabama State Department of Archives and History, 1922.

——. *From Frontier to Plantation in Tennessee*. Chapel Hill: University of North Carolina Press, 1932.

——. *Three Virginia Frontiers*. Baton Rouge: Louisiana State University Press, 1940.

——. *Western Lands and the American Revolution*. New York: D. Appleton-Century, 1937.

Coleman, R. V. *The First Frontier*. New York: Scribners, 1948.

Dick, Everett. *The Dixie Frontier*. New York: Knopf, 1948.

Eaton, Clement. *A History of the Old South*. New York: Macmillan, 1949.

Henderson, Archibald. *The Conquest of the Old Southwest*. New York: Century, 1920.

Turner, Frederick Jackson. "The Old West," in *The Frontier in American History*. New York: H. Holt, 1920.

Whitaker, Arthur Preston. *The Spanish-American Frontier, 1783–1795*. Boston: Houghton Mifflin, 1927.

PAUL W. GATES

Frontier Estate Builders
and Farm Laborers

*The Midwestern frontier has always been pictured as a simple
society where sturdy pioneers planted their corn in the clearings
or on the prairies and in time became owners of their "hundred and
sixties." These people were men of little means who gained a
middle-class status by hard work and unearned increment as the
country was settled.*

*Professor Gates, in his numerous writings on land speculation,
has been questioning this stereotype of the corn-belt frontiersman.
He believes that this frontier was not nearly so simple and unified
as we have long believed. In this essay, he calls attention to the
"early appearance of farm laborers and tenants, many of whom
were never to rise to farm-ownership status, and of great landed
estates, whose owners brought wealth with them and added much
to it" and states that this "did not make for 'a fundamental unity
in its [frontier's] social structure and its democratic ideals. . . .' " It
was these prairie landlords who helped enthrone the Republican
party and who kept the Democratic party in conservative hands
after the Civil War. It was not until the third-party movements
began to make inroads upon this system of privilege that the
democracy of the Midwest attained a status imputed to it by
Frederick Jackson Turner. This essay, like that of Professor Abernethy's on the South, indicates that American frontier society in*

143

the Mississippi Valley was much more complex than that envisioned in our previous thinking. These two suggest that the second and third waves of people who move into the frontier zone after the first generation deeply influence the character of the society that emerges there.

TO the simple democratic society of the American frontier consisting mostly of small farmers, as Frederick Jackson Turner described it, should be added two types, the one common, the other small in numbers but profoundly important in shaping land-ownership patterns, political action, and the beginnings of a cultured society. The first of these types includes the farm laborers, some of whom became farm tenants. The other type is the capitalist estate builder who took with him a "seemingly endless appetite for power and for land," as Arthur Moore put it.[1] It was these capitalist estate builders, whether cattle barons, land speculators turned developers, or men who went west with the set purpose of creating great plantations operated by tenants or hired hands, who made possible the employment of thousands of laborers.

The capitalist developer, big and little, was first revealed indirectly in 1860 when the Bureau of the Census presented statistics showing the number of farm laborers—statistics as noteworthy in their way as those showing the extent of farm tenancy in 1880 or the statement of the superintendent of the census in 1890 that the frontier was gone. Notwithstanding America's much-boasted opportunities, its seemingly limitless supply of public lands, its ever-expanding and newly opening frontier, the farm laborer, ordinarily a landless person whose economic status was less secure than that of the European peasant, was shown to exist in large numbers, not only in the older and well-developed communities, but in the new states and middle border territories.

Consider for a moment Iowa, only fourteen years a state, still but lightly touched by settlement, not able to boast two people to the square mile, with less than a third of its land in farms but the bulk of its public lands already in private ownership. Despite the slight development of this state, largely concentrated in the eastern counties, its obvious frontier status, its abundance of raw un-

[1] Arthur Moore, *The Farmer and Rest of Us* (Boston, 1945), 131.

improved prairie, Iowa in 1860 reported 40,827 farm laborers—
6 per cent of its population. More to the point, out of every hundred persons engaged in agriculture, twenty-three were farm laborers. Or look at Kansas, which had neither attained the dignity
of statehood nor acquired anything but a thin veneer of settlement along its eastern border in the six years since it had become
a territory. Census enumerators found here 10,400 farms and,
surprisingly, 3,660 farm laborers. Nineteen out of every hundred
persons engaged in agriculture were farm laborers. For the states
of the Old Northwest the percentage of farm laborers among the
total number of people engaged in agriculture ranged from
20 to 28.

Throughout the rest of the century, the number of farm laborers grew rapidly in the newer states of the Upper Mississippi Valley, while in the older states it fluctuated up and down and took a
violent upward turn in the last decade. In proportion to the total
number of persons engaged in agriculture, the number of farm
laborers reached a high point in 1870. The census for that year
shows that the percentage of farm laborers in the total number of
persons engaged in agriculture was 30 in Minnesota, 32 in Nebraska, 33 in Wisconsin, 34 in Kansas, and 37 in Iowa. All these
states had fairly stable and well-developed areas by 1870; but all
except Iowa also had portions not yet out of the frontier stage.
With so many farm laborers in new as well as old communities,
no picture of the West can be considered complete without attention to their social and economic background, the reasons why
they existed in such numbers. But Western historians have not
been concerned about them. The stereotype of the mortgaged
farmer is familiar to all students of Western lore, but the farm
laborer has not been the subject of rowdy ballads, he does not
appear in the fiction of the frontier, nor is he to be found in the
works of Turner, Paxson, Riegel, or Billington.

Statistics of farm labor for these years in new states and territories are so startling that it seems desirable to look into their
compilation to determine just who in the opinion of the census
enumerators fitted into this category. Analysis of the original
census schedules shows that older boys of farm families who were
over fifteen years of age and were living at home were not infre-
quently listed as farm laborers. Undoubtedly they performed

heavy routine work on the farm, but I have not thought of them as laborers, since they rarely drew wages and since they could expect to inherit a share of the farm some time in the future. Offsetting this factor was the exclusion of migratory workers who were employed for the harvest season but were not at the time of enumeration living with the farmers who had previously engaged them or were thereafter to do so. Clearly, the timing of the census was important in the matter of enumerating farm laborers. The first of June, the date for which information was collected, was not the busiest time for farmers in the Corn Belt, because crops were already in, haying had not begun, and wheat was not yet ready for harvest. A month or six weeks later, enumerators would have found greater numbers of hired hands to list.[2]

By 1870 the census takers were collecting information respecting the value of compensation, including board paid hired hands the previous year. True, this information was not processed and published, but a sample study of Poweshiek County in central Iowa shows that of 1,634 farmers owning land, 932 paid out for labor the previous year sums ranging from $5 to $2,000, the average being over $150. In nine townships in this county, payments to farm laborers, including the value of their board, amounted to $234,000.[3]

The census schedules also furnish information on the emergence of farm tenancy, a midway step from laborer to farm owner, which is particularly valuable since we have no specific data on tenancy as such until 1880. Some years ago in a colloquy on land specula-

[2] Information on the use of migratory laborers is meager, but the *Davenport Gazette* (Iowa), published in an important river port, is helpful in its issues of July 13 to 18, 1868. Daily mention is made of the demand for farm hands, for which as much as $3 and $4 per day was being paid. A stampede of city workers was reported which so depleted the community that construction projects could not be carried on. On the 18th, the steamer Dubuque was reported as bringing in 75 field hands, who within thirty minutes after arrival were engaged at $3.50 to $3.75 a day. Later reports of the movement north of wheat harvesters indicate that migratory labor was a major feature of agriculture in Illinois, Iowa, Wisconsin, and Minnesota.

[3] The original census schedules of Iowa and Wisconsin are in the Iowa Historical and Art Department, Des Moines, and the State Historical Society of Wisconsin, Madison, where they were used for this paper.

tion at a meeting of the American Historical Association, this writer ventured to suggest to Dr. Joseph Schafer, superintendent of the State Historical Society of Wisconsin, that in his examination of the profits and losses in speculation, he may have underestimated the rents speculators collected; this suggestion was scoffed at for intimating that tenancy existed on the frontier or that rents could have been collected for land use.[4] Dr. Schafer was a tartar in argument, but the fact remains that tenancy did exist on the frontier, it was not uncommon in Wisconsin in the fifties, and it does have to be taken into account in any consideration of the frontier process. In the absence of detailed census compilations, we can learn much about tenancy from earlier census schedules, the county deed records, local newspaper advertisements, and correspondence of land dealers and landlords.[5]

The censuses of 1850, 1860, and 1870 show a sharp increase in the number of farms in excess of five hundred acres, the expanding volume of hired hands previously alluded to, and numerous "farmers" and farm laborers who owned no real or landed property but did have personal property such as horses, mules, oxen, milch or beef cattle, and hogs. Some of these "farmers" and farm laborers may have been attempting to buy farms they were operating, but whether they were or not, they were at the time tenants. Analy-

[4] For his study of the land speculation of Charles Augustus Murray, who bought 20,000 acres in Grant and LaFayette Counties, Wisconsin, in 1836, Dr. Schafer used the conveyance records at the county seats to determine when the various parcels of land were sold and at what prices. He concluded that Murray had not done as well as if the money had been invested in gilt-edge securities. Since leases ordinarily were not recorded, he had no way of knowing whether any of the land had been rented or what income might have come from rents. In regard to farm tenancy in 1880, these two counties ranked close to the top among Wisconsin counties. The state figure for 1880 is 9 per cent; figures for Grant and LaFayette are 14 and 18 per cent. For Schafer's treatment see his *The Wisconsin Lead Region* (Madison, 1932), 148–154.

[5] Notices of Wisconsin farms for rent in the fifties were found in the *Janesville Gazette*, the Janesville *Democratic Standard*, the Baraboo *Sauk County Standard*, and the *Eau Claire Free Press*. The papers of Catlin and Williamson, Cyrus Woodman, and J. Richardson & Co. in the Wisconsin State Historical Society and of Allen Hamilton and George W. Ewing in the Indiana State Library are useful.

sis of the 1870 census listings of farmers and farm laborers in two lightly developed western Iowa townships and one well-settled central Iowa township shows that of 184 persons (excluding children) listed as engaged in agriculture, ninety-six owned land and eighty-eight owned no real property, but fifty-seven of these latter owned personal property and were presumably tenants. Thirty-one "farmers" and farm laborers listed no property of any kind. Of the agricultural population of these three townships (Belvedere, Ashton, and Shiloh), 53 per cent owned farms and 47 per cent owned no land.

Farm land was being rented to tenants in Ohio, Indiana, and Illinois as early as the 1820's, but the practice did not become common for nearly a generation.[6] After the frenzy of land speculation in the thirties, many investors, caught with heavy obligations in a falling market, with interest and tax costs growing, offered to rent their land to squatters or newly arriving immigrants too poor to buy, partly to protect their property but also to get at least the taxes out of them.[7] As early as 1842, Solon Robinson, the well-known agricultural writer, in describing the attractions of the flat lands of northwestern Indiana to immigrants, said: "No matter if you have no money, you can rent land very low, and will soon be in a condition to let land instead of hiring it." [8] By the middle of the century, tenancy was emerging everywhere in the prairies of Indiana, Illinois, and eastern Iowa and a little more slowly in Wisconsin. From northern and eastern Indiana, the Military Tract and the central prairie counties of Illinois, and the eastern counties of Iowa came many reports of persons renting land who lacked the means to buy. Renting was so common in La Salle County, Illinois, that the local newspaper in its price current listed farms as renting from $1.25 to $1.50 an acre. In eastern Iowa, where improved land also was renting at the same prices, a dealer in 1852 advertised thirteen farms for sale or rent.

6 Solon J. Buck, *Pioneer Letters of Gershom Flagg* (Springfield, Illinois, 1912), 22–46; *Indiana Oracle and Dearborn Gazette* (Lawrence, Indiana), Oct. 4, 1823. Nicholas Longworth had 27 tenants on his farms near Cincinnati in 1850. Ophia D. Smith, *The Life and Times of Giles Richards, 1820–1860* ("Ohio Historical Collections," Vol. VI [Columbus, 1936]), 45.

7 Paul W. Gates, *Frontier Landlords and Pioneer Tenants* (Ithaca, 1945), 3.

8 Herbert A. Kellar (ed.), *Solon Robinson, Pioneer and Agriculturist* ("Indiana Historical Collections," Vol. XXI [Indianapolis, 1936]), I, 351.

Elsewhere newspapers discussed the growing practice of share renting.[9]

In mid-century Indiana, a move to define the rights of landlords and tenants developed into a major political battle. Bills to give landlords a lien on crops raised by their tenants had the support of legislators from the prairie counties, where landlordism flourished, but were opposed by the Democratic representatives from the small-farm counties of southern Indiana. Opponents, perhaps not aware of how far landlordism had already developed in the richer counties of the north, said that any such measure would stimulate landlords to enlarge their domain, "increase their subordinate tenancies," and strike at "our true policy to encourage every man to become a land owner." It was legislation "in favor of capital, the rich, and against labor, the poor." Another Hoosier opponent of the measure proposed an amendment to give landlords liens on the furniture, the wife, and the children of the tenant! Session after session of the legislature gave consideration to the question from 1857 to 1881, but not until the latter year was action completed.[10]

The growth of tenancy was stimulated by the granting of lands to railroads to aid in their construction. Two early beneficiary railroads—the Illinois Central and the Burlington and Missouri —after making their selections of land, found squatters on them who could not easily be dispossessed without creating ill feeling, but who were not in a position to pay the price asked for their claims. The Burlington officials found that the easiest policy to follow in such cases was to rent the land to the squatters for one

[9] Letter of J. W. Schreyer, June 22, 1846, in *Indiana Magazine of History*, XL (Sept., 1944), 294; Anon., *A True Picture of Emigration: Of Fourteen Years in the Interior of North America* (London, 1838), 60; Florence E. Janson, *The Background of Swedish Immigration, 1840–1930* (Chicago, 1931), 141–142; Harvey L. Carter, "Rural Indiana in Transition, 1850–1860," *Agricultural History*, XX (April, 1946), 114; La Salle, Illinois, *Independent*, March 4, 1854; G. C. Beman, Croton, Lee Co., Iowa, Jan. 12, 1853, to D. Kilbourne (Kilbourne MSS. in the Iowa Historical and Art Department); *Davenport Gazette* (Iowa), Jan. 29, Nov. 25, 1852; Oct. 6, 1853; March 26, May 5, 1858; *Sioux City Register* (Iowa), March 17, 1860, and March 15, 1862.

[10] *Brevier Legislative Reports*, 1852, 1857, 1859, 1861, 1865, 1881; *Laws of Indiana General Assembly*, 1881, p. 565; *Indianapolis State Sentinel*, Jan. 14 and 23, 1857; *Monticello Herald*, April 1, 1875.

to three years at a nominal price of twenty cents an acre with the hope that such improvements as the squatters made would enable the land to bring a good price when the lease expired and legal action might be taken to evict, if necessary. In 1878, the Burlington was renting Nebraska land which had been farmed during the past year for $1 an acre and idle lands for fifty cents an acre; its land in Iowa was then being rented for as much as $1.25 to $2 an acre. Railroad land-grant policy, like the government policy of permitting—and, indeed, encouraging—extensive speculation in Western lands, hastened the coming of tenancy to the West.[11]

The rapid alienation of public land and swiftly rising land values helped to accelerate the renting of land in the sixties and seventies. In 1880, when statistics of tenancy were compiled, the figures for the public-land states, particularly those which still contained land available for homestead, alarmed land reformers. In Illinois 31 per cent and in Iowa 23 per cent of all the farms were tenant operated. The counties of greater land values and higher productivity had tenancy rates ranging into the high 30's and 40's. More surprising was the swift emergence of tenancy in the border counties of Kansas and Nebraska, where the land had been in private ownership no more than twenty-three years, much of it less than fourteen years. Here the tenancy figures ranged from 25 to 40 per cent. In the states of the Upper Mississippi Valley, the percentage of people engaged in agriculture who were either tenants or farm laborers ranged from 32 in Minnesota to 53 in Illinois.[12]

The early appearance of tenancy and agricultural labor in the

[11] Peter Daggy, Land Department, Illinois Central Railroad, Nov. 30, 1865, to C. E. Perkins; J. M. King, Clarinda, Iowa, June 21, 1865, to Perkins; J. D. McFarland, Lincoln, Nebraska, Nov. 25, 1868, to A. E. Touzalin; W. W. Baldwin, Land Commissioner, Burlington and Missouri, Aug. 23, 1879, to R. A. Crippen, Burlington Archives, Newberry Library. The correspondence of Edward Hayes of Oak, T. S. Goddard of Hastings, R. A. Crippen of Corning, Iowa, land agents of the B & M, contains allusions to numerous instances of the railroad's leasing to tenants on a cash or share-rent basis.

[12] To arrive at these percentages I added the number of tenant farms (presumably farmed each by one tenant) to the number of farm laborers and computed what percentage that total was of the number of people engaged in agriculture. The figures are from the *Tenth Census, Agriculture* (Washington, 1883), *passim.*

amount that has been shown in or close to frontier areas, together with their rapid increase, provides convincing evidence that government land policy was not producing the results its defenders claimed. In view of the oft-repeated objective of American land policy—to assure a nation of freeholders—how is it possible to account for the early appearance of farm laborers and tenants in frontier communities?

Paradoxically, the fact that cheap, and finally free, land was to be had in the American West has a direct bearing on the appearance of farm laborers and tenants in that section. Government land prices were progressively reduced from $2 an acre in 1800 ($1.64 for cash) to $1.25 in 1820, to 60¢ to $1 by the use of military bounty land warrants of 1847–55, to as little as 12.5¢ in 1854, until finally, in 1862, free land could be obtained. European peasants and debt-ridden farmers in older sections of America were lured west by the vision of cheap or free farms that they confused with cheap or free raw land.

Nor was it sufficiently noted that the cost of farm making was increasing as settlers moved into the tough-sodded, poorly drained, and timberless prairies, where in competition with construction and railroad building they either had to pay high wages for custom work such as breaking, harvesting, and threshing or buy expensive labor-saving equipment. Custom plowmen, using the heavy breaking plow pulled by a number of yoke of oxen, charged $2 and $3 an acre for breaking prairie. Lumber for the house, fencing, and perhaps a barn could no longer be "hooked" from neighboring government- or absentee-owned tracts and had to be brought in at heavy expense from the Mississippi River mill towns or Chicago. A yoke of oxen, wagon, plow, stove, chains, ax, shovel, grindstone, scythe or cradle, together with seed, funds to maintain the family until the first crop came in, fees for filing land-office papers, or money to make the down payment on a railroad tract, brought the amount needed to start farming to $500 at the minimum; safer estimates were two or three times that much. Land agents and representatives of the land-grant railroads warned prospective emigrants in the East and in Europe that they should bring some capital with them to the West.[13]

[13] *Guide to the Lands of the Northern Pacific Railroad in Minnesota* (New York, 1872), 22; Arthur F. Bentley, *The Condition of the Western Farmer as*

Notwithstanding these well-meant warnings, immigrants continued to reach the outer edge of settlement destitute, unable to start farm making. We need not probe their disillusionment when their scant resources proved insufficient to enable them to take advantage of the government's free homestead policy. They could still cherish the dream of owning a farm while they worked for others.

Immigrants newly arriving in the West soon learned that unless they quickly established a claim to land, their chances of making good selections would be minimized, perhaps lost to other more foresighted settlers or to speculators. The settler and the speculator were catching up with the surveyor, especially in Iowa, Kansas, and Nebraska, and land when offered or opened to entry was quickly snatched up. Consequently, a first step toward farm ownership was to select a tract, establish a claim upon it, and hope that it could be held for two or three years without cost even though the claimant was not actually living upon it or abiding by the provision of the pre-emption or homestead acts. Frontiersmen moving early into newly opened communities found they could sell their claims with but slight improvements for $50 to $100 to later comers and then go a little farther west and make another selection. Claim making, a species of land speculation, was indulged in by many who gradually acquired a little livestock and equipment through sales of claims or through outside earnings and were ready in a few years for more permanent farm making. A combination of claim speculation and temporary work on railroad construction jobs or building projects in growing urban centers was common. That many immigrants also took agricultural jobs as hired hands in areas close to, if not right in, the frontier is not as well known.

Some students and readers of fiction relating to Western pioneer life have entertained the notion that Western farmers never really prospered but were in a more or less chronic state of depression

---

Illustrated by the Economic History of a Nebraska Township ("Johns Hopkins University Studies in Historical and Political Science," Eleventh Series, No. 7 [July, 1893]), 28; Clarence H. Danhof, "Farm Making Costs and the 'Safety Valve': 1850–1860," *Journal of Political Economy*, XLVI (June, 1941), 317ff.; Paul W. Gates, *Fifty Million Acres: Conflicts Over Kansas Land Policy, 1854–1890* (Ithaca, 1954), 223.

that was aggravated by periods of unusually low prices and near crop failures with resulting acute distress. Perhaps more attention has been directed to the agrarian reaction to such distress and the causes thereof than to periods of favorable prices and bountiful crops that brought early prosperity to many. Certain it is that in no comparable period did such large numbers of immigrants to a new region gain ownership of the farms they were improving and live well upon those farms as in the fifty-year period from 1850 to 1900 in the Mississippi Valley. Boomer literature of the time tells of numerous cases of individuals in Illinois, Kansas, or Nebraska who made enough on one good crop to pay for their land and equipment. That there were such cases cannot be denied, but whether they were typical it is impossible to say. We do know that industrious, skillful farmers blessed by good fortune did succeed not only in subduing the usual 80- to 160-acre tract of wild land to grain production and livestock use, but in many instances in developing even larger farms. This was accomplished not alone by the head of the family and his children, but with the aid of hired men.

The census schedules of 1870 reveal thousands of instances of farmers with no more than 160 acres employing one or two laborers.[14] These farmers did not attract the attention of journalists or travelers of the time, and, consequently, it is more difficult to reconstruct their operations than those of the larger capitalist farmers, whose operations were on a much bigger scale and who individually employed numerous farm hands.

The American West proved attractive not only to poor immigrants but also to men of means interested in developing not single family farms but estates of thousands of acres worked by laborers and tenants. Large capitalistic enterprises in the pioneer West are not unknown to historians, but most attention has been centered on the bonanza wheat farms of the Red River Valley of Minnesota and Dakota and on cattle ranching in the Great Plains. Carried out on a grand scale and with a dramatic flourish, they drew the attention of journalists and other commentators

[14] Paul S. Taylor, "The American Hired Man: His Rise and Decline," *Land Policy Review*, VI (Spring, 1943), 3–17; LaWanda F. Cox, "The American Agricultural Wage Earner, 1865–1900: The Emergence of a Modern Labor Problem," *Agricultural History*, XXII (April, 1949), 94–114.

of the time and consequently found their way into most histories of the West.[15] Their day was short, their long-range influence not great, and they deserve a mere footnote in history compared with the quieter, more pervasive, and longer-lasting investments by masterful and aggressive capitalists in the Corn Belt, who came not merely to speculate nor to develop a bonanza farm but to create rent-producing estates composed of numerous farms operated either by hired hands or by tenants.

These estate builders were to be found in practically every portion, one can almost say in every county, of the Corn Belt. Their homes, in highly stereotyped and stilted engravings, the number of acres they owned, and the moral qualities of the owners all are presented in the numerous county atlases and biographical volumes that were the rage in the Gilded Age. Their investments ranged from a few thousand to hundreds of thousands of dollars and, for a score or more, to one or two millions.[16] That is not to say that they brought capital in this amount with them when they first ventured into the West. Much of their capital was made in the West.

The cattle ranchers and drovers who flourished in Indiana and Illinois in the forties, fifties, and sixties and in Iowa and Missouri a little later dominated great areas of the prairies for a time. They built upon their first investments by shrewdly buying the surplus stock of neighbors, fattening them on the prairie bluestem

---

[15] Harold E. Briggs, *Frontiers of the Northwest* (New York, 1940), 509–522; and Fred A. Shannon, *The Farmer's Last Frontier, Agriculture, 1860–1897* (*The Economic History of the United States,* David, Faulkner, Hacker, *et. al.* [eds.], Vol. V [New York, 1945]), 154–161.

[16] In Illinois alone a compiler found in 1892 the following "millionaires" whose wealth was largely made in farm lands: Matthew T. Scott, Orlando Powers, L. B. Casner, Estate of John Shaw Hayward, John C. Proctor, George Pasfield, Horatio M. Vandeveer, William H. Ennis, W. H. Bradley. In Missouri the outstanding millionaire landowners were David Rankin and five heirs of Milton Tootle; in Nebraska, Stephen Miles; in Minnesota, J. A. Willard and A. H. Wilder; in Indiana, William H. English and the Estate of Moses Fowler. Other identifiable millionaires in these states added materially to their wealth through farming operations and land improvement. *American Millionaires. The Tribune's List of Persons Reputed to be Worth a Million or More* (June, 1892), reprinted in Sidney Ratner, *New Light on the History of Great American Fortunes. American Millionaires of 1892 and 1902.* (New York, 1953).

with the addition of a little grain, and then driving them to Chicago, Indianapolis, or the East, wherever they could get favorable prices. Later they brought in cattle from Missouri and Texas. Their profits were invested in land when it could be bought "dirt-cheap" to assure an abundance of grass and grain for their operations. Slowly, they turned to grain feeding and grain production and improved livestock, using meantime an increasing number of hands. By mid-century the operations of the successful cattle kings were being conducted on a huge scale, with herds of cattle numbering in the thousands, fields of corn covering thousands of acres, and scores of hands to carry on the business. Their holdings in land increased to 5,000, 10,000, 20,000, even 40,000 acres.[17] For every giant farm of this size there were a score or more of smaller operators with holdings ranging from one to four thousand acres.[18]

These bonanza farms, located as they were in Corn Belt counties with high land values, soon became as outmoded as the sickle and cradle. Farm workers proved irresponsible when hired at low wages. They were careless with tools, they slighted their tasks, overworked or abused the draft animals, drank heavily, and often engaged in fisticuffs. On slight provocation they quit their jobs, knowing that equally good opportunities were available elsewhere, and they demanded high wages when the peak of employment was reached in the harvest season. Old Isaac Funk, who accumulated a fortune of two million dollars in his land and cattle business in McLean County, Illinois, said in 1861 that no one could afford to hire men to grow and market grain at prices then prevailing. Their wages were too high and they worked too little, thought Funk. Another Illinois landlord, in deploring the wage of two dollars a day being paid to harvest hands in 1862, held that "cheap farm laborers" were essential for the winning of the Civil War.[19] The best agricultural laborers wanted to become tenants or

---

[17] Gates, *Frontier Landlords and Pioneer Tenants, passim.;* "Hoosier Cattle Kings in the Prairies," *Indiana Magazine of History,* XLIV (March, 1948), 1–24; "Cattle Kings in the Prairies," *Mississippi Valley Historical Review,* XXXV (Dec., 1948), 379–412.

[18] The Census of 1880 shows 2,916 farms in excess of a thousand acres in the ten states of the Upper Mississippi Valley.

[19] *New York Tribune,* July 30, 1861 and Aug. 11, 1861; C. H. Moore to Dr. John Warner, July 21, 1862, Moore-Warner MSS., Clinton, Illinois; *Country Gentleman,* March 10 and May 5, 1864; July, 1865.

owners and would remain in employment only as long as was necessary for them to accumulate the resources for starting on their own.

Continuing immigration into the prairies with its resulting pressure upon the supply of land, skyrocketing values, taxes and assessments forced more intensive land use. Ranches with grain as a side issue could no longer be economically justified, and for a time the bonanza farms became grain farms with cattle as a side issue. Before long, central administration of the land was abandoned. The big farms were divided into small holdings and assigned to tenants. Though the workers might prove poor farm hands, it was seen that, given a share in the returns of farming, they were more responsible, more willing to exert themselves, more careful with their tools, horses, and oxen, and with their housing accommodations. In the transition to full tenancy the landlord might provide everything but maintenance for the operator and pay him eight or ten cents a bushel for the corn he produced. In 1870, a tenant who furnished his own team was paid fifteen cents for each bushel of corn, fifty cents for each bushel of wheat, and twenty-five cents for each bushel of oats he produced. A more common practice was for the tenant to pay the landlord one third to one half of the crops or a cash rent for each acre of cultivable land.[20]

The day of the Corn Belt cattle kings was short, as was their career as bonanza farmers. As entrepreneurs developing their estates they made jobs available for many workers who later were permitted, if not encouraged, to become tenants. In the tenant stage of land development some of the landlords continued to expend their surplus from rents in additional improvements, so that their constructive period lasted throughout the first generation and, indeed, well into the second. In the process of change,

[20] *Columbus State Journal* (Ohio) in *Davenport Gazette* (Iowa), Aug. 12, 1855; 1 Miscellaneous Record, 434, Logan County Recorder's Office, Lincoln, Illinois; James MacDonald, *Food from the Far West* (London, 1878), 142–148; Appendix, "Agricultural Interests Commission, Reports of the Assistant Commissioner" (London, 1880), *Parliamentary Papers*, 1880, XVIII, 18, 38–39; *Bloomington Bulletin* (Illinois), March 4, 1887. On the Fowler lands in Indiana, in return for breaking land and putting it in corn, tenants were paid 25¢ a bushel for the corn they raised in the first five crop years. *Benton Review*, June 11, 1885.

some land was sold; more, through inheritance diffusion, passed to a larger number of landlords. Analysis of the assessment records or the current platbooks of Corn Belt counties reveals a century later how tenaciously third- and fourth-generation descendants of the old cattle kings have clung to their possessions.

Side by side with these modern holdings are other equally large estates which sprang from another type of investment on the frontier, that of the capitalists who came west to create permanent estates like that of the Wadsworth family in the Genesee country of New York by buying and developing extensive areas. Some of these capitalists concentrated their attention entirely upon farm making, while others bought and sold real estate, acted as agents for eastern capitalists wishing to invest in the growing West, or perhaps ran a bank and made loans to squatters. Profits and fees they invested in land improvements. A number took construction contracts on railroads, receiving land instead of cash in payment. They were careful to keep their titles clear, to pay the taxes before liens were issued, and to protect their timber against the prevalent custom of "hooking." With all these side issues, they kept before them the goal of land development.

Extensive improvement of their holdings required these estate builders to seek out workers to break the prairie, fence, erect tenant houses for the families of workers and barracklike constructions for single men, to seed, cultivate, harvest, shuck, thrash, and haul the grain to market. To assure themselves an adequate labor supply, and subsequently to attract tenants, these entrepreneurs had at times to advertise, distribute handbills in eastern communities, and in a number of instances publish pamphlets describing the opportunities their lands provided to immigrants.[21] Workers could not save much from the low wages paid them, but many pioneers did make their start by accumulating small funds from such earnings and investing them, perhaps while still holding the farm job, in near-by land on which they might at the same time make some improvements.

For the Western immigrant who was anxious to have a farm of

[21] *Sioux City Register,* Jan. 12, 1861; Margaret Ruth Beattie, "Matthew Scott, Pioneer Landlord-Gentleman Farmer, 1855–1891" (Thesis, Cornell University Library, 1947), 58ff.; Jacob Van Der Zee, *The British in Iowa* (Iowa City, 1922), 57ff.

his own but who lacked the means to acquire it, it was distinctly better to be a tenant than a farm laborer. He could, when he attained this status, feel he was moving toward his goal. Now he shared with the capitalist proprietor the profits from farming, but he also shared the losses. Furthermore, he was usually required by his lease to make capital improvements upon the rented land, and the cost would be deducted from the rent. Every improvement he made raised the value of the land and pushed farther away the possibility of his buying it. If he paid cash rent, continued improvement of the land was certain to be followed by a higher rent charge; if he paid share rent, the landlord might— and in the eighties did—exact a larger portion of the grain. Tenancy was no happy choice to the immigrant looking for the free or cheap land about which he had heard so much, but unless he was willing to go far beyond the railroad into areas lacking social facilities and market opportunities, there was no other alternative.

Some landlords were willing to pay for much of the cost of breaking and fencing, to provide machines and even credit to carry their tenants through harvest. Others insisted on the tenants' making all the improvements, which they then might own or at least have the right to sell to other tenants, subject to the approval of the landlord. Advertisements for tenants were increasingly common in the prairie newspapers, but more ominous from the point of view of the tenant were advertisements of renters looking for land.[22] Eviction for sloth, failure to make required improvements, poor farming, and cheating the landlord increased as hordes of new immigrants looking for land to rent came in from central Europe. The pressure for places to rent made it possible for the landlord to exact more and to allow the tenant less. Farmers of older American stock found the role of tenant increasingly unbearable. Disillusioned by their meager returns and unwilling to compete with the new wave of European immigrants, they abandoned their rented places in Illinois and Iowa by the thou-

[22] The *Champaign Gazette* (Illinois), clipped in the *Bloomington Pantagraph* (Illinois), Jan. 23, 1879, reported "The demand for farms to rent far exceeds the supply, and men are compelled to seek other localities to get places." Monticello, Indiana, *Prairie Chieftain*, Nov. 4, 1852; *Bloomington Pantagraph*, Feb. 8, 1854 and Nov. 5, 1856; Watseka, Illinois, *Iroquois County Times*, Oct. 21, 1875; *Malvern Leader* (Iowa), Feb. 8, 1883; Feb. 26 and March 5, 1885.

sands in the seventies and eighties for a new try at ownership in western Kansas or Nebraska, or perchance in the Dakota country. It was this emigration of older American tenants from the Corn Belt that was responsible for the increasingly conservative character of agrarian politics in Illinois and Iowa. These disillusioned and frequently angry tenants who emigrated farther west carried their resentment with them and made the area in which they settled fertile ground for the Populist agitator.[23]

Meantime, the capitalist estate builders, having divided their holdings into small tenant farms, were emerging as farm managers. Where they had erected tenant homes, set out fences, and established orchards they needed to protect their investment by making certain that proper care and maintenance were provided. They naturally wanted for their tenancies good farmers who would keep the weeds down, get their crops in and harvested at the right time, protect the timber if any, and pay their cash rent promptly or turn in a fair landlord's share of the grain. Good tenants assured better yields and hence more share rent. Both landlords and tenants were driven to exploit the land by their need for high returns to meet costs of farm improvements, new implements, and perhaps livestock. Rotation, the use of alfalfa or clover, prevention of erosion were all subordinated to the production of grain, with declining fertility the natural—though not immediately apparent—result. Much the same thing can be said of farm owners who were struggling to raise funds out of their crops to purchase new equipment, to fence additional land, to drain the low places, or to enlarge their original two- or three-room houses to accommodate growing families. Economic circumstances were largely responsible for a pattern of land use that disregarded the lessons of the past in older states, was exploitative and destructive of values. In defense of the capitalist estate builders, it should be added that some of them early showed concern for proper land management by insisting upon rotation of crops; the use of alfalfa, clover, and lime; the elimination of weeds; and careful use of pastures.

Elsewhere the operations of capitalist estate builders, whose individual and family holdings ran as high as 60,000 acres and in one

---

[23] Chester McArthur Destler, "Agricultural Readjustment and Agrarian Unrest in Illinois, 1880–1893," *Agricultural History*, XXI (April, 1947), 104–116; Gates, *Fifty Million Acres*, 244ff.

case to 200,000 acres, have been described. Few of these "feudal lords," as George Ade called them, would sell unless faced with disaster.[24] They instilled in their children a deep respect for the land they had improved and sought by every possible legal device to restrict the right of alienation. Because of their great success in retaining ownership of their many farms, the names of Scully, Moore, Davis, Vandeveer, Ennis, Funk, Fowler, Wearin, Rankin, and Lawrence-Lowrie are as familiar today to the residents of the prairie states as were the names of the great planters of South Carolina and Georgia to the ante-bellum residents of those states.

With all the plethora of information the Bureau of the Census had gathered, the problem of multiple ownership of tenant farms received no attention until 1900. Something of the concentration of ownership of tenant farms, the heritage of the capitalist estate builder in the nineteenth century, may be seen in the census data of that year. The figures are not complete and are made less useful by the fact that they are compiled on the basis of residence of owner; but in the absence of anything better we must use them. For the states of the Upper Mississippi Valley, 3,800 landlords appear as owning 32,646 farms. Five hundred and fifty-one of these landlords had an average of 12.8 farms each, and 122 owners had an average of 35.5 farms each. In Illinois 34 landlords are shown owning 1,115 farms, or an average of 32 each.[25]

Ownership of Tenant Farms by Owners Living in Upper Mississippi Valley, 1900

	Number of Owners	Number of Farms Owned
Owned one farm	419,900	419,900
Owned two farms	39,124	78,248
Owned three to five farms	12,070	39,831
Owned five to ten farms	3,127	21,263
Owned ten to twenty farms	551	7,052
Owned twenty or more farms	122	4,331
Total (plural ownership)	54,994	150,725

[24] George Ade, "Prairie Kings of Yesterday," *Saturday Evening Post,* July 4, 1931, p. 14.

[25] *Census of 1900, Agriculture,* Part 1, lxxxviii; Howard A. Turner, *The Ownership of Tenant Farms in the North Central States* (United States Department of Agriculture *Bulletin,* No. 1433 [Sept., 1926]), 10.

Since one landlord owned 322 farms in Illinois and an additional 845 farms in Missouri, Kansas, and Nebraska but had his residence in the District of Columbia, it is easy to see how deceptive, how inadequate, the census data is.

The estate builder brought much-needed funds to the West, developed substantial areas, and provided early employment and housing facilities for many newly arrived immigrants who lacked means to begin on their own. He aided others in getting started by lending them funds to commence farming as a tenant or owner; by furnishing them the necessary farming implements, seed, and food until harvest; and by providing livestock on a partnership basis. Much of the risk in these operations was his. Frequently, he undertook such investments with borrowed capital on which he paid 10 to 15 per cent interest. Taxes bore heavily on him, as the residents of his community seeking better schools and roads raised his assessments on tangibles that could not be hidden. Poor crops or low prices or, worse still, a combination of both might so reduce his income as to make it impossible for him to meet his obligations. One bad year he could take, perhaps two, but a larger combination of bad years was disastrous. The late seventies marked the final defeat of a number of large farm operators, and this was the result of poor prices, unfavorable weather, high interest rates, and perhaps poor management.

This paper may have indicated that society on the frontier and in areas a generation beyond the frontier stage was more complex, had a wider range of economic well-being, than Frederick Jackson Turner thought. The early appearance of farm laborers and tenants, many of whom were never to rise to farm-ownership status, and of great landed estates, whose owners brought wealth with them and added much to it, did not make for a "fundamental unity in its [frontier's] social structure and its democratic ideals . . . ." Concepts of the homogeneity of frontier society, similarity of frontier outlook, common addiction to democratic principles, may well be questioned.

Ante-bellum Democratic senators of the Upper Mississippi Valley appeared to be more concerned with their own land speculation schemes or the welfare of fur, lumber, mining, and railroad companies than with the fortunes of their farmer constituents; and they did little to loosen the reactionary control southern slave owners had over their party. The land-owning aristocracy early moved into politics via the Whig and Republican parties and fought as vigorously for privilege as did eastern conservatives. It was a combination of prairie landlords—Isaac Funk, Jesse Fell, Asahel Gridley, and David Davis—who had an important share in bringing the Republican nomination to Lincoln in 1860. Their activities contributed to fasten protection, the gold standard, land subsidies to railroads, and an incongruous land system upon the country. When the Democratic party in the Middle West recovered from its debacle, it was in the hands of Bourbons no more liberal in their outlook than the Republican officeholders they sought to displace.

The appearance of the Greenback and Populist parties seemed for a time to offer promise of effective agrarian leadership, but a combination of upper-class landowning families that directed the Greenback and Granger parties and a will-of-the-wisp search for a magic commodity price formula by the Populist party offered no aid to the farm laborer searching for a route to ownership or to tenants struggling to retain their step on the ownership ladder. While Western newspapers were bewailing the fate of Irish tenants, they gave no heed to the emergence of the tenant class at home whose rights were less secure, whose plight as serious. The landlords and successful farmers were in the saddle politically, and though they might erupt in condemnation of financial lords of the East, railroad magnates, or tariff-minded manufacturers, they did nothing to assure fixity of tenure, fair rent and compensation for improvements to tenants; in Illinois they joined together to beat down levels of wages paid to farm workers.[26]

At the close of the nineteenth century the agricultural laborers and tenants outnumbered full owner-operators of farms in five of the states we have studied, and in all the Upper Mississippi Valley the numbers of farm laborers and tenants were fast growing. Agrarian reform movements offered nothing to improve their

[26] A Farmers Union meeting in Mason County, Illinois, in 1885 resolved "not to exceed fifteen dollars per month, by the year, for the best farm labor, ... that for the limit of six months, the limit of wages be eighteen dollars per month ... that we pay no more than $1.50 per day for driving header wagon in harvest; $1.50 per day for labor in haying, and from 50¢ to $1.00 for common labor, to be regulated by time and circumstances." *Mason County Democrat*, Jan. 16 and Feb. 6 and 20, 1885.

lot. It was not until the twentieth century that the status of the tenant was substantially bettered with his gradual accumulation of livestock, equipment, and investment in improvements, which has made him a substantial farmer with an equity worth thousands of dollars.

SELECTED READINGS

Briggs, Harold E. *Frontiers of the Northwest.* . . . New York: D. Appleton-Century, 1940.

Cox, LaWanda F., "The American Agricultural Wage Earner, 1865–1900: The Emergence of a Modern Labor Problem," *Agricultural History,* XXII (April, 1949).

Destler, Chester McArthur. "Agricultural Readjustment and Agrarian Unrest in Illinois, 1880–1893," *Agricultural History,* XXI (April, 1947).

Gates, Paul W. *Fifty Million Acres: Conflicts Over Kansas Land Policy, 1854–1890.* Ithaca: Cornell University Press, 1954.

————. *Frontier Landlords and Pioneer Tenants.* Ithaca: Cornell University Press, 1945.

Shannon, Fred Albert. *The Farmer's Last Frontier, Agriculture, 1860–1897.* (*The Economic History of the United States,* David, Faulkner, Hacker, *et al.* [eds.] Vol. V.) New York: Rinehart & Co., 1945.

Taylor, Paul S. "The American Hired Man: His Rise and Decline," *Land Policy Review,* VI (Spring, 1943).

WALTER R. AGARD

Classics on the Midwest Frontier

The American frontier stripped the emigrant of his European culture, said Frederick Jackson Turner, and made him into a materialistic and practical man devoid of artistic appreciation. To modify that point of view, a classical scholar presents evidence in this essay to show that the ancient world laid its hand across the vastness of space and time upon the Midwest frontier. This influence is seen particularly in architecture, education, churches, libraries, and the press. It kept alive the conviction, says Professor Agard, that the United States still belonged to the traditions of Western Europe. What Midwestern state does not have an Athens or a Sparta, public buildings graced by the beautiful Doric columns, or a college once founded by a church that believes Christianity the true religion and the classics the road to true knowledge? Still, the classical influence was principally felt through the students educated in these 182 colleges founded between 1830 and 1860 who became politicians, ministers, and leaders of the Midwestern pioneers.

Professor Agard does not argue that the ancient world was a dominant influence in the early Midwest, but he does hold that it was the classics that furnished the "sweetness and light" to a hardworking people and thus helped keep alive the traditions of Western Europe. Strange as it may seem, Turner himself was trained in the classics!

"WITH the past we have literally nothing to do," declared
B. Gratz Brown, a Missouri Fourth of July orator in 1850. "Its
lessons are lost and its tongue is silent. . . . Precedents have lost
their virtue and all their authority is gone." Such was the spirit
of the pioneering Midwest, which, according to Frederick Jackson
Turner, had stripped its sons of European culture and transformed them into a people "strong in selfishness and individualism, intolerant of administrative experience and education," with
"that coarseness and strength combined with acuteness and ac-
quisitiveness; that practical, inventive turn of mind, quick to find
expedients; that masterful grasp of material things, lacking in the
artistic . . . that restless nervous energy." [1]

Did the Midwest frontier have "literally nothing to do" with
the past of Greece and Rome? We may assume that B. Gratz
Brown was guilty of oratorical overstatement in view of the important role which classical education played on the eastern seaboard, from which many of the settlers came. Turner's appraisal,
however, raises the question as to whether the classics made any
great contribution to the development of the Midwest frontier.
Let me state at once my conclusion that their influence was a
minor one. But as we examine the evidence furnished by architecture, education, and the churches, libraries, and the press, we
may find that they provided, at least for those pioneers who entered professional careers, intellectual and artistic nourishment
to supplement a diet which was for the most part ascetically practical. And they may have helped to keep alive the conviction that
America, for all its exciting new enterprises, still belonged in its
ultimate aspirations to the traditions of Western Europe, and
could not be intellectually or spiritually isolated from those traditions.

Let us take as a picturesque introduction to this inquiry a survey of place names in the twelve states defined by Turner as com-
prising the Midwest. Along with those inherited from the Indians
and the French, and those recalling the pioneers' native towns,
Biblical sites, and leading settlers, or those descriptive of natural
phenomena, there are a surprising number of places which in
their initial ambition claimed kinship with classical antiquity.

[1] Frederick Jackson Turner, *The Frontier in American History* (New York,
1920), 355, 32, 37.

Probably ministers and teachers were often responsible for choosing such names, although many were inherited from the eastern United States; and as railroads were constructed, officials tried to build up the prestige of some whistle-stops by giving them classical titles. One such list, made for the state of Washington by a Chicago, Milwaukee and St. Paul railroad official, includes Corfu, Laconia, Marcellus, and Pandora! That his classical training was somewhat scanty is indicated by his notation: "Laconia—on account of its location at the summit—was named after what I thought was Laconia in Switzerland located high up among the Alps, but in looking over the Swiss map this morning I am unable to find a place of that name there." [2] In the case of towns founded in the 1820's, names such as Athens, Sparta, and Arcadia evidence the warm sympathy and admiration felt by Americans for contemporary Greeks in their victorious war of independence.

Ohio leads the Midwestern list with thirty-five, followed by Michigan with fourteen, twelve in Indiana, eleven in Wisconsin, ten in Illinois, eight in Missouri, seven in Minnesota and Kansas, five in Iowa and Nebraska, three in South Dakota, and two in North Dakota. The most popular names are, as one would expect, such famous ones as Athens, Sparta, Rome, Troy, and Carthage; but Arcadia also rates high (Ohio, Indiana, Michigan, Iowa, Wisconsin, Kansas, Missouri), probably a continuing sentimental inheritance as pioneers moved westward. Personal names often repeated include Homer, Euclid, Seneca, and Virgil. Mythology supplied Aurora, Minerva, Neptune, Atlas, and Orion. And there is a sprinkling of whimsical ones such as Antiquity (Ohio), Elysian (Minnesota), Eureka (Minnesota, Wisconsin, and Kansas), Mirabile (Missouri), and River Styx (Ohio).

Such place names obviously have little significance beyond showing that some of the pioneers knew their Homer and Virgil and ancient history and had cultural aspirations for their new homes. If some city claimed to be the "Athens of the Middle West," here actually *was* an Athens. But in the public buildings and homes of the frontier, classical influence took a more substantial form and, insofar as people look carefully at architecture and are affected by it, Greek precedent played a role of some value in determining public taste. It happened that the rapid develop-

[2] G. R. Stewart, *Names on the Land* (New York, 1945), 324.

ment of the Northwest Territory occurred during a period when Georgian architecture (itself deriving its ornamentation from Greek designs) was yielding to the Greek Revival, which decorated homes, churches, and courthouses with massive Doric and Ionic porticos and continued the use of classical pediments, entablatures, and moldings. This was distinguished architecture. As Talbot Hamlin, our foremost historian of American architecture, says, "American settlers of these new lands brought with them and sometimes preserved that basic tradition of strong, simple compositions, large scale, and decorations based on classic sources." [3]

So we find scattered throughout the country in cities, villages, and the countryside, from Ohio to Puget Sound, pioneer-period buildings with the fine proportions and restful dignity of Greek temples. Many were built by local contractors who used the manuals published in New England by Asher Benjamin; in certain instances, the actual carving was done in the East and the products were shipped west from Buffalo on Great Lakes cargo boats. Thoroughgoing regional studies of this architectural achievement —one of the finest, certainly, in our history—remain to be made for most of the states of the Midwest. [4] They will reveal how thoroughly Greek decorative motifs, in large scale for the façade of buildings, in small scale for enriching window, cornice, and fireplace surfaces, were employed in the buildings erected from 1820 up to the time of the Civil War. Ohio boasts many towns rich in such homes, churches, and public buildings, for example, the stately Doric of the Matthews and Guthrie houses in Zanesville; the Painesville Courthouse; St. Luke's Church, Granville; and the delicate Ionic of the Kinsman house, Warren; the Avery house, Granville (with its lovely Doric side porch); and the Congregational Church at Tallmadge. Many such structures were built in Michigan in the 1840's, notably Gordon Hall, Dexter, with its impressive six Doric columns, and the Ionic portico of Frost

[3] Talbot F. Hamlin, *Greek Revival Architecture in America* (New York, 1944), 314.

[4] It has been done for northern Ohio by I. T. Frary, *Early Homes of Ohio* (Richmond, 1936). J. F. Kienitz, of the University of Wisconsin, to whom I am indebted for the use of his manuscript and photographs, has a volume on Wisconsin architecture nearly ready for publication. Considerable architectural material was made available by WPA projects.

House, formerly in Ann Arbor and now removed to the Ford Village at Dearborn. In Indiana, the fine Paoli Courthouse with its massive Doric portico was built about 1850. In Illinois, the graceful Doric columns of the Hildrup house, Belvidere (1855), the Anson Rogers house at Marengo, and the courthouse portico at Knoxville, may be cited.

In Wisconsin, the earlier small-scale Greek decoration of small front porches with Doric columns, and often an entablature and pilasters framing the doorway and the fireplaces, is represented by the Indian Agency house in Portage (1832), the John Harris cottage at Mineral Point (1835), the Lowell Damon house, Wauwatosa (1845), and the Vanderpool farmhouse at Prospect (1848). The larger-scale Greek Revival porticos (sometimes called "cottage temple" form) appear in many substantial homes, in the villages as well as cities. Three that deserve special mention are the majestic William Hunt house in Racine, built about 1850, with its four great Ionic fluted columns (copies of those on the Erechtheum North Porch in Athens), a beautiful grille of palmette design in the pediment, and Doric pilasters framing both the main and dormer windows; the Cotton house (1845) south of Green Bay, with two monumental Doric columns and a corresponding large-scale dignity throughout its planning; and the Lain-Estburg house (1848) in Waukesha, having four austere fluted Doric columns and a severe pedimental roof, with pilasters framing the main doorway, the sides of the house, and the living room fireplace, which has an entablature with triglyph decoration.

The effect of such buildings as these on the people who lived in and among them has not been recorded, as far as I know; but Talbot Hamlin is certainly right in calling attention to the very high standard of craftsmanship and taste represented by them, the "new vivid aesthetic sensitiveness and love of beauty" which they realized in the frontier wilderness. He also indicates how this architecture was later a victim of the brutal economic stresses of the frontier and the resulting aesthetic vulgarity that replaced the sensitiveness and dignity of Greek architectural elements.[5] But up to the time of the Civil War, the frontier had re-created many classic architectural forms and profited from the re-creation. After that period, throughout the Midwest hundreds

[5] Hamlin, *Greek Revival Architecture . . .* , 315–317.

of such buildings remained, to continue whatever beneficent influences residents would permit them to exercise.

But the chief influence of the classics was exerted, of course, through schools and colleges. Largely because of the efforts of various religious denominations eager to extend their influence in the new territories, numerous so-called "colleges"—most of them actually at the start little more than academies—were established wherever the frontier extended. Many were aided with personnel, advice, and money by the Society for the Promotion of Collegiate and Theological Education at the West, organized in New York in 1843. Wealthy men in the East were solicited for funds on grounds not only of patriotism and religion but also of sound business advantage; as Lyman Whiting said in an address in 1855, "Like the pillars of Hercules, Education and Religion define and defend the path of trade." [6]

Prior to the Civil War, the amazing number of 182 permanent colleges had been established in this country, a majority of them frontier colleges in the period from 1830 to 1860; and many more had sprung up for only an ephemeral existence.[7] Never had there been such a touching faith in the power of democratic education. And there was no doubt in the minds of the members of the SPCTEW that the frontier desperately needed education. According to a report of the Society in 1855:

The quality of Western society ... exposes it to vehement and brief excitements, to epidemic delusions and agitation.... The West is, therefore, peculiarly perturbed with demagogues and popular agitation, not only in politics, but in religion and all social interests. Amid these shifting social elements we want principles of stability, we want a system of permanent forces, we want deep, strong and constant influences, that shall take from the changefulness and excitability of the western mind by giving it the tranquility of depth, and shall

[6] *Address Before the Society for the Promotion of Collegiate and Theological Education at the West* (New York, 1855), 15–18.

[7] This development is traced in detail by D. G. Tewksbury, *The Founding of American Colleges and Universities Before the Civil War* ... (New York, 1932), and C. B. Goodykoontz, *Home Missions on the American Frontier, with Particular Reference to the American Home Missionary Society* (Caldwell, Idaho, 1939). For data on the early history of their institutions, I gratefully acknowledge my indebtedness to Thomas Dietrich, of Lawrence College; Paul R. Murphy, of Ohio University; and the late Mars M. Westington, of Hanover College.

protect it from delusive and fitful impulses by enduing it with a calm, profound and pure reason.[8]

The founders of these colleges knew how such "stability," "tranquility of depth," and "pure reason" were to be inculcated. It was by the twin forces of the Christian religion and classical culture. That the two were indeed regarded as twins is indicated in the famous Yale Report of 1828, which asserted that "the single consideration that divine truth was communicated to man in the ancient languages ought to put this question [the importance of the study of Greek and Latin] at rest and give to them perpetuity." [9] The Beloit College motto, "Scientia vera cum fide pura," summed it up concisely: Christianity provided the pure faith, Greece and Rome the true knowledge.

This happy family relationship was not, however, always maintained. At colleges where religious conviction was intolerant of any rivalry, the classics were regarded as decidedly inferior in position to the Bible and were sometimes even banned. In 1827, Bishop Philander Chase, founder of Kenyon College, declared it improper to study "heathen authors" except as "they were subservient to the truths of the gospel," and instructed his faculty not altogether to "extinguish the lamps of Heathen literature," but to "outshine them by the splendour of the *Sun of Righteousness.*" [10] In the decade following 1836, the opposition at Oberlin was more violent, including a student petition for the elimination of Latin, the substitution of Church Latin for Plautus, Seneca, Livy, and Horace, and even a public burning by students of many classical texts. "The heathen classics," it was urged, were unnecessary because "the poetry of God's inspired prophets is better for the *heart*, and at least as good for the head as that of Pagans." [11]

[8] *Twelfth Annual Report* (New York, 1855), 46. In Merle Curti's *The Growth of American Thought* (New York, 1943), 259–292, there is an excellent summary of the anti-intellectualism, and the crudities are described in picturesque detail in R. C. Buley, "Glimpses of Pioneer Mid-West Social and Cultural History," *Mississippi Valley Historical Review*, 23:4 (March, 1937), 481–510.

[9] "Original Papers in Relation to a Course of Liberal Education," *American Journal of Science and Arts*, XV (1929), 297–351.

[10] G. F. Smythe, *Kenyon College* (New Haven, 1924), 67.

[11] R. S. Fletcher, *A History of Oberlin College from Its Formation through the Civil War* (Oberlin, Ohio, 1943), I, 364ff., 209.

But the violence of such opposition soon burned itself out, and
the traditional classical curriculum was restored at Oberlin in
the 1850's.

   The dominance of Greek and Latin in the course of study of
the frontier colleges, copied from their eastern prototypes, seems
to us now almost incredible. However small the faculty may have
been, there was inevitably a teacher of Greek and one of Latin.
The leading professor for Beloit's opening class in 1847 was
Joseph Emerson, called "Zeus" by the students.[12] Of the six
members of the first faculty of the University of Wisconsin, one
taught ancient languages, and Chancellor Lathrop insisted that
Latin and Greek be the center of the curriculum.[13] The first
University of Minnesota faculty consisted of nine members, two of
whom taught Greek and Latin; and in his inaugural address
President Folwell gave generous praise to language study. Folwell
had been deeply stirred by a visit to Greece in 1860, during his
student days in Europe; after watching an Acropolis sunset, he
wrote, "It is no wonder that the arts flourished under such a sky
and in the midst of such scenery." [14]

   There is a surprising uniformity in the classical entrance requirements and courses of study in these frontier colleges. In
general, they followed the pattern of the Brown University *Laws*
of 1827: "Every person admitted into this University must be able
to construe and parse Cicero's *Orations,* Virgil's *Aeneid* and the
Greek Testament, and to write good Latin. He must know the
rules of Arithmetic, and have a good moral character." [15] In many
college catalogues of the 1840's, students seeking admission were
instructed to have an accurate knowledge of Greek and Latin
grammar, since this knowledge was indispensable to their subsequent progress.

   As representative of the standard classical course of study and
its formidable continuity, we may cite three curricula: those of

[12] E. D. Eaton, *Historical Sketches of Beloit College* (New York, 1928), 33.
[13] M. Curti and V. R. Carstensen, *The University of Wisconsin* ... (Madison, Wis., 1949), I, 73.
[14] T. C. Blegen, *The Land Lies Open* (Minneapolis, 1949), 182, 187. I am
further indebted to Dean Blegen for many helpful suggestions.
[15] L. F. Snow, *The College Curriculum in the United States* ... (New York,
1907), 122.

Ohio University in 1820–21, of Hanover College (Indiana) in 1840–41, and of Lawrence College (Wisconsin) in 1867–68. In all of them, Latin, Greek, and mathematics were the "core" subjects of the freshman and sophomore years, and the courses offered were remarkably similar. The Greek included the New Testament, Xenophon, Herodotus, Homer, the writing of Greek prose, and the study of Greek History; the Latin included Sallust, Livy, Horace, Cicero, Latin prose, and "Roman antiquities." In the last two years, only a few Greek and Latin courses were required, such as the tragedies and orations in Greek, and Tacitus and Juvenal in Latin; and many courses in rhetoric, the sciences, and the social studies were offered, including Evidences of Christianity, History, Philosophy, Political Economy, Chemistry, Botany, and Astronomy. Here is obviously a standardized curriculum, with little change in pattern over a period of fifty years. It was in effect not only in the denominational colleges but also, with the exception of courses in religion, in the new state universities. An examination of the classical curriculum of the University of Michigan in 1840 and the University of Wisconsin in 1868 reveals a similar pattern.

As time wore on, this course of study came under increasing attack, but it was stoutly defended by many leading educators up to 1870, and continued to be the core material in most of the colleges. As late as 1885, President Northrop in his inaugural address at Minnesota declared it was "midsummer madness" to emphasize "utilitarian subjects at the expense of mathematics and languages." [16] In the denominational colleges, the classical curriculum continued to dominate much longer. Dean Theodore C. Blegen informs me that as late as 1910, classes at Augsburg College were described not as Freshman, Sophomore, etc., but as First, Second, Third, and Fourth Greek.

The arguments for classical training, stemming from the historic document issued by the Yale faculty in 1828, were repeated with conviction by administrators, teachers, trustees, and boards of visitors. The study of Latin and Greek, it was claimed, is uniquely valuable in disciplining the mind, forming the taste, providing a standard of literary merit, and giving the best intellectual prepara-

[16] James Gray, *The University of Minnesota, 1851–1951* (Minneapolis, 1951), 85.

tion for the ministry, law, and medicine. W. T. Harris, United
States Commissioner of Education from 1889 to 1906, while
serving earlier as superintendent of schools in St. Louis argued
that since Greece and Rome furnish our chief cultural heritage
and can be known intimately only through their languages, their
prescription as the chief studies for our youth is a wise one.[17] The
Board of Visitors of the University of Wisconsin as late as 1891
declared that no other subjects could better prepare a student to
be an intelligent and influential member of society, and it was a
pity, in their opinion, that only 10 per cent of Wisconsin students
elected Greek compared with 25 per cent at Michigan and 23 to
60 per cent in the private colleges of Wisconsin.[18]

Conclusions drawn from such arguments varied from modest
statements approving the ancient languages and literatures to such
extravagant claims as these: "Experience has shown that with the
study or neglect of the Greek and Latin languages sound learning
flourishes or declines. It is now too late for ignorance, indolence,
eccentricity, or infidelity to dispute what has been ratified by the
seal of ages." [19] A writer in 1820 feared that "Should the time ever
come when Latin and Greek should be banished from our
universities, and the study of Cicero and Demosthenes, of Homer
and Virgil should be considered as unnecessary for the formation
of a scholar, we should regard mankind as fast sinking into absolute barbarism, and the gloom of mental darkness as likely to increase until it should become universal." [20] Testimonials less extreme but none the less earnest could be endlessly quoted, many
of them by teachers of the languages, but others by administrators,
ministers, and former students in various fields. One of the most
reasonable and cogent statements was that made by Professor
William F. Allen before the Wisconsin Teachers' Association in
1873 on "The Utility of Classical Studies as a Means of Mental
Discipline." [21] Professor Allen, an able Latinist, won greater re-
nown later at Wisconsin as a teacher of history; Frederick J.

[17] W. T. Harris, *The Place of the Study of Latin and Greek in Modern
Education*, n.d., n.p.

[18] University of Wisconsin Regents' *Report*, 1891–1892, 50.

[19] J. Van Vechten, *Memoirs of John M. Mason* (New York, 1856), 239.

[20] In the *Western Review*, III (Cincinnati, 1820), quoted in F. L. Mott,
A History of American Magazines (Cambridge, Mass., 1938–1939), I, 146.

[21] *Essays and Monographs* (Boston, 1890), 155–164.

Turner served as his assistant and was profoundly influenced by his teaching, especially by a "frontier" theory which Allen formulated.[22]

This emphasis on "mental discipline" as the primary value of the study of the classics, by even as sensitive and dynamic a teacher as Professor Allen, is indicative of the way in which the classics were generally taught. The amount of literature read was relatively small and the humanistic interpretation was limited. Instead, minute attention was given to grammar and syntax, to moods, tenses, and particles, to accurate translation. A rather touching student comment on the aridity of this method of teaching is perhaps typical. A Kenyon graduate, paying tribute to his various teachers, wrote: "For three years (1859–62) I sat under the teaching of Professor Trimble. We read with him the usual Greek and Latin authors, with as much thoroughness as they were read anywhere at that time . . . . I think we felt that Professor Trimble was quite competent to have done something for us in the higher walks of classical culture . . . [if he had gone] beyond the routine required of him."[23] It is indeed a pity that teachers of Greek and Latin did not often allow themselves to share with their classes a wider range of ideas, literary and artistic forms, and institutions. Sometimes, of course, they did. The University of Michigan claimed in announcing its courses for 1852–53 that it taught the comprehensive study of classical culture and "a constant comparison between the ancient and modern world"; and an indication that the claim was justified can be found in the tribute later paid by President Angell to one of Michigan's great teachers of that period, Henry S. Frieze: "Contact with this inspiring teacher formed an epoch in my intellectual life."[24] And even when teachers concentrated on "mental discipline," doubtless many of the values of Homer and Virgil, Sophocles, Plato, and Tacitus were woven into the fabric of the abler students' lives. The discipline itself, when well taught, was invigorating. Lucien Price, writing of a "Hardscrabble Hellas" experience at the end of

[22] "The Place of the North West in General History," in *Papers of the American Historical Association*, III (New York, 1889), 251, 331–348.

[23] Smythe, *Kenyon College*, 177.

[24] *The University of Michigan—An Encyclopedic Survey* (Ann Arbor, Mich., 1944), IV, 628–629.

the century, speaks of "the thrilling grind of Greek," as well as the challenging appeal of "that stalwart Hellenic tradition." "We could hear," he concludes, "on the salt strand of the ages the surge and thunder of the *Iliad*." [25]

How did other students react to this course of study, so far divorced from the conditions of frontier daily life? Apparently, they usually took it in their stride. Typical is the testimony of Dean John G. Coulter of Purdue, who, reminiscing about student days at Hanover College in the 1870's, said: "The classical curriculum was all prescribed except for an option in the sophomore year between calculus and Hebrew .... The subjects prescribed were not to be evaluated by the students; they were medicine that had to be taken .... Those who dropped out were looked down upon as lacking the fortitude to endure a scholastic regime whose efficiency for the development of intellectual power was never challenged." [26] Of course most of these students were preparing for the ministry or another of the learned professions for which the classics had been traditionally the normal training. Occasionally, signs of decreasing regard appear, as in a letter written in 1857 by a former Wisconsin student, who praised the education of the frontier in comparison with that of the effete eastern colleges, and asked, "Need, then, our poets go back to the mouldy piles of poor jaded Greece and Rome?" [27] But for the most part, student editorials and letters of the period show favorable references to classical topics. For example, a Beloit graduate, reminiscing over his experience as a freshman in 1850, wrote as a matter of course: "Tea and coffee were unknown luxuries to us, but we were as well off in this respect as Croesus was. Sugar was scarce, but we had more of it than Julius Caesar had"; and a Beloit commencement speaker in 1873 took his cue from Cato to further a popular local cause in declaring, "Gymnasium aedificandum est." [28] At Oberlin in 1858, the Phi Delta Society recorded a debate on the subject "Resolved, that the revival of athletic sports of the ancient Greeks would be beneficial to the mental and moral condition of the present age," and a later literary club subject

[25] *Atlantic Monthly,* CXXXIX (February, 1927), 153–166.
[26] J. G. Coulter, *The Dean* (Lafayette, Indiana, 1940), 44.
[27] Curti and Carstensen, *The University of Wisconsin ...* , I, 199.
[28] Eaton, *Historical Sketches of Beloit College,* 52, 79.

was "Whether the times of ancient Greece and Rome were more favorable to the production of poetry than the present." Scores of similar instances could be cited.

Since the classics had such a central place in the curriculum of the colleges and universities up to 1870, and even after that yielded their position only gradually, it might seem that their influence on frontier development was considerable. But we must bear in mind that only a small fraction of the population ever went on to an academy or high school, let alone a college; up to 1870, the college population was largely confined to students headed for the learned professions. For example, in 1839 the enrollment at Miami, at that time the largest college west of Pennsylvania, was only 250; in 1841 there were only 140 enrolled at Western Reserve; in 1850 only 27 at Ohio University; in 1853 only 123 at Hanover; and in 1867 only 90 at Kenyon. The early days of the state universities also gave little evidence of their later growth. In 1851, there were only 57 college students at Michigan; in 1866, only 41 at Wisconsin; and as late as 1883, only 223 at Minnesota. Moreover, as educational opportunity broadened, notably with the development of the state universities, emphasis was shifted from the classical course of study and placed on meeting the ordinary needs of plain people; courses of study centered upon science, English, and social studies, and studies vocational in type were provided. The University of Michigan, under the leadership of President Henry Tappan, led the way. The trend was greatly accelerated by federal grants starting in 1862, which resulted in the rapid development of agricultural and mechanical courses.

For several years before any radical change took place, criticism had been voiced by the general public, especially members of the state legislatures who were concerned about practical education to meet the needs of their constituents who had careers in business, farming, or industry in mind. As early as 1858, a committee of the Wisconsin legislature had criticized the requirement of Latin and Greek and proposed that a classical education be left to the private colleges, and that the state university meet the more practical needs of students. "It is not by pouring [*sic*] over the dreamy and mystical pages of classic lore," said the report of this committee, "that the student is to develop the energy of character and strength of purpose to enter manfully into the great battle of life." [29]

As for adult education, public libraries, later to be a leading agency in this respect, began to appear only toward the close of the pioneer period. Until nearly the middle of the nineteenth century there were few libraries in the Midwest except those of the colleges, which of course were well stocked with classical books. Miami boasted a library of about four thousand volumes in 1840. But in the well-established towns, subscription libraries began to spring up, with ancient and English classics, novels, travel books, and current magazines available, many of them imported from England. By 1825, at least thirty communities in Ohio had such libraries, and in 1837 there was a St. Louis subscription library which had over four thousand volumes. It cannot be claimed, however, that the classics were in great demand; novels of romance and adventure and accounts of exploration and travel were apparently most popular.

As we have seen, the classical curriculum was long regarded as the proper training for the learned professions. A certain number of graduates of the colleges and universities became teachers of Greek and Latin in academies, high schools, and higher institutions. When the frontier classics teachers wrote books, like their colleagues in the East they chiefly made adaptations of German scholars' grammars and texts, such as *The Greek Verb* by William Nast of Kenyon College, in 1835, and O. M. Mitchell's *Works of Quintilian,* published about 1833. There were occasionally less conventional efforts, such as a biography of George Washington in Latin by Francis Glass, an Ohio schoolteacher.

But professional men other than teachers contributed in giving the classics some influence in frontier life. Foremost, of course, were the ministers, who mingled the Hellenic tradition with the Hebraic in their sermons and quoted Aristotle as well as St. Paul. Lawyers who were delegates to the constitutional conventions of frontier states, members of territorial assemblies and state legislatures, and pleaders before the higher courts, often cited classical authorities. One spirited declaration deserves to be remembered. General William R. Smith, addressing the Wisconsin Constitutional Convention of 1846, said he "would tell the gentlemen he

[29] *Wisconsin State Journal,* II (Madison, Wis., 1858), 1280–1290.

acted upon one principle—the gentlemen had read it at school—
'Nullius addictus jurare in verbum magistri'—in plain English—
I put my faith to no man's sleeve, I follow no party leader's call." [30]

Politicians referred to ancient Greece and Rome as a model or a
warning in stating their own policies. For example, Governor
Lewis Cass of Michigan, in a speech advocating better living conditions for ordinary people, declared the "boast of Augustus that
he had found Rome a brick and left it a marble city was the boast
of a tyrant" who had no concern for the welfare of most of his
subjects.

Even in the rough-and-ready newspaper world, the classics
played a picturesque and sometimes significant role. A casual
inspection of frontier newspapers reveals frequent references to
them. Often mythological allusions are found in the editorials or
the "culture column" the newspapers ran, consisting of original
essays and verse or reprints from eastern publications. A typical
example is the New Year's ode in the January 3, 1845, issue of the
Milwaukee Daily Sentinel, praising the American prairies with a
simile reminiscent of Virgil:

> Like the huge billows, on old Ocean's form,
> Evoked from rest by Eolus' rude storm.

A writer in the *Ohio Daily Gazette* of June 20, 1838, declared
that the West would combine the old with the new, to make "a
nation which has, like Hercules, shown all the giant in the cradle."
And the *Madison* (Wisconsin) *Argus,* named after the mythical
many-eyed Argus, used one of its eyes on October 24, 1844, to
admire moral courage, which, it declared, brings peace of mind
more satisfying than "the fleeting glories of a Roman triumph."
Countless allusions of this sort could be cited.

Most often of all, ancient history was invoked to help prove a
thesis, as when the *Miners' Free Press* of Mineral Point, Wisconsin,
on July 31, 1838, contributed to workers' education "A Few
Thoughts on the Importance of Literary Associations," reprinted
from the *Gentleman's Magazine,* which included the following
grim warning: "History attests the assertion that a wane of litera-

[30] The original quotation comes from Horace, *Epistle I.* See Milo M. Quaife
(ed.), *The Convention of 1846* (Madison, Wis., 1919), 99 and 156, for classical
allusions by General Smith.

ture is one of the most certain presages to national decay. The fate of Greece and Rome avouch the verity of this." The advantages of society blessed by a democratic free press over a newspaperless past, as described in a Yale Phi Beta Kappa address and reprinted in the January 9, 1844, *Green Bay Republican,* were pointed up in this rousing statement: "When Demosthenes thundered and Virgil sung [*sic*] it was for the few and not for the many; and their lofty productions were indebted even for the limited circulation to the dogged labors of the transcriber." It need hardly be said that such interpretations of the classics were not always on the highest scholarly level.

Several well-known editors in the developing Middle West continued this tradition in less extravagant terms and became famous for the way in which they pointed with pride or viewed with alarm in terms of classical allusion. James M. Goodhue, product of a classical education at Amherst College, who founded the *Minnesota Pioneer,* the first newspaper in that state, and William R. Nelson, fearless editor of the *Kansas City Star,* deserve special mention. Nelson's great campaign for good roads in Missouri had as its keynote this statement: "Great as was the greatest of the Caesars, greatest was he as a roadbuilder." [31] It is worthy of note that Frank Reilly, a *Chicago Daily News* editorial writer, stimulated Eugene Field's imagination by quoting from the *Odes* of Horace.[32] According to Ralph Nafziger, director of the University of Wisconsin School of Journalism, there were many such newspapermen in the Middle West who were well versed in the classics and were famous for quoting from classical sources. Among them was Roger C. Craven of the *Omaha World-Herald,* who signed many of his early columns with such pseudonyms as "Omega" and "Brutus," made frequent references to Roman history and mythology in his editorials, and penned notes to his friends in Latin. The influence of newspapers was considerable, especially in the early years, when many of the pioneers read nothing except the

---

[31] *William Rockhill Nelson, the Story of a Man, a Newspaper and a City . . .* (Cambridge, Mass., 1915), 25. In Mary W. Berthel's biography of Goodhue, *Horns of Thunder* (St. Paul, 1948), 13, she quotes an amusing excerpt from an editorial in which Goodhue compared himself, as pilot of a newspaper, to Aeneas trying to steer safely between Scylla and Charybdis.

[32] C. H. Dennis, *Victor Lawson, His Time and His Work* (Chicago, 1935), 88.

Bible, the almanac, and their local paper. As Mrs. Trollope had remarked, "They are all too actively employed to read, except at such broken moments as may suffice for a peep at a newspaper." [33]

The homes that subscribed to magazines had to rely on England and the East or on ephemeral publications like the *Western Review* (Lexington, 1812–21); the *Western Magazine and Review* (Cincinnati, 1827–30); the *Western Monthly Magazine* (Cincinnati, 1830–36); and the *Western Messenger* (Cincinnati, 1835–40). Often the poetry in them was classically inspired; and the *Messenger* could boast of one veritable triumph: Keats' "Hymn to Apollo" was first published in it.

The classical training of doctors occasionally resulted in the picturesque use of allusions, such as the series of medical articles in *Liberty Hall and Cincinnati Gazette* of 1821, signed "Hippocrates."

Furthermore, although little proof can be offered, it is fair to assume that certain of the most intellectually and artistically acute among public-spirited businessmen owed something of their outlook to their classical training. Among them may be cited Henry H. Sibley, the leading figure in the early cultural development of Minnesota, and Horace W. S. Cleveland, pioneer landscape architect and city park designer in many states of the Midwest. In his engaging account, *Olympians in Homespun*, Lucien Price tells of his admiration for Mr. Willetts, owner of the local glass factory, "a graduate of Yale [who] for his recreation read Greek." [34] Doubtless many such instances could be found.

From the evidence here presented, we may draw two conclusions: that the classics served to introduce some sweetness and light into the brutally pragmatic frontier, and that they helped keep vital the traditions of Western Europe, supplementing the ones forged by the challenging new environment.

There are several ironic touches in the juxtaposition of the classics and the frontier. One is the fact that Turner himself was classically trained and was an assistant to a Latin scholar. Another is the fact, largely ignored, I believe, by Turner, that waves of

---

[33] Frances M. Trollope, *Domestic Manners of the Americans* (London, 1832), I, 128. The "lavish imitation of the classics" in frontier poetry is further discussed in Logan Esary, "Early Ohio Valley Literature," *Mississippi Valley Historical Review*, V (Sept., 1918), 143–157.

[34] *Atlantic Monthly*, CXXXVII (April, 1926), 433–447.

foreign migration from northern Europe shortly before and following the Civil War brought to the Middle West, rather than the eastern United States, many professional men who became farmers or who served their fellow immigrants as preachers, teachers, and lawyers. Trained in the gymnasia and universities of Germany, Switzerland, and Scandinavia, they gave cultural distinction to the pioneer scene. For example, as a result of the abortive 1830 revolution in Germany, "men of property and education, substance and social standing" began to come to Ohio, Indiana, Illinois, Wisconsin, and Missouri, where they were often called "Latin farmers." As Carl Wittke said, many a German farmer in the West "was more familiar with Virgil than with guiding a plough through a furrow in prairie soil; and there were German workers on the railroads and in the shops who knew Homer in the original." [35] Finally—perhaps the most ironic part of all—today in the United States, one of the strongest bastions of the classics is in that part of the country which used to be the Midwest frontier, and in which they seemed so incongruous an element a hundred years ago. Let us hope that they will continue to play a useful role in helping to make Americans wise in the ways of Western culture.

SELECTED READINGS

Allen, W. F. *Essays and Monographs*. Boston: G. H. Ellis, 1890.

Curti, M. and Carstensen, V. R. *The University of Wisconsin*....
2 vols. Madison, Wis.: University of Wisconsin Press, 1949.

Eaton, E. D. *Historical Sketches of Beloit College*. New York: A. S. Barnes Co., 1928.

Fletcher, R. S. *A History of Oberlin College from Its Formation through the Civil War*. Oberlin, Ohio: Oberlin College, 1943.

Frary, I. T. *Early Homes of Ohio*. Richmond, O.: Garrett and Massie, 1936.

Gray, James. *The University of Minnesota, 1851–1951*. Minneapolis: University of Minnesota Press, 1951.

[35] C. Wittke, *We Who Built America; the Saga of the Immigrant* (New York, 1940), 189. For the picturesque and sometimes pathetic story of the "Latin farmers," see also Albert B. Faust, *The German Element in the United States* (New York, 1909), I, 442 and 584; also, *The Memoirs of Gustave Körner*, ed. by T. J. McCormack (Cedar Rapids, Iowa, 1909).

Hamlin, T. F. *Greek Revival Architecture in America.* New York: Oxford University Press, 1944.

Rusk, R. L. *The Literature of the Middle West Frontier.* 2 vols. New York: Columbia University Press, 1925.

Snow, L. F. *The College Curriculum in the United States....* New York: Columbia University Press, 1907.

Stewart, George R. *Names on the Land.* New York: Random House, 1945.

Tewksbury, D. G. *The Founding of American Colleges and Universities Before the Civil War....* New York: Columbia University Press, 1932.

Wittke, Carl F. *We Who Built America; the Saga of the Immigrant.* New York: Prentice-Hall, Inc., 1940.

Wright, Louis. *Culture on the Moving Frontier.* Bloomington, Indiana: University of Indiana Press, 1955.

FREDERIC G. CASSIDY

Language on the American Frontier

When the English language was brought to the American colonies by the pioneers from all parts of the British Isles, it lost its moorings and literally ran wild through the American experience as these people saw new objects and met new situations. Indian and European words were added, new combinations of words were made, and old words were given new meanings. In the opinion of some purists, the language was debased. After the Revolution, men like Noah Webster argued that an independent country needed a new language as much as a new government, and he proceeded to nurture this movement away from the old.

The frontier was important in this evolution, says Professor Cassidy, and he shows that even journal writers of the Lewis and Clark expedition used 1,107 Americanisms of different kinds, of which 583 were unrecorded before. As a result of this historic experience out at the edge of the world, the English language in America has gone from a semicolonial position to the autonomy of a national language with many regional peculiarities. In this development one constant and powerful factor has been the frontier.

IT is currently fashionable, and has been for some years, to refer to the language we speak in the United States as "the American language." This phrase may, of course, be produced in several tones of voice—a patriotic tone, a tone vibrating with manifest destiny, a naïve tone, or a chauvinistic one. A quite recently published dictionary has rushed forth with the clamorous title of the *New World Dictionary of the American Language*—betraying clearly the tone of voice of its business office, which is out to make Americanism pay.

The student of language, however, uses this phrase in the tone of voice indicating quotation marks. By no acceptable *linguistic* definition can our language be called "the American language"; it is not a separate speech unintelligible to speakers in the British Isles, Australia, or Canada; it is merely one variant form of the language which already has an established name: the English language. Not even the sturdiest isolationist can deny the historic connections.

The term "the American Language" was given currency, as we all know, by the great popular success of H. L. Mencken's book, first published in 1919, of which it was the title. Mencken was nothing if not bold; he had an ax to grind; he enjoyed telling the English where to get off *at*. Evidently this struck a note of welcome to many American ears, for his book became surprisingly a best seller. Scholars, therefore, even while rejecting the linguistic validity of his phrase, owe Mencken a considerable debt of gratitude for at last making the public intelligently aware—as many a better scholar before him had failed to do—that among the most interesting achievements of our new nation has been a characteristically different idiom. The colony which grew away from the homeland politically and has since come of age has also developed its own ways of speech. It is fair to say that if the English language had only one pole or center a hundred years ago, today it has two. And this bipolarity is the direct result of what happened on the American frontier.

To begin with, of course, America itself was the frontier: so are all colonies with respect to their parent lands. The most striking characteristic of a frontier society is its fluidity. True enough, there is considerable carry-over of habits, customs, institutions, ideals from the homeland, insofar as these are desirable and possible under the new conditions. But the important thing is that the fixity, the settled and confining structure of society in the old country, is shaken loose. Thus the new country gives a new chance. It demands fresh ways—and it makes fresh ways possible.

The migrations of humanity that take place from time to time, seen through the long eye of history, are like the flowing of a stream of volcanic lava. Driven by an outburst from a center of pressure, this stream pours out, running wherever it may, over the unresisting flats, around the rockier protuberances, picking up and incorporating many things in its path, ever cooling and hardening as it goes, but always with that glowing, fluid edge. This edge is the frontier.

So in the past three centuries the pressures of Europe flung out the crowd of adventurers and refugees, the rebellious and the ambitious, the disinherited and the farsighted. To America they flowed, thinly at first, spreading along the coast, trickling inland in the lower places, slowed by the mountains and resistance of Indians, but always with the hot edge rising and creeping on. At last, after a century and a half the lava stream broke into the plains and rolled westward ineluctably. In some places it eddied to a stop, cooled and became sluggish; but there was always the hot edge, the frontier, flowing on and on, taking many new shapes, swallowing many things that it came upon, some of its own currents mingling with others or overflowing them wholly—molten, hungry, seething with bubbles of humanity.

What of language in all this? It would be impossible to imagine such a movement of peoples as taking place without the use of language. Language is at once the exclusive and the most characteristic property of human beings: in the movement to the world frontiers, language went along. The first comers, of course, spoke some variety of their European tongue as it existed at the time. Limiting ourselves to English, we may say that on the ships of the explorers probably every sort of local or dialectal speech could have been heard. Settlements, when those were made, were sometimes less miscellaneous linguistically, but they were never "pure." Mixture, a characteristic of the frontier, was present too in the settlers' speech.

In a valuable study of New England pronunciation published in 1927, Professor Anders Orbeck looked into the places of origin of some 680 early English-speaking settlers of the towns of Plymouth, Watertown, and Dedham, Massachusetts.[1] He discovered that

---

[1] *Early New England Pronunciation as Reflected in Some Seventeenth Century Town Records* (Ann Arbor, Mich., 1927), 119ff.

among the number there was one settler each from Scotland, Wales, and the Isle of Man; less than ten each from nineteen shires of England; and that the greatest number clearly came from Norfolk, Suffolk, Essex, and London. Stated in terms of the major language areas of England, this is to say that 7 per cent came from the North, 4 per cent from the West Midlands, 9 per cent from the Southwest, 5 per cent from the Southeast, and 75 per cent from the East Midlands. If this may be generally taken as representing the early settlement of New England, it means that the pronunciation and usage which furnished the basis of standard British English clearly predominated also on the New England frontier.

Evidence for the Virginia colony is not as satisfactory, but the language of the East Midlands seems also to have predominated there. Nevertheless, there was the other 25 per cent not from the East Midlands—an admixture which left its effect—and the compromise speech of the colonies was thus begun with elements deriving from the homeland even before elements newly acquired by the settlers could make themselves felt.

As this first flow of settlement in eastern New England began to cool, there came another of a somewhat different sort, deriving more from the North and West of England than from the East Midlands. Since lands along the coast were by now taken up, the new settlers moved inland, and eventually their speech became dominant in New England west of the Connecticut River, in the upper Hudson River Valley, and in eastern Pennsylvania. Then this current spread out farther to the south and west, and so the speech differences of these later comers took their place on the new frontier and rolled across the plains and mountains to the Pacific.

To note only the most striking linguistic effect of this, one may look at the loss or retention of post-vocalic *r* in such words as *bar* and *barn* in the United States today. Following the pattern of London and British standard pronunciation, the Atlantic coastal strip both north and south generally drops the *r—baa, baan*. The inland area, following the pattern of the North of England, which eventually covered most of the rest of the country, retained the *r—bar, barn*. This latter wave has flowed so strongly that there appears to be a backwash today toward the East. It may even be that within a few generations the *r*-usage of the country at large may engulf the *r*-less areas of the East.

The American colonies, then, were the linguistic frontier of the motherland, with two main currents of regional influence flowing in. And from a mingling of these, the colonies soon produced their own linguistic frontier. The development of the language in the old country and in the new seems indeed to have moved, for a time, in opposite directions. In Britain, a certain local type of speech—that of London and the near-by shires—was becoming more and more accepted as a standard for educated, literary, and official use, emerging steadily as the upper-class language in a very class-conscious society. In contrast, in America generally and especially on the frontier, the dominant speech was of middle-class origin, and in its relatively classless society, there was nothing really parallel to British upper-class speech. The language has been refined and spread by education—and that not without continuing British influence—but the historic differences established in colonial days have not disappeared.

The separation between American English and British English did not go unnoticed. Travelers had commented on the colonial ways of speech before the Revolution, but the emotions which that event aroused brought the matter into greater prominence. The first list of Americanisms, that of John Witherspoon, appeared in 1781; the next, collected by John Pickering, in 1816.[2] Rather than quote from these, however, I turn to the Diary kept by the English novelist, Captain Frederick Marryat, who visited the new United States in 1837–38. Marryat's account shows keen observation of features which we still use daily. He writes: [3]

Many English words are used in a very different sense from that which we attach to them; for instance: a *clever* person in America means an amiable good tempered person, and the Americans make the distinction by saying, I mean English clever.

Our clever is represented by the word *smart*.

The verb *to admire* is also used in the East, instead of the verb *to like*.

[2] H. L. Mencken, *The American Language* (4th rev. ed., New York, 1936), Ch. II; *Supplement I* (1945), Ch. II.

[3] *A Diary in America, with Remarks on its Institutions* (Philadelphia, 1839), II, 33–38.

"Have you ever been at Paris?"

"No; but I should *admire* to go."

A Yankee description of a clever woman:— "Well, now, she'll walk right into you, and talk to you like a book"; or, as I have heard them say, "she'll talk you out of sight."

The word ugly is used for cross, ill-tempered. "I did feel so *ugly* when he said that."

Bad is used in an odd sense: it is employed for awkward, uncomfortable, sorry:—

"I did feel so *bad* when I read that" —awkward.

"I have felt quite *bad* about it ever since" —uncomfortable.

"She was so *bad,* I thought she would cry" —sorry.

And as bad is tantamount to *not good,* I have heard a lady say, "I don't feel *at all good,* this morning."

Mean is occasionally used for ashamed.

"I never felt so mean in my life."

"We reckon this very handsome scenery, sir," said an American to me, pointing to the landscape.

"I consider him very truthful," is another expression.

"He stimulates too much."

"He dissipates awfully."

And they are very fond of using the noun as a verb, as—

"I *suspicion* that's a fact."

"I *opinion* quite the contrary."

The word *considerable* is in considerable demand in the United States. In a work in which the letters of the party had been given to the public as specimens of good style and polite literature, it is used as follows:—

"My dear sister, I have taken up the pen early this morning, as I intend to write *considerable.*"

The word *great* is oddly used for fine, splendid.

"She's the *greatest* gal in the whole Union."

"Are you cold, Miss?" said I to a young lady, who pulled the shawl closer over her shoulders.

"Some," was the reply.

The English *what?* implying that you did not hear what was said to you, is changed in America to the word *how?*

"I reckon," "I calculate," "I guess," are all used as the common English phrase, "I suppose." Each term is said to be peculiar to different states, but I found them used every where, one as often as the other . . . .

The verb "to fix" is universal. It means to do any thing.
"Shall I fix it right away?"—*i.e.* "Shall I do it immediately?"....
brush your coat, or *get ready* your breakfast first?"
Right away, for immediately or at once, is very general.
"Shall I fix it right away?"—*i.e.* "Shall I do it immediately?"....
"I'm a *gone 'coon"* implies "I am distressed—*or* ruined *or* lost."
I once asked the origin of this expression, and was very gravely told
as follows:—

"There is a Captain Martin Scott in the United States army who is
a remarkable shot with a rifle. He was raised, I believe, in Vermont.
His fame was so considerable through the State, that even the animals
were aware of it. He went out one morning with his rifle, and spying
a raccoon upon the upper branches of a high tree, brought his gun
up to his shoulder; when the raccoon, perceiving it, raised his
paw up for a parley. "I beg your pardon, mister," said the raccoon
very politely; "but may I ask you if your name is *Scott?"*—"Yes,"
replied the captain.—*"Martin Scott?"* continued the raccoon.—"Yes,"
replied the captain.—*"Captain* Martin Scott?" still continued the
animal.—"Yes," replied the captain, "Captain Martin Scott."—"Oh!
then," says the animal, "I may just as well come down, for I'm a
gone 'coon."

Marryat sums up his impressions by saying that in provincial
use the language has become "debased"—which is not surprising.
Even the upper classes of Americans, however, he remarks, "do
not ... speak or pronounce English according to our standard;
they appear to have no exact rule to guide them .... In fact, every
one appears to be independent, and pronounces just as he pleases.

"But it is not for me to decide the very momentous question, as
to which nation speaks the best English. The Americans generally
improve upon the inventions of others; probably they may have
improved upon our language."

Judging by his general tone, I do not think that Marryat is
sneering here. Certainly there were plenty of Americans, flushed
with revolutionary ardor, who believed that they *could* improve
on the English language. One of these, of course, was the man who
taught America to spell, the great lexicographer, Noah Webster.
In 1789, Webster proclaimed his eagerness for a new language in
the following words: [4]

[4] *Dissertations on the English Language* ... (Boston, 1789), I, Introduction.

As an independent nation our honor requires us to have a system
of our own, in language as well as government. Great Britain, whose
children we are, and whose language we speak, should no longer be
our standard; for the taste of her writers is already corrupted, and
her language on the decline. But if it were not so, she is at too great
a distance to be our model and to instruct us in the principles of
our own tongue.

Several circumstances [he continues] render a future separation of
the American tongue from the English necessary and unavoidable.
[These he next discusses, then concludes:] We have therefore the
fairest opportunity of establishing a national language and of giving
it uniformity and perspicuity, in North America, that ever presented
itself to mankind. Now is the time to begin the plan.

Webster's prediction, of course, has not come true. The separation between British and American speech has grown no greater
than it was in his time, at least at the standard level. If anything,
modern communication and cultural interchange have reduced the
breach. What the prediction signified in its time, however, was
that the differences had become too striking to ignore; that the
newly independent nation was in no disposition to imitate what
now seemed a foreign model; that, on the contrary, some fruits of
the linguistic frontier seemed desirable and defensible. Webster's
separatism is a rationalization of a real situation.

We may now look in some detail at the elements of which the
new American English was formed. When the words which the
colonists had brought proved inadequate to the new environment,
they responded in three chief ways: they borrowed from the
Indians or from other Europeans, they gave new meanings to old
words, they made new combinations. It is interesting to notice at
what time the various Indian words, for example, came in.
Naturally enough, the first of these were the names of animals and
plants of the new world, especially those valuable for food.

Even before 1620, *moose, raccoon, opossum, terrapin, persim-
mon, moccasin, tomahawk,* and *totem* had entered the English
language. Within the next thirty years, by the middle of the century, *muskrat, sachem, papoose, quahog, hominy, powwow, skunk,
squash, squaw, wampum,* and *wigwam* had followed. Still other
seventeenth-century borrowings were *hickory, manitou, woodchuck,* and *Tammany.* Eighteenth-century additions are *pecan,*

muskellunge, Catawba, succotash, catalpa, caucus; and the nineteenth century saw the adoption of *chipmunk, sequoia, tamarack,
mugwump, mackinaw, teepee, cayuse,* and climactically, at the
very end of the century, *hooch.*

Some of these Indian words did not come directly: both *bayou*
and *cisco* came through French—*bayou* in Louisiana from Choc-
taw *bayuk,* and *cisco* in the Great Lakes area. The name of this
fish, *cisco,* is in fact an abbreviation of French *ciscoette,* itself an
abbreviation of the Ojibwa *pemitewiskawet.* Thus, these Indian
words have been naturalized first into French, then into English,
the *-ette* suffix probably due to analogy with the common suffix
that we have also borrowed in such words as *cigarette* and *quar-
tette,* and the first syllable of *bayou* probably recalling French
baie. The French habit of abbreviating long Indian words for
simplicity is seen not only in *ciscoette,* but also in *caribou,* which
they reduced from Algonkian *buccarebou.* They also shortened
Indian tribal names: *Sioux* is all that they left of *Nadouessioux,*
and the *ark* of *Ozark* is their abbreviation of *Arkansas.*

Another thing to notice is the succession of borrowings as the
moving frontier brought the whites into contact with different
tribes. Early loans were mostly from Algonkian languages, a few
from Iroquois; across the Mississippi, more words were taken from
the Sioux; still later the languages of the Northwest and Southwest were levied upon. We have two well-known words for an
Indian dwelling: *wigwam* taken before 1628 from Algonkian, and
teepee taken before 1872 from Siouan. *Hooch* is a western word,
abbreviated from Tlingit *hootsnuwu.*

Indian terms have entered strikingly into our political language. The *powwows* of the red men, with their big meetings,
deliberations, oratory, and dances—aided often enough by the
white men's firewater—struck a responsive chord. Not only *powwow,* but *mugwump, Tammany, sachem,* and others testify to
this influence. Nor should we forget that from Indian sources
have come into the language a host of American place names,
some euphonious, like *Ohio* and *Missouri,* others that fall less
comfortably upon the ear, like *Ogunquit, Walla Walla, Keokuk,
Puyallup,* and the now proverbial *Podunk.*

In the process of naturalization, words are not only abbreviated
and otherwise simplified in pronunciation, but many are frankly

made over and suited to English word patterns. The notorious
example of this process is *woodchuck,* which makes us think of
an animal which lives in the *woods,* and *chucks.* Everybody
knows, of course, *what* it chucks, though nobody is certain how
much it would if it could. All this accretion of nursery lore is due
entirely to the naturalization of the word by speakers of *English:*
its original in Algonkian has no such implications—it is simply
the name for a kind of marmot, *wejack,* mistakenly applied.

As to the words which English-speakers on the American frontier borrowed from other Europeans, the chief sources were, of
course, French and Spanish, though Dutch and German have also
added their bit. The far-flung French outposts and colonies in the
Great Lakes and Mississippi system have furnished several geographical terms: *butte, coulee* (probably first adopted in Wisconsin), *sault (Sault Ste. Marie* is the best known), *rapids, prairie.*
From the intrepid *voyageurs* and *coureurs de bois* who made first
contacts with the Indians of the interior come *portage* and *cache,*
calumet and *lacrosse.* But the French loans have entered at
every cultural level from the most homely upward: *shivaree* and
sashay, pumpkin and *chowder, bureau* and *depot, cent, dime,* and
picayune, and the word that has become utterly American in
atmosphere of song and story—*levee.*

The direct Spanish influence came somewhat later but has
been very marked and is still continuing. Few of our state names
show the influence of French—*Vermont, Louisiana, Illinois,*
possibly some others; many more are Spanish—*Florida, California,*
Nevada, Colorado, Arizona, Montana. From Spanish have come
the topographic terms *arroyo, mesa, canyon, sierra,* and *savannah,*
to say nothing of *tornado.* Spanish names for plants and animals
are particularly numerous: *alfalfa, marijuana, mosquito, bonito,*
palomino, armadillo, alligator are purely Spanish, but the
Spaniards have also passed on to us such originally Indian words
as *avocado, yucca, mesquite, coyote,* and now *peyote.* We have
discarded the name of the fish *tunny,* which came into British use
through French, and have substituted the American word *tuna,*
which came to us from the Spanish—who, by the way, got it from
the English to begin with!

I will not attempt to go through the whole list of Spanish
loans—it is too long; but let me at least suggest the fields to which

these words belong. Food and drink—*tamale, barbecue, chili con carne, cafeteria;* building—*adobe, patio, plaza, pueblo;* clothing —*chaps, poncho, sombrero,* ten *gallon* hat; ranch life—*rodeo, stampede, corral, lariat, bronco, buckaroo, mustang;* legal and penal—*hoosegow, calaboose, desperado, vigilante;* mining—*bonanza* and *placer.*

Let me touch next, rapidly, on the Dutch and German loans. The Dutch, of course, had a successful colony centrally placed in the lower Hudson valley. From this point, their influence spread into southeastern New England, up the Hudson, and into New Jersey. Overrun by superior numbers, they nevertheless left several words that are essential to American English—some of which, indeed, have gone around the world—so *Yankee, boss,* and *Santa Claus.* Others in daily use are *cookie, cole slaw, caboose, scow, snoop,* and *spook.* German loans came considerably later and mostly refer to foods—*delicatessen, frankfurter, hamburger, wiener, noodle, pretzel, sauerkraut,* and so on; but some relate to education—*kindergarten, semester, seminar;* and to various other things less uplifting—*loafer, bum, dumb* (in the sense of stupid), *pinochle,* and *spiel.* Even the exclamation *ouch* is German, and the new suffix *-fest,* used in popular combinations such as *slug-fest* in boxing, *run-fest* in baseball, and *talk-fest,* which may be found at any *coffee-clutch.*

So much for foreign elements—there is no time to mention others taken from the Africans, the Irish, the Chinese, the Jews. All were incorporated in the flowing lava of the frontier and have become an inseparable part of it. We turn next to the English words which acquired a new meaning under frontier conditions. One remarkable example is the word *lumber.* In England it had meant, and still means, castoff material of any sort—what most Americans would call *junk.* The first task of the settlers in the new land, however, was to make clearings in the forest primeval. Trees were in the way; when cut down, they lay about everywhere. The wood from them, in fact, was so much lumber, in the old sense of the word. So it naturally acquired the new sense of *wood,* and by now *lumber* has displaced *timber* as the general term.

One other notorious example: *corn* in the old country had meant grain of any sort—wheat, barley, oats. On the American frontier, the new grain which was the most accessible and best suited to the climate, upon which the Indians depended and which they taught the white man to grow, was *maize*. The settlers began by calling it *Indian corn*, but that was immediately abbreviated to plain *corn*. From it was made *pone, hominy, suppawn, succotash*. American settlers adopted all of these—they even made it the basis of a drink. In Dr. Mitford Mathews' *Dictionary of Americanisms,* published in 1951, are listed no less than 151 words and phrases in which corn is used in its new sense—*cornbread, cornsilk, corn belt, cornbird, corn-cracker* are just a few of the commoner ones.

Then there is the third way in which the vocabulary has been increased: by forming new combinations. These too are very numerous, but a few of the more striking may be offered in approximately the order of their creation. From the seventeenth century: *log house, snowshoe, pine knot, bayberry;* from the eighteenth century: *salt lick, mountain laurel, horse-thief, minuteman, cotton gin;* and from the nineteenth century: *cocktail, gerrymander, sod fence, Indian giver, know-nothing, stern-wheeler, cowboy, mail order,* and *sideburns.*

The intimate connection of language with the frontier cannot be better demonstrated, however, than by showing the additions made in the course of a single exploration. Fortunately, the most famous one has been studied in Dr. E. H. Criswell's work entitled *Lewis and Clark: Linguistic Pioneers.*[5] The expedition lasted some twenty-eight months, from May, 1804, till September, 1806, and went from St. Louis through the Louisiana Territory to the Pacific and back. Of the 29 regular members of the group, nine are believed to have kept journals, and seven of these journals survive. Dr. Criswell has digested these painstakingly and offers the following conclusions: The seven writers, among them, used 1,107 Americanisms of all kinds, of which 583 were unrecorded before. In addition, their use of 301 words, meanings, and combinations is the earliest on record. As to the source of the words, 143 were new adoptions, 86 were words that were going out of use in Britain, and 91 were survivals of words already obsolete in Britain but still alive in America. A large number are names of fauna and flora newly encountered, and many relate to

[5] *University of Missouri Studies,* XV (April, 1940), 2.

Indians, but there are all kinds. Examples of fresh combinations
are *beaver pond, council lodge, tow-cord, Indian mush, melon-
bug*. Some old words that acquire new meanings are *goldfinch,
apron, button, run, bear claw*. The additions to the language
made by this one expedition are impressive. Yet they represent
only one small record, one small insight into what was a continuous, ebullient language activity by millions of others—scouts,
Indian fighters, trappers, miners, settlers—a vast part of which
went *un*recorded. There can be no question that hundreds of
the verbal creations that bubbled up along the hot fringe of the
frontier are now irrecoverably lost.

So far, we have been treating of the language chiefly in terms of
words. But this is not enough. Language is not a mere collection
of single items—it is an articulate thing varying in its style of
expression; and this style as much as anything else goes to reflect
the fluidity of the frontier, its infinite variety and unceasing
change. In the general flow, some currents become strong enough
to gain at least a temporary identity. They follow a course and
leave a definite impress. The regional types of American English
today reflect such larger currents, though time, widespread education, easy transportation and communication, and the restlessness
of our population have done much to level out differences in the
last fifty years. Only in the more isolated places where industrial
society has not yet triumphed, where national broadcasting,
national distribution of movies and reading materials have not
swept everything before them, are local characteristics strongly
preserved in present speech. Fortunately, however, American literature can furnish us quite accurate representations of some of
the local types of language that mingled on the frontier a hundred
years ago.

For New England, the *Biglow Papers* of James Russell Lowell
may be taken.[6] Lowell describes what he was attempting in them
as follows: "I imagined to myself such an up-country man as I had
often seen at anti-slavery gatherings, capable of district-school
English, but always instinctively falling back into the natural
stronghold of his homely dialect when heated to the point of self-

[6] Quotations are from the preface to the second series of the *Biglow Papers*
and from Paper No. 1 of the first series. Horace E. Scudder (ed.), *The Complete Poetical Works of James Russell Lowell* (Boston, 1924).

forgetfulness . . . . To me the dialect was native, and spoken all about me when a boy."

Hosea Biglow has written a poem against war. His father, Ezekiel, writes an explanatory letter to the editor of the *Boston Courier,* to whom he is submitting the poem for publication. This is part of the letter:

MISTER EDDYTER:—Our Hosea wuz down to Boston last week, and he see a cruetin Sarjunt a struttin round as popler as a hen with 1 chicking, with 2 fellers a drummin and fifin arter him like all nater. the sarjunt he thout Hosea hed n't gut his i teeth cut cos he looked a kindo's though he'd jest com down, so he cal'lated to hook him in, but Hosy woud n't take none o' his sarse for all he hed much as 20 Rooster's tales stuck onto his hat and eenamost enuf brass a bobbin up and down on his shoulders and figureed on to his coat and trousis, let alone wut nater hed sot in his featers, to make a 6 pounder out on.

wal, Hosea he com home considerabal riled, and arter I'd gone to bed I heern him a thrashin round like a short-tailed Bull in fli-time. The old Woman ses she to me ses she, Zekle, ses she, our Hosee's gut the chollery or suthin anuther ses she, don't you Bee skeered, ses I, he's oney amakin pottery, ses i, he's ollers on hand at thet ere busynes like Da & martin, and shure enuf, cum mornin, Hosy he cum down stares full chizzle, hare on eend and cote tales flyin, and sot rite of to go reed his varses to Parson Wilbur bein he haint any grate shows o' book larnin himself, bimeby he cum back and sed the parson wuz dreffle tickled with 'em as i hoop you will Be, and said they wuz True grit.

Hosea ses taint hardly fair to call 'em hisn now, cos the parson kind o' slicked off sume of the last varses, but he told Hosee he didn't want to put his ore in to tetch to the Rest on 'em, bein they wuz veery well As they wuz, and then Hosy ses he sed suthin a nuther about Simplex Mundishes or sum such feller, but I guess Hosea kind o' didn't hear him, for I never hearn o' nobody o' that name in this villadge, and I've lived here man and boy 76 year cum next tater diggin, and thair aint no wheres a kitting spryer 'n I be.

The most characteristic quality of the pronunciation, as we can see, is a sort of choppiness, an emphatic accentuation which reduces words to their essentials, unstressed syllables tending to disappear entirely—thus *recruiting* becomes *cruetin; calculated* becomes *cal'lated; always* is *ollers; dreadful, dreffle; something, suthin; potato, tater;* and so on. Present participles "drop their g's," but by compensation they usually have the syllable "a" prefixed: *a drummin, a bobbin, a thrashin.* This syllable "a" is used in other places too; it serves as a link between strongly stressed words: "he looked *a* kindo's though . . . ."

The old pronunciation—it goes back to Shakespeare's day—of "ar" where we would say "er" is found here in such words as *varses,* book *larnin,* and of course *parson,* where, however, it has become standard. Other old pronunciations are *riled* for *roiled,* and *nater* and *feater* for *nature* and *feature.* Final "a" becomes "y" in *chollery* for *cholera,* and *Hosy* for *Hosea.* "E" becomes "ee" in *skeered, eend, veery.*

But more characteristic even than details of pronunciation or the choppy emphatic delivery is the use of lively popular metaphor, usually drawn from the immediacies of life, often becoming almost proverbial, and often with a dry irony: "as popler as a hen with 1 chicking," "hed n't gut his i teeth cut," "a thrashin round like a short-tailed Bull in fli-time," "woud n't take none o' his sarse," and of course such words as *spry, eenamost, sot, hisn, hearn* for *heard.* This then is the down-East Yankee manner of speech that went west with the frontier, and which in a milder form can be heard still in Wisconsin from the oldest generation in a few places where the strong New England settlements were made.

By way of comparison, let us turn to the South. Following is part of a conversation from *Woodcraft,* a novel of William Gilmore Simms, first published in 1856.[7] It represents the speech of a South Carolinian named Millhouse, who is helping Captain Porgy to rehabilitate his plantation after the Revolution. Millhouse is urging the Captain to marry the widow Eveleigh, who, he says, is *willing.* The Captain speaks first:

"Ha! ha! ha! Delightful! 'Pon my soul, Millhouse, you put the case in quite a new and striking point of view. You think I should speak in time to prevent the widow from addressing me, and so spare her blushes."

"In course, I does! That's jest the thing—spar' her blushes!"

"But, suppose she were to propose to me, and I were to—refuse her?"

"Lord love you, cappin, and be merciful to your onderstanding; but you wouldn't be so onkind and outright redickilous, as to do that—and arter all that she's been a-doing for you."

"It would be rather hard-hearted, I confess."

[7] Quotation is from Ch. LVI, "The Sheriff in Limbo."

" 'Twould be most monstrous redickilous! But, cappin, you mus'n't
wait for her to do the axing. It mout-be she'd come arter awhile, and
when she couldn't stan' keepin' in her feelin's any longer; but then it
mout-be—it would be—too late, then, to help your sarcumstances. Ef
the property was to be sold by the sheriff, what would it bring, I want
to know, now, when thar's so little money guine about. Not enough,
by half, to pay this warmint, M'Kewn. But, ef 'twas only on account
of the lady, it's your business to speak quick. The man has no right
to keep the poor woman a-waiting on him. He has no right to keep
a-thinking, with pipe in his mouth, while she's a-weeping and pining
away a-most to nothin'."

"But I don't see that Mrs. Eveleigh shows any such signs of suffering, Millhouse."

"It's all innard, cappin. She's got too proud a stomach, to show
outside, in her flesh and sperrits, how much she suffers innardly.
Many's the woman that's looked fat and hearty, while her heart's
been a-breaking in her buzzum . . . ."

There are many obvious similarities here to the speech of the
Biglows, though the rendering of Millhouse's speech is somewhat
less accurate: Simms has given it a literary turn. Nevertheless it
contrasts clearly with the language of the educated Captain and
shows a few local characteristics. In common with the Yankee
speech, we find the "dropping of g's" and the prefixing of "a":
keepin', feelin's, a-waiting, a-thinking, a-weeping. There is the
Elizabethan "ar" in *sarcumstances* and *warmint.* There are such
pronunciations as *ef* for *if, jest* for *just,* and such reduced forms as
arter for *after, a-most* for *almost, innard* for *inward,* and so on—
none of these specifically local, but merely indicating the general
character of uneducated speech at the popular level.

Local features, in the selection read, are few, but one may point
to *spar'* for *spare* and *thar* for *there,* which Zekle and Hosy Biglow
would not have said. *Mout-be,* repeated twice, is still a notable
South Carolina feature today, and *ax* for *ask* and *monstrous* as an
emphatic adverb were probably more favored in this region than
elsewhere.

Let us next skip to the frontier itself, to Nevada in the "flush
times" of the silver fever, and read a bit out of Mark Twain's
Roughing It,[8] first published in 1872. Of this time and place,
Twain has written: "As all the peoples of the earth had represent-

[8] Quotation is from Vol. II, Ch. VI.

ative adventurers in Silverland, and as each adventurer had brought the slang of his nation or his locality with him, the combination made the slang of Nevada the richest and most infinitely varied and copious that had ever existed anywhere in the world, perhaps, except in the mines of California in the early days. Slang was the language of Nevada."

Our scene depicts a rough named "Scotty," whose fellow rough, Buck Fanshawe, has died, attempting to tell the minister about it and to get him to preach at Buck's funeral. Scotty's slangy talk is put side by side with the sober formality of the clergyman.

But to return to Scotty's visit to the minister. He was on a sorrowful mission, now, and his face was the picture of woe. Being admitted to the presence, he sat down before the clergyman, placed his fire-hat on an unfinished manuscript sermon under the minister's nose, took from it a red silk handkerchief, wiped his brow and heaved a sigh of dismal impressiveness, explanatory of his business. He choked, and even shed tears; but with an effort he mastered his voice and said in lugubrious tones:

"Are you the duck that runs the gospel-mill next door?"

"Am I the—pardon me, I believe I do not understand?"

With another sigh, and half-sob, Scotty rejoined:

"Why you see we are in a bit of trouble, and the boys thought maybe you would give us a lift, if we'd tackle you—that is, if I've got the rights of it and you are the head clerk of the doxology-works next door."

"I am the shepherd in charge of the flock whose fold is next door."

"The which?"

"The spiritual adviser of the little company of believers whose sanctuary adjoins these premises."

Scotty scratched his head, reflected a moment, and then said:

"You ruther hold over me, pard. I reckon I can't call that hand. Ante and pass the buck."

"How? I beg your pardon. What did I understand you to say?"

"Well, you've rather got the bulge on me. Or maybe we've both got the bulge somehow. You don't smoke me and I don't smoke you. You see, one of the boys has passed in his checks and we want to give him a good send-off, and so the thing I'm on now is to roust out somebody to jerk a little chin-music for us and waltz him through handsome."

"My friend, I seem to grow more and more bewildered. Your observations are wholly incomprehensible to me. Cannot you simplify them in some way? At first I thought perhaps I understood you, but I grope now. Would it not expedite matters if you restricted yourself to categorical statements of fact unencumbered with obstructing accumulations of metaphor and allegory?"

Another pause, and more reflection. Then, said Scotty:

"I'll have to pass, I judge."

"How?"

"You've raised me out, pard."

"I still fail to catch your meaning."

"Why, that last lead of yourn is too many for me—that's the idea. I can't trump nor follow suit."

The clergyman sank back in his chair perplexed. Scotty leaned his head on his hand and gave himself up to thought. Presently his face came up, sorrowful but confident.

"I've got it now, so's you can savvy," he said. "What we want is a gospel-sharp. See?"

"A what?"

"Gospel-sharp. Parson."

"Oh! Why did you not say so before? I am a clergyman—a parson."

"Now you talk! You see my blind and straddle it like a man. Put it there!"—extending a brawny paw, which closed over the minister's small hand and gave it a shake indicative of fraternal sympathy and fervent gratification.

"Now we're all right, pard. Let's start fresh. Don't you mind my snuffling a little—becuz we're in a power of trouble. You see one of the boys has gone up the flume—"

"Gone where?"

"Up the flume—throwed up the sponge, you understand."

"Thrown up the sponge?"

"Yes—kicked the bucket—"

"Ah—has departed to that mysterious country from whose bourne no traveler returns."

"Return! I reckon not. Why, pard, he's *dead!*"

This is, of course, a "set piece" in which exaggeration has had its role. One should not fail to notice, however, that the speech of the minister is also under scrutiny. His unctuous polysyllabism, his unbending rejection of even the most ordinary conversational informality—he refuses to say "can't" or "I'm"—and withal his repeated use of the "How?" rather than "What?" on which, we recall, Captain Marryat commented—all these Mark Twain has observed quite as carefully as he has the slang.

We conclude with another selection from Mark Twain, *Life on the Mississippi,* published about 1852.[9] It is an example of the very tall talk of a boaster of a type that had his day on the frontier a hundred years ago. Mark Twain is not the only writer to depict this kind of hyperbolic blowhard, but his picture is an eloquent one. The speaker is winding himself up verbally for a fight with all comers, if he is to be believed, and seeks to warn the beholders of the devastation which he will wreak:

Whoo-oop! I'm the original iron-jawed, brass-mounted, copper-bellied corpse-maker from the wilds of Arkansaw! Look at me! I'm the man they call Sudden Death and General Desolation! Sired by a hurricane, dam'd by an earthquake, half-brother to the cholera, nearly related to the small-pox on the mother's side! Look at me! I take nineteen alligators and a bar'l of whiskey for breakfast when I'm in robust health, and a bushel of rattlesnakes and a dead body when I'm ailing. I split the everlasting rocks with my glance, and I squench the thunder when I speak! Whoo-oop! Stand back and give me room according to my strength! Blood's my natural drink, and the wails of the dying is music to my ear. Cast your eye on me, gentlemen, and lay low and hold your breath, for I'm 'bout to turn myself loose!

These few short samples cannot possibly give a balanced view of the state of language on the frontier. Suffice it to say that there was to be heard every *local* type of pronunciation and idiom which had become established in the more settled parts of the country, that the contacts of these variant types led forever to compromises of one kind and another, that interlingual contacts with Indians and non-English-speaking Europeans were ever-present, that certain types of adventurers—the roaring boys, the crackers and bullies and slingers of extravagant talk—were loosing their tongues on all sides. On the seething frontier, everything went— the turbulence of life in general was inevitably reflected in language. There was an enormous appetite for words, an admiration for words: a man who could bring out a salty phrase or an apt comparison would smash the cracker-barrels.

Reflections of this ebullience are with us still. Americans pay less attention to "rules" of language, written or unwritten, than devoted schoolteachers would like them to. Our authors are less

[9] Quotation is from Ch. III.

afraid of linguistic innovation than those of many other nations; we set more value upon vigor of expression than upon control. These things, no doubt, are reflections of the recency of the frontier experience. In addition to this, the language we speak, while not "the American language," is definitely our own, a type of English enlarged and, in general, enriched by the retention of older elements, the development of many new meanings and combinations, and the seasoning of numerous foreign acquisitions. It has a smack of its own, a strength of its own. It is no longer a semiattached colonial speech: it has achieved autonomy, even polarity, side by side with the original pole of British English. A great deal—the fundamental part—these two poles share in common; their difference has come about as a direct result of the tremendous experience that made this nation. And in that experience, a most vivid and creative part was played by the frontier.

SELECTED READINGS

American Speech. New York: Columbia University Press, 1925—.

Eggleston, Edward. *The Transit of Civilization*. New York: Peter Smith, 1933. Orig. pub. New York, 1901.

Kurath, Hans. *A Word-Geography of the Eastern United States*. Ann Arbor, Mich.: University of Michigan Press, 1949.

Marckwardt, Albert H. *American English*. New York: Oxford University Press, 1955.

Mathews, Mitford M. (ed.). *A Dictionary of Americanisms on Historical Principles*. Chicago: University of Chicago Press, 1951.

―――. (ed.). *The Beginnings of American English, Essays and Comments*. Chicago: University of Chicago Press, 1931.

Mencken, Henry L. *The American Language*. 4th rev. ed. New York: A. A. Knopf, 1936. *Supplement I*, 1945. *Supplement II*, 1948.

Pyles, Thomas. *Words and Ways of American English*. New York: Random House, 1952.

Stewart, George R. *Names on the Land*. New York: Random House, 1945.

HENRY NASH SMITH

Mark Twain as an Interpreter of the Far West: The Structure of Roughing It

In the literary world the American frontier has occupied a position of importance, especially in this past century since writers have found the pioneers interesting people instead of uncouth ne'er-do-wells. As a discoverer of the frontier, Mark Twain was himself one of the literary pioneers, and his semiautobiographical novel, Roughing It, *stands as his interpretation of the westward advance. In this volume the West is interpreted through comic devices, showing how a person from the East is transformed by the West into an "old-timer," accepting a country where "Sam Slade is more feared than the Almighty."*

In this essay, Professor Smith analyzes Roughing It *to show how Mark Twain approached the task at hand and then raises the question of the influence of the West upon our literature. He shows that Clemens finally rejected the frontier in favor of a more genteel society, though he affirmed the Western virtues of comradeship and freedom, which the transitory frontier held for all. Mark Twain's sympathetic treatment of the frontiersmen, the influence of their vernacular upon his style, and the major literary device of using a tenderfoot in a frontier settlement—these have deeply influenced the writing of American fiction down to the present. Though Professor Smith doubts if the American West had much influence upon the development of our democracy, he indicates that the West has influenced the themes and methods of treatment used in our literature to a degree still unknown and unappreciated.*

MARK TWAIN used materials drawn from his experiences in the Far West, in Nevada and California, on many occasions. In Chapter XII of *Innocents Abroad,* for example, a railway trip through the Rhone valley calls up the memory of his stagecoach journey out to Nevada; and Jim Baker's blue jay yarn in Chapter III of *A Tramp Abroad* has its setting in the Mother Lode country of California. *Roughing It,* however, is the only book of Mark Twain's which deals with the Far West at length. It interprets his experiences there more fully than any other and gives him a unique opportunity to investigate this material by means of a narrative structure larger in scope than the self-contained anecdote. I shall confine my attention almost entirely to the problem of structure in *Roughing It,* because I think this is the best way to arrive at Mark Twain's imaginative interpretation of the Far West.[1]

It is true, of course, that many passages in the book interpret the West in the sense that they employ comic devices characteristic of Washoe journalism and indeed of frontier journalism in general. The extravagant jokes, the wild exaggerations (such as the description of the Washoe zephyr which bears through the air a neatly stratified miscellany of objects), the burlesques and parodies

[1] In addition to such standard works as Bernard De Voto's *Mark Twain's America* (Boston, 1932), Gladys C. Bellamy's *Mark Twain as a Literary Artist* (Norman, Oklahoma, 1950), J. DeLancey Ferguson's *Mark Twain: Man and Legend* (Indianapolis, 1943), and Vernon L. Parrington's *The Beginnings of Critical Realism in America* (New York, 1930), this lecture draws heavily upon two unpublished dissertations: Paul S. Schmidt, "Samuel Clemens' Technique as a Humorist, 1857–1872," University of Minnesota, 1951, and Martin B. Fried, "The Composition, Sources, and Popularity of Mark Twain's *Roughing It,*" University of Chicago, 1951. *Roughing It* is cited in the edition published by Harper & Bros., 2 vols. in 1, New York, 1913, and passages are quoted with the permission of Harper & Bros. and the Mark Twain Estate. The references to rites of initiation in preliterate societies are based on Hutton Webster's *Primitive Secret Societies: A Study in Early Politics and Religion* (2nd ed., New York, 1932).

(such as the description of the serial romance composed by various hands for the literary weekly in Virginia City) are continuous with, although almost always technically superior to, the standard fare of Nevada newspapers in the days of the mining boom.

But I should like to raise a question about the book as a whole rather than about its component parts. Does it have an over-all structure which can be recognized as an imaginative rendering of the author's Far Western experience? The usual answer to this question is no. William Dean Howells, reviewing the book upon its first appearance in 1872, found the plan of it "very simple indeed, for it is merely the personal history of Mr. Clemens during a certain number of years . . . ." After listing the various materials which the book contains, he says that they "appear in kaleidoscopic succession"—that is, without plan, at random. Subsequent critics have reached substantially the same conclusion about the structure of *Roughing It*. Martin B. Fried, in an unpublished dissertation devoted to the book, says it is constructed according to the plan for a lecture which Mark Twain explained to his wife in 1871: "*Any* lecture of mine ought to be a running narrative-plank, with square holes in it six inches apart, all the length of it, and then in my mental shop I ought to have plugs (half marked 'serious' and the other marked 'humorous') to select from and jam into these holes according to the temper of the audience."

Mark Twain's early lectures were obviously put together in this fashion. And it is beyond question that *Roughing It* often exhibits the same strategy of opportunism, especially in the later chapters, where the author was straining himself to spin out his materials to the length demanded by the conventions of subscription publishing. There is biographical evidence also that Mark Twain was not fully conscious of writing to an organically unified plan. He had never before constructed a book. The Jumping Frog volume published in 1867 had been a collection of sketches which had previously appeared in periodicals, and *Innocents Abroad,* which was having sensationally good sales while Mark Twain was writing *Roughing It,* was based in large part on letters written for newspapers without a thought of book publication. Soon after Mark Twain began work on *Roughing It,* he informed his sister Pamela that he was writing "a book like the 'Innocents' in size and style." Finding his memory of the overland stage journey dim, he asked for his brother Orion's journal of the trip, which Orion sent him; and he had with him also a scrapbook of articles from the Virginia City *Territorial Enterprise,* which he evidently drew upon, even to the extent of reprinting eight of them. Eventually he was forced to use the dispatches he had sent from the Sandwich Islands to the Sacramento *Union.* This was a step he had not contemplated when he began writing, for he had intended making a separate book of the Sandwich Islands material. Furthermore, Mark Twain expressed dissatisfaction with the chapters describing the overland journey and at one time meant to leave out half of them; but in the end he did not because he needed the pages to fill up his stint. He does not say why he disliked the overland chapters; perhaps he would have preferred not to rely so heavily on material procured from Orion. His opinion seems the more strange because this sequence is one of the most satisfactory parts of the entire narrative—a reminder that the wise critic will be very cautious in accepting a writer's estimate of his own work.

The composition of *Roughing It* was interrupted for long intervals, sometimes for months on end, by the death of Livy's father, the birth of the Clemenses' first child, Livy's slow convalescence, and the long illness and death in the Clemens household of Emma Nye, a friend of Livy's. Years afterward, Mark Twain remembered this period as the blackest of his life.

Nevertheless, the first half of *Roughing It* (covering the journey across the plains and the narrator's experience in Nevada) has a coherent and powerful narrative structure despite occasional falterings and waverings of intention. As is so often the case with Mark Twain's work, we have to face the possibility, even the probability, that this structure proceeds from deeper sources than the author's conscious intention. There are indications that he was at least intermittently aware of an upsurge of power in the act of composition. Even though he said that he was writing a book like *Innocents Abroad,* Mark Twain did set out deliberately to write an entire book rather than merely to rework previously published newspaper correspondence. In the work as originally planned, he had relatively little newspaper material upon which he could draw. The journal Orion sent him has not been discovered, but at the one point where we can compare the finished narrative with Orion's notes (the account of the outlaw Slade), Mark Twain's creative development of the bare bones of Orion's remembered fact is strikingly apparent. Furthermore, despite Albert B. Paine's assertion that in July of 1870, Elisha P. Bliss, president of the American Publishing Company, suggested to Mark Twain the idea of describing his experiences in Nevada and California, there is some evidence that as early as 1864, when he was working as a journalist in San Francisco, he had intended writing such a book. It may be significant that in March of 1870 Mark Twain had acknowledged to his sister the receipt of a "coffin of Enterprise files," which had apparently been shipped at his request from St. Louis to Elmira. And on May 29 he had written to his friend Mrs. Mary M. Fairbanks, ". . . the publishers are getting right impatient to see another book on the stocks, and I doubt if I could do better than rub up old Pacific memories and put them between covers along with some eloquent pictures." Bliss encouraged him to go ahead with this project, but the idea was the author's own.

Despite the misfortunes that darkened the Clemens household while *Roughing It* was in gestation, Mark Twain more than once speaks of his delight in writing it. When he had finished the first four chapters, he wrote to Bliss: ". . . I tell you the 'Innocents Abroad' will have to get up early to beat it.—It will be a book that will jump right strait [sic] into a continental celebrity the first month it is issued. . . . I see the capabilities of my subject." Seven or eight months later, when he was perhaps halfway through the book, he declared: ". . . I am writing with a red-hot interest. Nothing grieves me now—nothing troubles me, nothing bothers me or gets my attention—I don't think of anything but the book, and I don't have an hour's unhappiness about anything and don't care two cents whether school keeps or not. It will be a bully book."

These indications of a happy flow of inspiration, extending through hundreds of pages of manuscript, authorize a careful scrutiny of *Roughing It* for the purpose of discovering a continuous and significant structure. The imagination that was to prove capable of producing *Huckleberry Finn* was always there from the beginning, and even in Mark Twain's apprentice period we have to keep in mind the power that had not yet made itself fully apparent. I believe that this power can be felt pervasively in the first half of *Roughing It*.

In seeking for evidences of an over-all design in the book, we may profit from the efforts that have been made to classify it, to assign it to a genre. It has been called both a work of autobiographical reminiscence and a travel book. These categories are not mutually exclusive, but they imply different emphases. I should like to explore each in turn.

If the continuity of the work arises from its being autobiographical, we must seek its structural principle in the rendering of the self, the personality whose experiences are recorded. It has been recognized that the "I" of *Roughing It* is a predominantly fictitious character, differing markedly from the actual Samuel L. Clemens. Martin Fried says the narrator is "sometimes Mark Twain, the inspired idiot, romantic, gullible, and ridiculous, and sometimes Samuel Clemens, the inspired reporter, who describes what he saw." When the author had written at least nine chapters, he wrote to Orion: ". . . right in the first chapter I have got to alter the whole style of one of my characters and re-write him clear through to where I am now. It is no fool of a job, I can tell you, but the book will be greatly bettered by it."

The character who was to be altered was the narrator. He undergoes an important development in the course of the narrative; the revision must have been made to this end. But Mr. Fried's suggestion that this change is simply disillusionment about prospecting and mining hardly seems weighty enough to warrant so large a term as "dynamic." A more useful proposal is advanced by Paul Schmidt, who introduces the convenient phrase "narrative persona" to designate the mask, the fictitious role assigned to the "I" of the narrative. Mr. Schmidt believes that in *Roughing It,* the "handling of the narrative persona is the only structural device which claims attention." He finds two sharply contrasted roles for the narrator: "the first pose is that of the tenderfoot in the West, and the second is that of the shiftless bum who is too lazy to help his pardners dig on their mining claim." This seems to me highly suggestive, and I should like to apply the distinction to *Roughing It* in some detail. Both tenderfoot and old-timer, or, as Mr. Schmidt calls this second persona, the "vernacular character," are clearly present in the book. But he does not offer very much light on the subject of their relation to each other.

In order to understand the relation of the persona of the tender-foot to the persona of the vernacular character, we may profitably consider what is implied in the classification of *Roughing It* as a travel narrative. This suggestion places the book in an interesting context of other narratives of travel in the early Far West. There can hardly be any question here of the evolution of a genre (although certain points of contact between *Roughing It,* Albert D. Richardson's *Beyond the Mississippi,* and Ross Browne's *Adventures in the Apache Country* have been pointed out). But associating *Roughing It* in our minds with such earlier books of travel as Washington Irving's *A Tour on the Prairies* or Francis Parkman's *The Oregon Trail* enables us to see certain generic traits in it. The first of these is the predominance of movement in the narrative plan. Movement was the inevitable form of the white man's contact with the early Far West. The region had not been settled long enough for stable societies to develop; there were no native writers to interpret the region. Everyone who wrote about the Far West was an outsider, a traveler. What he saw was inevitably new and strange. Nothing could be taken for granted— not the landscape, for the very contours of the land, the climate, the plants and animals were unlike those of the settled portion of the country; not the people, who were either completely strange Indians or an almost equally strange heterogeneous population of new arrivals from the four corners of the earth; and certainly not the social patterns of the wilderness, the overland trail, or a mining boom. All writers of travel narratives in the frontier period were describing new and strange experiences for the audience back home, for whom the Far West bore a completely exotic character.

Irving and Parkman, although different from each other in many ways, are alike in that they have come voluntarily to see the sights—they are prototourists, without a serious purpose which commits them to the trail. The Far West does not have any personal meaning for either of them. They are not involved; what they see is a spectacle. In *A Tour on the Prairies* (1835), Irving goes about manufacturing literature by recording the trains of association set in motion within him by what he observes during his excursion beyond the frontier. Imaginatively, he is living in a private universe, or rather in a universe of stereotyped images and emotions which is implicit in his prose style and has nothing to do with the West. Parkman, spending a summer on the Plains in 1846 while the invading columns march westward to the conquest of Mexico, California, and Oregon, is fascinated by the barbaric splendor of the Sioux, but in the American emigrants sees only rude peasants suffering from jaundice and clad in crude garments of homespun. He observes the Indians as an anthropologist, the Pikes and Mormons as a Boston Brahmin.

Roughing It likewise describes a journey; and in the opening sequence Mark Twain adopts the narrative persona of a tourist. But the persona is deliberately exaggerated for the purpose of burlesquing it. The narrator says he originally intended merely to spend three months in Nevada on a pleasure jaunt. His head is filled with adolescent dreams of "Indians, deserts and silver bars." (I, 2.) The themes of movement and novelty, and the tone of exoticism, are given great prominence. Yet the reader quickly becomes aware that the narrative technique in this book is extremely complex—so complex, in fact, that beside it Irving's and Parkman's technique seems primitive. For although the principal character, the tenderfoot tourist, tells the story in the first person, it is evident that the pronoun "I" links two quite different personae: the tenderfoot setting out across the Plains and the old-timer, the veteran, who has seen the elephant and now looks back upon his own callow days of inexperience. Both these personae are present in the narrative from the start. The contrast between them, which is an implied judgment upon the tenderfoot's innocence and a corresponding claim for the superior maturity and sophistication of the old-timer, is the consequence of precisely that journey which the book will describe. Thus, in a sense, the whole plot is implicit in the management of point of view from the first paragraph.

From this fact several consequences flow. First, we recognize that the movement which formed the narrative pattern of all accounts of Far Western travel has for the first time acquired a moral significance. The West is no longer mere spectacle, mere landscape or potential wealth or theater of Manifest Destiny, but a source of transforming experience. The traveler who enters the region described by Mark Twain is certain to be changed into a different person, as earlier travelers were not. In the second place, it is affirmed implicitly from the outset in the management of the narrative that the criterion of judgment, the standard by which good is distinguished from bad and wisdom from foolishness, is no longer to be found in the settled society which the traveler is on the point of leaving behind but resides in that as-yet-unknown Far West toward which his journey is taking him.

The basic situation which *Roughing It* develops is presented in a condensed version in Chapter V. Three days out of St. Joseph, Missouri, the passengers on the stagecoach see their first coyote:

... he was not a pretty creature [says the narrator], or respectable either, for I got well acquainted with his race afterward, and can speak with confidence. The coyote is a long, slim, sick and sorry-looking skeleton, with a gray wolf-skin stretched over it, a tolerably bushy tail that forever sags down with a despairing expression of forsakenness and misery, a furtive and evil eye, and a long, sharp face, with slightly lifted lip and exposed teeth. [I, 31–32.]

This does not seem at first glance to be an attractive portrait; but the perceptive reader will have noticed that the moral universe of *Roughing It* is somewhat paradoxical, and he may therefore be prepared to discover that the sad-looking coyote is really a triumphant and heroic figure, endowed with supernatural powers. This coyote explains, indirectly, what the author calls "the gladness and the wild sense of freedom that used to make the blood dance in my veins on those fine overland mornings!" [I, 31.]

The coyote's hidden power begins to appear when you "start a swift-footed dog after him ... —especially if it is a dog that has a good opinion of himself, and has been brought up to think he knows something about speed." The coyote seems to make no effort at all, yet the dog cannot come closer than the twenty feet which the coyote chooses to leave as a proper interval between them. The dog

... begins to get aggravated, and it makes him madder and madder to see how gently the coyote glides along and never pants or sweats or ceases to smile; and he grows still more and more incensed to see how shamefully he has been taken in by an entire stranger, and what an ignoble swindle that long, calm, soft-footed trot is; and next he notices that he is getting fagged, and that the coyote actually has to slacken speed a little to keep from running away from him—and *then* that town-dog is mad in earnest, and he begins to strain and weep and swear, and paw the sand higher than ever, and reach for the coyote with concentrated and desperate energy. This "spurt" finds him six feet behind the gliding enemy, and two miles from his friends.

But presently the coyote turns and smiles blandly, with a polite apology for having to hurry away:

...and forthwith there is a rushing sound, and the sudden splitting of a long crack through the atmosphere, and behold that dog is solitary and alone in the midst of a vast solitude! [I, 33–34.]

Thereafter, the dog takes no interest at all in chasing coyotes.

This anecdote summarizes Mark Twain's imaginative interpretation of the Far West. It involves a tenderfoot with a higher opinion of himself than he can make good in the frontier environment; a veteran who looks disreputable (and is disreputable, by town-bred standards) but is nevertheless in secure command of the situation; and the process by which the tenderfoot gains knowledge, quite fresh and new knowledge, at the cost of humiliation to himself. The anecdote presupposes a transvaluation of values as the traveler passes from the accustomed life of towns to the strange life of the Far West. The conventional attitudes and accomplishments brought from back home are shown to be ridiculous in comparison with the coyote's secret—a secret that seems actually to release him from the operation of the customary laws of nature.

Here, I think, is to be found the relation between the two narrative personae which Mr. Schmidt has identified. *Roughing It* describes the process by which the tenderfoot is transformed into the old-timer, the vernacular character. The process can best be described as an initiation. The narrative is not everywhere controlled by this theme, but the pattern of initiation is sufficiently clear in the first half of the book to constitute an expressive structure.

The opening chapters emphasize the callowness and ignorance of the two tenderfeet (the narrator and his brother) who are setting out upon their adventure. "I was young and ignorant," says the narrator. "I never had been away from home." He has a childish daydream of what travel to the remote West will mean for the elder brother who has just been appointed Secretary of Nevada Territory:

Pretty soon he would be hundreds and hundreds of miles away on the great plains and deserts, and among the mountains of the Far West, and would see buffaloes and Indians, and prairie-dogs, and antelopes, and have all kinds of adventures, and maybe get hanged or scalped, and have ever such a fine time, and write home and tell us all about it, and be a hero. [I, 1–2.]

In addition to the naïve content of this fantasy, the ignorance and inexperience of the narrator are emphasized by the linking of sentence elements with the loose conjunction "and." The consciousness depicted here is incapable of discrimination. It is a chaos of stereotypes and clichés.

At St. Joseph, starting point of the stage route, the travelers discover they cannot take with them the ludicrously inappropriate clothing they have brought along ("swallow-tail coats and white kid gloves to wear at Pawnee receptions in the Rocky Mountains ... stove-pipe hats ... patent-leather boots") but they do hang on to a six-pound unabridged dictionary: "for we did not know— poor innocents—that such things could be bought in San Francisco on one day and received in Carson City the next." [I, 4–5.] That is, they simultaneously overestimate and underestimate the wildness of the West. The dictionary is mentioned repeatedly on the journey—so often, in fact, that it becomes a kind of symbol of the useless pedantries and proprieties which these neophytes are trying to take with them into the wilderness. [I, 5, 19, 20, 148.] Their real education begins when they are introduced to the strange status system of the West as it is exhibited in the attitudes of the driver of the stage coach toward other employees and the attitudes of the other employees toward him. The driver enjoys a prestige that could be approximated nowhere else save on the river, in the exalted position of a steamboat pilot. It is a system of status which does not depend on conventional social distinctions or on economics, since the passengers, presumably much wealthier than any of the employees of the stage line, are viewed by the driver with as much contempt as he shows toward his hostlers. [I, 22–23.]

Very early in the journey—in fact, on the evening of the first day—the travelers encounter a woman who describes herself as "a sociable heifer" and in her unself-conscious volubility and general good will stuns them with the vision of a female who is neither a

lady of rank nor a deferential servant, but a self-confident individual who is perfectly sincere in inviting them to "lay over a couple
o' days" at her home town to meet the folks. [I, 9.] Next morning,
the narrator is all but blasted from the earth by the indignation of
a station keeper at his naïveté in expecting to find coffee to drink;
he is jolted by the profanity of this strange new world beyond the
frontier and is humiliated in Salt Lake City when Brigham Young
"put his hand on my head, beamed down on me in an admiring
way and said to my brother: 'Ah—your child, I presume? Boy or
girl?' " [I, 97.] The education includes also the withering scorn of
a bootblack when the narrator hands him a five-cent piece in payment for a shoeshine. [I, 122–123.]

These passages are characteristic of Mark Twain's humor in that
the narrator is the comic butt. It is an engaging device in its own
right, and it enables the author to deal in violent effects without
the cruelty that is often distressing to the twentieth-century reader
of frontier humor. But the exaggeration of the youth and callowness of the narrator has the primary function of making the tenderfoot's innocence unmistakable.

During the westward journey on the stagecoach, the travelers
are slowly emancipated from the system of values they are leaving
behind and familiarized with the true state of affairs in the new
life toward which they are moving. The preposterous jackass rab-
bit sits "thinking about his sins" [I, 14]—a suggestion which, reinforced as it will be by other touches in the course of the narrative,
suggests that the conventional morality and theology of respectable
society are not applicable to a region where, in a phrase from
Thomas J. Dimsdale's *Vigilantes of Montana* that Mark Twain
quotes with delight, the desperado Slade is feared "a great deal
more than the Almighty." [I, 73.] The freedom of the wilderness
confers a marked exhilaration on the passengers: ". . . as we lay
and smoked the pipe of peace and compared all this luxury with
the years of tiresome city life that had gone before it, we felt that
there was only one complete and satisfying happiness in the
world, and we had found it." [I, 12–13.] But the transit from one
world to another is not to be made without hardship and even
suffering. As the travelers move out over the Plains, they receive
intimations of the violence which is the price of their new freedom: at first comically, when old-timers pump the tenderfeet full

of tall tales about an Indian massacre (one of the alleged survivors said "he was stuck so literally full of arrows that after the Indians were gone and he could raise up and examine himself, he could not restrain his tears, for his clothes were completely ruined"); but then seriously, in the account of the one authentic survivor who dragged himself with his wounds to seek aid, "for more than forty hours suffering unimaginable anguish from hunger, thirst, and bodily pain." [I, 56.] The stories of dangers faced by earlier travelers are reinforced in Chapter IX by a skillfully rendered episode in which the sleeping passengers are awakened by confused cries for help; shouts of "Kill him! Kill him like a dog!"; pistol shots; pleas for mercy; and "Then a fainter groan, and another blow, and away sped the stage into the darkness, and left the grisly mystery behind us." This "dark occurrence" is never fully explained to the tenderfeet; the new driver and conductor are not very much interested in the subject. Violence is so common in this wilderness that only the unsophisticated pay much attention to it. [I, 59–61.]

These premonitions lead up to the two chapters (X and XI) given over to Slade, the paradoxical bad man whose bloody exploits and death at the hands of the vigilantes are described at length but do not lead to any clear explanation or judgment. By the end of this sequence, however, it is thoroughly established that the Far West is not a Sunday School picnic.

In Utah the tenderfeet feel themselves to be in "a land of enchantment, and goblins, and awful mystery." [I, 93.] But they continue their penetration of the West. Bemis, a fellow passenger who can conveniently undergo experiences not appropriate for the narrator or his brother, gets himself hilariously drunk on the "exclusively Mormon refresher, 'valley tan.'" [I, 94.] In a mildly documentary mood, Mark Twain includes "the customary inquisition into the workings of polygamy," but instead of the usual moral indignation, the passage reaches its climax in a fictitious monologue of Brigham Young burlesquing the sacrosanct institutions of matrimony and the family.

As the travelers set out upon the last leg of their journey, the author prepares the reader for their entrance into Carson City by an explicit restatement of the Western attitude toward newcomers from the East:

...many a time in Nevada, afterward [he says], we had occasion to remember with humiliation that we were "emigrants," and consequently a low and inferior sort of creatures. Perhaps the reader has visited Utah, Nevada, or California, even in these latter days, and while communing with himself upon the sorrowful banishment of those countries from what he considers "the world," has had his wings clipped by finding that *he* is the one to be pitied, and that there are entire populations around him ready and willing to do it for him— yea, who are complacently doing it for him already, wherever he steps his foot. Poor thing! they are making fun of his hat; and the cut of his New York coat; and his conscientiousness about his grammar; and his feeble profanity; and his consumingly ludicrous ignorance of ores, shafts, tunnels, and other things which he never saw before, and never felt enough interest in to read about. And all the time that he is thinking what a sad fate it is to be exiled to that far country, that lonely land, the citizens around him are looking down on him with a blighting compassion because he is an "emigrant" instead of that proudest and blessedest creature that exists on all the earth, a "FORTY-NINER." [I, 123–124.]

The first real physical discomfort for the travelers comes appropriately just as they draw near their goal—in crossing the alkali desert west of Great Salt Lake, where the monotony of blistering heat and choking dust is not relieved by even "a sob from the lost souls that doubtless people that dead air." [I, 128.] After frankly digressive (and inferior) chapters on the repetition of the same story about Hank Monk and Horace Greeley, and about the Goshoot Indians, the emigrants reach their destination, Carson City, the territorial capital of Nevada. At once they witness a wildly exaggerated shooting scrape in the street, which is evidently a burlesque of Eastern stereotypes concerning Western violence. [I, 146.] The narrator reaches a distinctly more advanced stage of his initiation when he joins a male community variously called "The Brigade" or, more tellingly, just "the boys"—inhabitants of the attic of Bridget O'Flannigan's boardinghouse. [I, 149.] He adopts the costume of the country [I, 155]; and during a camping trip to Lake Tahoe, he begins to exhibit conspicuously the traits that Mr. Schmidt calls attention to in the vernacular character—laziness, irresponsibility, irreverence. Having set fire to the mountainside, the narrator and his companion give up a half-hearted attempt to stake out timber claims that has occasioned a satiric thrust at the cult of landownership. [I, 159.] Back in Carson City, the narrator undergoes further education in the ways of the West when he buys a worthless bucking horse. [I, 168–174.] On a backbreaking trip to the Humboldt, the delight of campfire comradeship by night awakens the "nomadic instinct" that "countless ages of growth toward perfect civilization" have failed to root out of the modern male. [I, 192.] The tenderfoot exhibits his naïveté again by expecting to find silver lying about in huge nuggets on the ground and by being deceived by "fool's gold." [I, 195–199.] Then follows the episode at the inn where the travelers encounter the bully Arkansas. This would-be bad man is less formidable than Slade and can be vanquished by the landlord's wife brandishing a pair of scissors. [I, 218.] The initiation of the tenderfeet culminates in the magnificent incident of the snowstorm, which I should like to examine in some detail.

The four chapters which follow here—XXXI–XXXIV—seem to me the high point of the book, both in the skill with which the individual episodes are rendered and in the arrangement of the events with respect to the whole narrative pattern. The snowstorm episode is a brilliant climax to the rejection of genteel assumptions which must take place before the tenderfoot can be admitted to the vernacular community; and the symbolic death of the narrator, coming as it does at the end of his probation, evokes the archetypal pattern of all initiations.

In the immediately following episode of the Buncombe trial, the narrator is no longer the comic butt but writes from the point of view of an anonymous, undifferentiated member of the group which he characterizes as "the older citizens of a new territory." [I, 234.] A fresh comic butt, belonging as it were to the next generation of emigrants, is introduced in the person of General Buncombe. For the first time, the narrator and the reader view the tenderfoot from without instead of from within.

The point of the snowstorm episode is that the three companions, lost in the storm and believing themselves to be facing certain death, solemnly renounce their respective wickednesses in language which is an incandescent parody of the sanctimonious rhetoric of the nineteenth-century evangelical pulpit. The invulnerable self-deception of the men who believe themselves about to die and, above all, the absurdly trivial nature of the "sins" they abjure (whisky, cards, and, as a climax, the narrator's tobacco pipe) constitute a devastating attack on the distorted ethical system of the genteel tradition:

[Ollendorf] . . . said he had given up all hope of life, and although ill-prepared, was ready to submit humbly to his fate; that he wished he could be spared a little longer, not for any selfish reason, but to make a thorough reform in his character, and by devoting himself to helping the poor, nursing the sick, and pleading with the people to guard themselves against the evils of intemperance, make his life a beneficent example to the young, and lay it down at last with the precious reflection that it had not been lived in vain. He ended by saying that his reform should begin at this moment, even here in the presence of death, since no longer time was to be vouchsafed wherein to prosecute it to men's help and benefit—and with that he threw away the bottle of whisky. [I, 228.]

One would think this burlesque could not be carried to a higher pitch; but Mark Twain has a further resource in Mr. Ballou's malapropisms:

He said he never gambled, but still was satisfied that the meddling with cards in any way was immoral and injurious, and no man could be wholly pure and blemishless without eschewing them. "And therefore," continued he, "in doing this act I already feel more in sympathy with that spiritual saturnalia necessary to entire and obsolete reform." [I, 228.]

The narrator himself, finally, casting away his pipe, maintains the malicious exaltation of the rhetoric:

While I yet talked, the thought of the good I might have done in the world, and the still greater good I might *now* do, with these new incentives and higher and better aims to guide me if I could only be spared a few years longer, overcame me and the tears came again. [I, 229.]

Next morning, of course, they discover they are within fifteen steps of a comfortable inn and are annoyed at the thought that their horses, having taken shelter at once, "must have overheard and enjoyed all our confessions and lamentations." Each man is soon drawn back to his abandoned vice, and they shake hands on an agreement to say no more about "reform" and "examples to the rising generation." [I, 232.] It is their formal entrance upon the rights and privileges of members of the Washoe vernacular community.

The elaborate practical joke played on General Buncombe, which follows, is again noteworthy for the sustained and searching brilliance of its burlesque of genteel theology and the pompous rhetoric of the bar. The "impassioned effort" of the deluded General, confident in the rightness of his cause, winds up "with a grand war-whoop for free speech, freedom of the press, free schools, the Glorious Bird of America and the principles of eternal justice! [Applause.]" [I, 238.] Governor Roop's judicial opinion mocks the standard injunctions to humility based upon the doctrine of original sin:

Gentlemen, it ill becomes us, worms as we are, to meddle with the decrees of Heaven. It is plain to me that Heaven, in its inscrutable wisdom, has seen fit to move this defendant's ranch for a purpose. We are but creatures, and we must submit. If Heaven has chosen to favor the defendant Morgan in this marked and wonderful manner ... it ill becomes us, insects as we are, to question the legality of the act or inquire into the reasons that prompted it .... It is for us to submit, without repining. [I, 239.]

Immediately after the Buncombe trial, the narrator leaves for Esmeralda and another fling at prospecting. His full membership in the community of old-timers is taken for granted; one of the party is Captain John Nye, brother of the governor, who is a genius at making himself and everyone around him comfortable —a man, indeed, who might almost stand as the personification of vernacular poise and competence. But the narrative is now tinged with foreshadowings of disappointment and frustration. Whatever may be the pleasures of life in the mining camps, the economics of the boom are far from satisfactory. The narrator is reduced at last to taking a job "as a common laborer in a quartz-mill, at ten dollars a week and board." [I, 244.] This interlude lasts only a week, and he tries his luck once again at prospecting. Now, however, he is not a novice going into raptures over fool's gold, but an initiate sharing a general craze for the mythical Whiteman "cement-mine," a will-o'-the-wisp just as devoid of substance but one which goads the imagination of the entire community. [I, 251.]

The writing begins to reflect the aimless character of the narrator's wanderings. He is evidently trying hard to find something to describe, and in an effort to be funny he is reduced to the spectacle of a dog smarting in the alkali water of Mono Lake [I, 260], to feeble puns, and to pointless tall tales about how cold it is in the town of Mono. [I, 263.] The better part of a chapter is given over to telling how the narrator and his partner were almost marooned on an island in Mono Lake. [I, 264–268.] The account of the narrator's experiences as a prospector ends with two chapters devoted to the story of the "blind lead," when he and his friend thought themselves millionaires for ten days but forfeited their claim through accident and carelessness. The narrator is persuaded to try working one more claim but quits in disgust after his first shovelful of dirt lands on the back of his neck. [II, 3.] He has had enough of prospecting.

Such an outcome is entirely correct as a commentary on the mining boom. Many men fancied themselves millionaires for a time, yet in the end had nothing to show for their spree. But to accept this outward fable as the narrative line of the book, as Parrington does, for example, is to reduce the meaning of *Roughing It* to a thin and obvious sociological parable. If failure to make a million in the mines and build a mansion on Nob Hill constitutes the definitive frustration for the narrator, then the story cannot be read as having contained promise of anything beyond exactly this consummation, and it means no more than that the narrator tried to get rich quick but (in common with nearly everyone else) failed. This is not a plot capable of holding serious interest, then or now. It is certainly an underestimate of Mark Twain's imaginative depth to assert that he could have found himself absorbed by such a story over a period of time, as we know he was in the writing of *Roughing It*. The book itself, in fact, provides a definitive critique of the get-rich-quick mania in its stories of what happened to the lucky few who did, by accident, make their killing, only to be destroyed by it even more completely than their unlucky companions were destroyed by failure. Mark Twain saw the mining boom in perspective. His only anecdote of nabobs not ruined by sudden wealth, the story of Colonel Jack and Colonel Jim in New York, makes the fact of their wealth quite incidental to the charm of their expansive generosity and innocence. What Mark Twain finds memorable in his Washoe experience is a quality of character, an attitude, that is more accessible to the Jim Gillises who failed than to the men who made their fortunes.

It is thus a serious mistake on Parrington's part to find the "lesson" of Mark Twain's Far Western experience in a cynical code of absolute self-interest. Parrington quotes one passage, and one only, from *Roughing It;* and he makes this passage a pivotal text for his discussion of Mark Twain. It occurs in a chapter describing the speculative mania in a community that had, quite literally, "gone crazy." "Everybody's head was full of such 'calculations' as those," says Mark Twain, ". . . such raving insanity, rather. Few people took *work* into their calculations—or outlay of money either; except the work and expenditures of other people." The passage quoted by Parrington comes in the next paragraph:

We never touched our tunnel or our shaft again. Why? Because we judged that we had learned the *real* secret of success in silver-mining—which was, *not* to mine the silver ourselves by the sweat of our brows and the labor of our hands, but to *sell* the ledges to the dull slaves of toil and let them do the mining! [I, 209.]

Parrington comments: "It was the great lesson of his generation, and thus instructed he proposed to sell his brains in the best market. Exploitation was the royal road to wealth and he was eager to exploit both himself and his fellows."

No one familiar with Mark Twain's biography would deny that he had in him the impulses of a speculator. To mention only one example, he earnestly desired to establish a world-wide monopoly with the Paige typesetting machine and in this fashion to make himself a multimillionaire. But the passage Parrington quotes from *Roughing It* does not mean what he takes it to mean. The ironic intention of the passage is evident from its context; it is evident also in the phrase "the dull slaves of toil," a burlesque of the clichés which Mark Twain would have us understand govern the thinking of the deluded speculators. The passage, in other words, is a satire (and thus a rejection) of the very attitude which Parrington takes to be expressed seriously in it.

The lesson which Mark Twain says he drew from his experience as a prospector is not so portentous. He begins the second volume with the nonchalant question "What to do next?" and surveys with some amusement the list of vocations he had attempted and abandoned in the past. His problem, as he presents it, was simply how to make a living (not a fortune, just a living) with the least possible exertion. The answer comes with perfect timing in a letter offering him a reporter's job on the Virginia City *Territorial Enterprise.* He says he took the job despite misgivings on the score of inexperience, because if he refused he must "presently become dependent upon somebody for my bread, a thing necessarily distasteful to a man who had never experienced such a humiliation since he was thirteen years old." [II, 4.]

The second half of *Roughing It* is, in my opinion, structurally distinct from the first. Henceforth the narrative scheme is loosely autobiographical, and the narrative is merely a framework within which more or less fully developed anecdotes are placed. The second half, that is, answers closely to the description of the entire work given by Mr. Fried and other critics. Fourteen chapters cover the period of Mark Twain's work as a reporter on the staff of the *Enterprise.* As is appropriate to this new status, the point of view is that of a spectator not deeply involved in the life of the community, yet perfectly at home in it. Two elaborate anecdotes— "Scotty Briggs and the Parson" [II, 42–53] and "Jim Blaine and his Grandfather's Ram" [II, 98–104]—and a number of shorter pieces appear in this section of the book, and there is a good deal of more or less documentary attention to mining, to gunplay, and to such other matters as the sale of Gridley's floursack for the benefit of the Sanitary Commission. But there is no sense of direction, and when the narrator leaves for California, one has the impression he has simply grown bored with Virginia City.

The second half of *Roughing It* records the early stages of a completely new career for Mark Twain, the career that took him to San Francisco and eventually to the East with his rapidly developing fame as journalist, lecturer, and writer. But when he was writing the book, he was still too fully involved in the career to be able to perceive its outlines or estimate its direction. This second story was potentially just as full of meaning as the fable which gives structure to the first half of the book, but is was not a simple meaning, and we may wonder whether Mark Twain ever achieved enough objectivity concerning himself to enable him to see his career in perspective. At any rate, from this point onward he was not able to impose narrative form on his materials. But he was in effect leaving the frontier when he boarded the stage for San Francisco; he was a backtrailer on his way to New York, Hartford, and Europe. The later chapters of *Roughing It* are therefore not directly relevant to the problem of literary interpretation of the Far West. They bear upon quite a different theme—the story of the young man from the provinces coming to the metropolis to make his way in the world, and succeeding, and then finding that success does not bring him happiness, but disillusionment. This is a myth that belongs to an urban, an industrial, a capitalist world, not to the frontier.

If we separate the plots of the two parts of *Roughing It* in this fashion, must we conclude that the second half throws no light at all on the first? This is hardly the case. The tenderfoot undergoes his period of probation, passes the tests imposed on him, and earns his way into membership in the vernacular community. He is rewarded by being allowed to acquire a new set of criteria, ethical and social, which give him a new perspective on the culture he has left behind. He experiences an exhilarating sense of freedom and, for a time, finds ample matter for literature in various modes of burlesquing the culture he seems to himself to have abandoned. But no sooner is his initiation complete than he faces a crisis in his personal life and also (since this tenderfoot is Mark Twain) in his art—a crisis indicated in George Santayana's shrewd analysis: "The humorists . . . only half escape the genteel tradition; their humour would lose its savour if they had wholly escaped it. They point to what contradicts it in the facts; but not in order to abandon the genteel tradition, for they have nothing solid to put in its place." As the problem arises in *Roughing It*, it may be stated simply as the question whether the vernacular community of the Far West produces any solid affirmations. The course of the narrative implies that after identifying himself with that community, Mark Twain found he could not remain satisfied with it very long. Not only was the milieu of a frontier community, even the most sophisticated of frontier communities, confining in a social and economic sense; it seems to have ceased nourishing his imagination. It did not give him enough to write about.

Mr. Schmidt tries to identify the affirmations arising from Mark

Twain's imaginative identification of himself with the vernacular community. *Roughing It* undoubtedly makes some affirmations, and they are important. They provide the energy which sustains Mark Twain's career as a writer, at least through *Huckleberry Finn*. Mr. Schmidt lists the vernacular values under the general headings of color—a sheer delight in the texture of experience; brotherhood—a comradeship that disregards the social and economic distinctions of older and more stable societies; and freedom—the absence of inhibition, the autonomy of the spontaneous human being not coerced by traditional codes and institutions. These headings serve to remind us of the sources of power in Mark Twain at his best.

But what happens in the second half of *Roughing It* suggests that the affirmations of the first part are in some way lacking in ultimate force or durability. They neither are enough in themselves to serve as a point of consummation, nor do they clearly lead to something else that might so serve. In recounting his departure from Virginia City, Mark Twain says it had "afforded me the most vigorous enjoyment of life I had ever experienced." This note of nostalgia for a frontier life can be heard often in writing about the West through the nineteenth century, and for that matter, down to the present. The emotion underlies the belief that the basic virtues of the American character and American institutions are derived from the frontier past which is still current, not merely among historians in the school of Frederick Jackson Turner, but quite generally in the population at large. Yet there was something paradoxical about all American frontiers. They were, by definition, transitory. You could not commit yourself to the frontier permanently even if you wanted to, for the frontier changed out from under you. And it has been a grievous question whether the passing of the frontier leaves behind some permanent and durable value, some insight or enlargement of the imagination which is relevant to the different way of life that comes afterward.

This question bears especially upon the virtual nihilism of Mark Twain's last years, as expressed, for example, in *The Mysterious Stranger*. But there is obviously not time enough on this occasion to deal with a problem of such magnitude. I shall conclude by suggesting that the wavering of intention and of narrative pattern in the second part of *Roughing It,* as the narrator passes beyond his frontier phase, is strangely similar to the problem posed for the historian by the effort to apply Turner's hypothesis to the interpretation of American history after the closing of the frontier of free land. The democracy which Turner believed to have been born on the frontier seemed to have no basis in American society after the free land was gone. But if this were indeed the case, then the historian was faced with a formidable dilemma: either he must give up the effort to find democratic values in an industrial-urban society, or he must reject the thesis that democracy is an effect of free land. Turner, like Mark Twain, gives us an intensely attractive picture of an earlier, simpler America which unfortunately seems unrelated to the America of our own day.

But the artist is perhaps not so vulnerable to the ruins of time as is the historian. Mark Twain the writer certainly derived from the West—from the older West of Missouri and the newer West of Nevada—the two bases of his achievement as an artist: his style, formed upon the vernacular speech of the river and the mining camps, and his major strategy, which consisted in a prolonged exploration of the imaginative consequences of the new perspective provided by the persona of the vernacular character, outside the official culture and with no apparent stake in it. Although the consequences of this alienation from the dominant cultural tradition are still felt to their cost by American writers, the energies released by the revolution in language and in attitude which is foreshadowed by the initiation of the narrator of *Roughing It* into the vernacular community are far from being spent. On the contrary, they have contributed to the formation of American literature in the twentieth century to an extent still not fully explored by literary critics or historians. The secret to which the tenderfoot was admitted at the end of his initiation is even yet not entirely understood and assimilated. But there can be no doubt that his journey was made to some purpose.

SELECTED READINGS

Bellamy, Gladys C. *Mark Twain as a Literary Artist.* Norman: University of Oklahoma Press, 1950.

Benson, Ivan. *Mark Twain's Western Years.* Stanford: Stanford University Press, 1938.

Blair, Walter (ed.). *Native American Humor.* New York: American Book Co., 1937.

Branch, Edgar M. *The Literary Apprenticeship of Mark Twain.* Urbana: University of Illinois Press, 1950.

De Voto, Bernard. *Mark Twain's America.* Boston: Little, Brown, 1932.

Ferguson, J. DeLancey. *Mark Twain: Man and Legend.* Indianapolis: Bobbs-Merrill, 1943.

Paine, Albert B. (ed.). *Mark Twain's Letters.* 2 vols. New York: Harper & Bros., 1917.

Wecter, Dixon. *Sam Clemens of Hannibal.* Boston: Houghton Mifflin, 1952.

A. IRVING HALLOWELL

The Backwash of the Frontier:
The Impact of the Indian
on American Culture

The restless hordes of men who left their homes to seek a new world usually found a primitive people lying athwart their advance. These people were called barbarians or savages by the white men and were to be destroyed or pushed aside to make way for progress. Turner argued that the white pioneer living at the edge of American civilization became an Indian in dress and behavior, but he never held that the influence was permanent or important. Since most history has been written by the conquerors, the influence of the primitive people upon American civilization has seldom been the subject for dispassionate consideration.

With the anthropologist's eye, Professor Hallowell in this essay takes a look at the long shadow cast by the American Indian in our culture. He comes to quite a different conclusion than Professor Boardman did about the influence of the barbarian in China. He finds that the Indian had a deep influence on "our speech, our economic life, our clothing, our sports and recreations, certain indigenous religious cults, many of our curative practices, folk and concert music, the novel, poetry, drama, even some of our basic psychological attitudes, and one of the social sciences, anthropology." This philosophical essay shows that the contribution of the Indian was greater than what has been assumed and that American

society has been greatly enriched rather than impoverished by this
aspect of the frontier experience.

ALTHOUGH Frederick Jackson Turner and his disciples have
made little point of the influence of the American Indian upon
our civilization, it is the Indian's continuing presence throughout
our whole colonial and national history that has given many
aspects of our culture a special coloring. In this respect, our
national experience differs from that of any western European
nation, though our culture is continuous with that of Europe.
Recently, Bernard De Voto has stressed the manifold nature of this
unique historical situation and its neglect by historians: [1]

Most American history has been written as if history were a function
solely of white culture—in spite of the fact that till well into the
nineteenth century the Indians were one of the principal determinants
of historical events. Those of us who work in frontier history—which
begins at the tidal beaches and when the sixteenth century begins—
are repeatedly nonplused to discover how little has been done for us
in regard to the one force bearing on our field that was active everywhere. Disregarding Parkman's great example, American historians
have made shockingly little effort to understand the life, the societies,
the cultures, the thinking, and the feeling of the Indians, and disas-
trously little effort to understand how all these affected white men
and their societies.

It is discernible Indian influences of this sort that have formed
what I have called "the backwash of the frontier," fertile silt
carried on the currents and eddies left by the turmoil on the
borderlands. Many other factors beside frontier conditions were
involved in the further development of these influences—factors
too complex to analyze here. And the problem is complicated by
the extreme diversity of America's reactions to the Indian and his
cultures; by the manner in which Indian influences have been
mediated, the varying forms they have assumed at different
periods of our national existence, and their depth. Most often
they have been manifested at the vernacular level of American
culture, one expression of our cultural provincialism, which is
perhaps the reason so little systematic attention has been paid to

[1] Joseph K. Howard, *Strange Empire* . . . (New York, 1952), 8.

them. Our contacts with the Indians have affected our speech, our economic life, our clothing, our sports and recreations, certain indigenous religious cults, many of our curative practices, folk and concert music, the novel, poetry, drama, even some of our basic psychological attitudes, and one of the social sciences, anthropology.

To the outside world there is a closer association of the Indian with the image of America than perhaps we are aware of. For example, Cooper's *The Last of the Mohicans* is not only read by every American schoolchild, it has been said to be the best known American novel in the world. So too, *Hiawatha*, Longfellow's poetic image of the Indian, is widely read and translated in other countries. Ivan Bunin, the Russian poet and novelist, "is probably as well recognized for his translation of *Hiawatha* as for any of his original works." [2]

Americans have created a whole succession of images of the Indian, some literary and interpretative, some growing out of direct contact of particular types of white men with him and changing with historical circumstances. Although the Pope declared as far back as 1512 that the natives of America were descended from Adam and Eve, in colonial New England, Cotton Mather thought that "probably the *Devil* decoy'd . . . [them] . . . hither, in hopes that the gospel of the Lord Jesus Christ would never come here to destroy or disturb his absolute empire over them." As God's elected agents and under his "wonder-working Providence," the colonists must convert these "tawney serpents" or annihilate them. However, the Indian was never simply The Enemy. On the earliest frontiers, the colonists were befriended by the natives. Who has not heard of Squanto? White men from the beginning profited in many practical ways from the Indians' knowledge of their own country and through intimate contacts learned about their customs, manner of thought, and character, and were influenced by them.

During the eighteenth century, when in England and on the Continent a literary image of the Noble Savage, partly derived from ideas about the Indian, was being created, the colonists

[2] Clarence Golides, "The Reception of Some Nineteenth Century American Authors in Europe," *The American Writer and the European Tradition,* ed. Margaret Denny and W. H. Gilman (Minneapolis, 1950), 116.

greatly deepened their firsthand knowledge of the American natives. Trading activities brought tribal groups over a wider range into contact with the colonists. The Indians were not always fought against; on occasion they were comrades-in-arms, and aboriginal methods of fighting influenced the colonists. The speeches made by Indians in treaty negotiations aroused so much interest in native oratory that a novel literary form, with no prototype in Europe, emerged. Verbatim reports of these conferences were widely circulated and read in printed form. It has even been said that information about the organization and operation of the League of the Iroquois, which Franklin picked up at various Indian councils, suggested to him the pattern for a United States of America. In any case it was Franklin whose appreciation of the attitude of the Indians toward their own culture led him to express the anthropological principle of the relativity of culture norms when, in 1784, he wrote: "Savages we call them, because their manners differ from ours, which we think the Perfection of Civility: they think the same of theirs." [3]

As the eastern frontier receded westward and for most Americans the contemporary Indians could be viewed at a comfortable distance, it was their decline that became a romantic literary theme. As expressed in poetry, drama, and the novel, it was an early backwash of the frontier. But it was by no means always the Noble Savage that was depicted; a double image was created—the savage as ignoble as well as noble. During this period, the first half of the nineteenth century, when the Indian was such a popular figure in American literature, it is particularly significant that most of the authors who dealt with Indian themes derived their information from written sources rather than from direct observation. Cooper depended on Heckewelder's writings, and Longfellow on Schoolcraft's *Algic Researches* (1839). It has been said that "Cooper poured the prejudices of John Heckewelder into the Leather-Stocking mold, and produced the Indian of nineteenth century convention." [4] The authors who were busy writing about the Indians were far removed from the men who faced them on the new frontiers.

[3] Alfred O. Aldridge, "Franklin's Deistical Indians," *Proceedings of the American Philosophical Society*, XCIV (1950), 398.

[4] Paul A. W. Wallace, "John Heckewelder's Indians and the Fennimore Cooper Tradition," *ibid.*, XCVI (1952), 500.

Two and a half centuries after Englishmen on the eastern frontier faced the Indian, American frontiersmen in the Mississippi Valley and the Far West found themselves in a parallel situation and regarded him in much the same hostile light—the Indian blocked the path of America's "manifest destiny." In 1867, the Topeka *Weekly Leader* spoke for the West when it characterized the Indians as "a set of miserable, dirty, lousy, blanketed, thieving, lying, sneaking, murdering, graceless, faithless, gut-eating skunks as the Lord ever permitted to infect the earth, and whose immediate and final extermination all men, except Indian agents and traders, should pray for." [5] Cotton Mather's terser characterization of the "tawney serpents" seems almost mild and dignified beside this scathing blast.

Wrestling with his own day-to-day problems, with the Long Hairs not far off, the trans-Mississippi frontiersman was in no position to appreciate the extent to which the Indians *already* had affected American culture. And it would be interesting to know how many Americans on this frontier had read *Hiawatha*. Certainly, few of them could have imagined that, when the West was won and the Indians were safely settled on reservations, native arts and crafts would be appreciated for their aesthetic values and widely exhibited, musicians and poets would visit these remaining enclaves of Indian culture to study their music and songs at first hand, and a museum devoted exclusively to the preservation and exhibition of Indian objects would be established in the largest city of the nation. What would have surprised them more, perhaps, if they could have looked at a Boy Scout Handbook of the twentieth century, is the statement that it "is a pity that most boys think of head-dresses, war whoops, tomahawks, and scalps the instant Indians are mentioned. . . . There are so many thousands of beautiful and desirable things in their lives that it is safe to say that they can offer boys a mighty good code of sport and happiness." And among the other things that would strike the frontiersman forcibly would be the requirement that, in order to win a merit badge in Indian lore, the Boy Scout must learn the Omaha Tribal Prayer. Yes, the Omaha, one of those dastardly Siouan tribes—the gut-eating skunks!

But if the Midwestern frontiersman had been interested enough,

[5] Robert Taft, *Artists and Illustrators of the Old West, 1850–1900* (New York, 1953), 66.

he would have discovered that the word *skunk,* which he could so glibly hurl at the Long Hairs as a derogatory epithet, was derived from an Indian language and had entered American speech in the seventeenth century. The borrowing of words as well as traits of Indian culture, like the use of corn, had been going on for a long time. Referred to by anthropologists as cultural diffusion, this kind of cultural borrowing is a process that has been occurring throughout the entire history of man. It has been one of the main stimuli of cultural change. When people of different cultures meet and social interaction takes place, this situation inevitably eventuates in some cultural borrowing on the part of either or both peoples.

In the past two decades, cultural anthropologists in this country have devoted increasing attention to detailed studies of the effects of Euro-American culture upon the Indians, that is, acculturation, rather than confining themselves, as was once the case, primarily to the collection of data that would make it possible to reconstruct an ethnographic picture of aboriginal life in its undisturbed form. On the other hand, although recognizing that in principle acculturation is seldom if ever a one-way process, anthropologists have paid scarcely any attention to the total effects upon American culture of our continuing contacts with Indians.

One of the things that anthropologists have discovered is that while Indians may "clothe" themselves, so to speak, with many of the accouterments of white man's culture, this is often no more than skin-deep. Even when the Indian is brought into close contact with the white man for more than a generation, and despite missionary efforts and educational opportunities, there is a psychological lag to be taken into account which indicates a dimension of the acculturation process about which we know too little.

In contrast to this side of the acculturalization picture in the United States, it is interesting to recall, when white adults, and especially children, were captured in the seventeenth, eighteenth, and early nineteenth centuries by many different groups of Indians and lived among them in daily intimacy, the apparent ease with which these individuals adjusted themselves to Indian culture. Turner speaks of the "occasional instances of Puritans returning from captivity to visit the frontier towns, Catholic in religion, painted and garbed as Indians and speaking the Indian tongue, and the half-breed children of captive Puritan mothers." While there were many hundreds of white captives taken, we have detailed and reliable information on only a few cases, including individuals who were abducted as children. These "white Indians" often refused to return to the mode of life into which they had been born, even when given an opportunity.[6] In the eighteenth century Crèvecoeur asked: "By what power does it come to pass, that children who have been adopted when young among these people, can never be prevailed on to readopt European manners?" Such individuals sometimes forgot their native speech, like Cynthia Ann Parker, captured by the Comanches in 1836 at the age of nine. When recaptured by the whites as a grown woman, all she could remember was her name. Other captives praised Indian character and morals and some of them adopted an Indian world view and religious beliefs. It was said of Mary Jemison, abducted in 1758 at the age of fifteen, that "she was as strong a pagan in her feelings as any Indian," that all her religious ideas conformed to those of the Senecas, and that "the doctrine taught in the Christian religion she is a stranger to." Of William Failey, abducted in 1837, his brother-in-law and biographer wrote: "In fact, his long residence among the Indians has made him an Indian." Don Ryan in *The Warriors' Path* (1937) and Conrad Richter in *The Light in the Forest* (1953) have given this theme modern novelistic treatment. The latter book was soon republished in paper-back form (1954), and Walt Disney is planning a movie version of it.

Benjamin Franklin must have been highly impressed by the attitude which the Six Nations assumed towards the values of their own culture as compared with that of the whites. An anecdote, in several forms, appears in his writings which presumably was derived from the considered response these Indians made when, during the Lancaster conference in 1744, it was suggested that if they so desired some of their boys might be sent to Williamsburg for a white education. The Iroquois countered with the proposition that "if the English Gentlemen would send a Dozen or two of their children to Onondago, the great council would take care of their Education, bring them up in really what was the best Manner and make men of them." [7]

---

[6] Erwin H. Ackerknecht, "White Indians," *Bulletin of the History of Medicine*, XV (1944), 26, 30.

[7] Aldridge, "Franklin's Deistical Indians," 399; A. Irving Hallowell, "American Indians, White and Black: The Phenomenon of Transculturalization," *Current Anthropology*, IV (1963), 519-530.

These Indians not only felt secure in their own values; they felt free to appraise those of the white man. And the captives who became "white Indians" discovered that the actual manner of life of the natives was something other than the literary images of the Noble Savage or the fiendish red man. The Indian cultures contained values which the white child could assimilate, live by, and in adulthood refuse to relinquish. Old White Boy and all his sons became Seneca chiefs. Even aside from captives, there were white men on the frontier who became semiacculturated to Indian ways. Sam Houston, in his early days, lived with the Cherokees. It has not been sufficiently stressed that *Leatherstocking,* the most famous internationally of all characters in American fiction, falls into this category. Although a white man by "natur," he had Indian "gifts." He is said to have "acquired some knowledge of most of the Indian dialects." During his early life, he lived among the Delawares and long before they called him Deerslayer, he had successively borne three other Indian nicknames. On occasion, he identified himself with the Delawares and their aboriginal values. When contemplating torture by the Hurons, he says he will strive "not to disgrace the people among whom I got my training." And the Huron chiefs, uncertain about his return from the brief furlough granted him, entertained "the hope of disgracing the Delawares by casting into their teeth the delinquency of one held in their villages." While they would have preferred to torture his Indian comrade Chingachgook, they thought the "pale face scion of the hated stock was no bad substitute for their purposes." Quite aside from his characterization as the honest, resourceful, intrepid frontiersman and scout, the uniqueness of Leatherstocking as the first white man in fiction represented as acculturated in his youth to Indian languages, customs, and values, should not be overlooked.

From a contemporary vantage point, I believe that our relations with the Indians involve one distinct peculiarity which might have been difficult to predict at an earlier period of our history. Despite our achievement of political dominance, considerable race mixture, and the effects of acculturation on the native peoples, neither the Indian nor his culture has completely vanished from our midst. The question arises, have the Indian cultures of the postfrontier period completely ceased to influence us? The answer is no.

One effect of the reservation system has been the conservation of those aspects of the native cultures that had survived all the vicissitudes of previous contacts with the white race. A new potential source of influence on our twentieth-century culture was created. Before we can turn to the nature of this influence, however, it is necessary to obtain the wider historic perspective that a more systematic consideration of the older lines of influence will provide us.

In the first place, it could have been predicted that, as a result of the colonization of the New World, loan words would appear in various Indo-European languages that could be traced to aboriginal American languages. Besides the nouns borrowed to designate objects unknown in England, there are many expressions in American English that reflect Indian influence—*burying the hatchet, Indian summer, Indian giver, happy hunting ground,* and *war-paint,* used by the American woman. *Buck* as a slang expression for *dollar* harks back to the Indian fur trade when prices had reference to beavers or buckskins. Place names of Indian origin are, of course, legion—the names of twenty-six states, eighteen of our largest cities, thousands of small towns, most of the long rivers and large lakes, and a few of the highest mountains are of Indian derivation.

Having come to a country new to them, it was inevitable that the colonists, whose traditional culture had not prepared them to live as they had to live here, should be influenced by those aspects of Indian culture that had immediate practical advantages in daily life. In any case, the determinative importance of the fact that this was not in any sense a virgin land must not be forgotten. The countless generations of Indians had left their imprints upon the landscape. Without the plow, the soil had been cultivated, and the raising of native crops was as typical over wide areas as was hunting and fishing. It is still debatable how far the actual virgin terrain had been radically modified by burning, girdling, and tilling. There were narrow forest trails, trodden by moccasined feet, that were already old, and the whites made use of them in their own system of overland communication, developing some of them into highways eventually connecting great centers of American civilization. Then there were the earthworks of an older Indian population in the Old Northwest Territory which influenced the patterning of some early white settlements. The "pilgrims" who founded Marietta, Ohio, found it convenient to moor their flatboats "at the foot of a raised terrace the Mound Builders had once used as an avenue between their temple and the river." Circleville takes its name from the fact that in the laying out of the original town, concentric circles of aboriginal earthworks were closely followed by the outlying streets. An octagonal courthouse, surrounded by a circular green, became the hub of the town. And it is said that "in the Wabash River bottoms, in the early spring, many farm houses stand high and dry on a wooded burial mound while all the fields are under water." [8]

Among the early settlers, communication by water was everywhere the most important. While they were familiar with certain types of watercraft in their own culture, they and their descendants have been influenced by at least two types used by the Indians, the Chesapeake Bay log canoe and the bark canoe of the north.

From a European point of view, the Indians wearing moccasins, leggings, and breechclouts were considered to be relatively naked compared to themselves. However, considered in a very broad culture-historical perspective, their own style and that of the aborigines shared a generic train in common: throughout the boreal regions of the Northern Hemisphere, clothing of the fitted or tailored type prevails, standing in marked contrast to the untailored style once found in the ancient Mediterranean region, Africa, and Central and South America. In all these latter regions, for example, nothing like the fitted footgear represented by the boot, shoe, or moccasin is found. While the practice never spread beyond the frontier itself, nevertheless there were white men who adopted the wearing of not only Indian moccasins, but leggings and a breechclout as well. The moccasin, of course, is the most noted item of Indian clothing that was used by white men very early. It was a fitted type of footgear, and if the colonists had been Romans, this item of clothing might not have been borrowed so quickly, or its use continued. Turner has noted that the General Court of Massachusetts once ordered five hundred pairs each of snowshoes and moccasins for use in the frontier counties. Much later, footgear of this type was used by lumbermen. In the back-

[8] Walter Havighurst, *Land of Promise, the Story of the Northwest Territory* (New York, 1946), 24–25, 158.

woods of Manitoba in the 1930's, a clergyman of my acquaintance always wore a pair of his best beaded moccasins in the pulpit on Sundays. It would be interesting to know more about the commercialization of the moccasin type of shoe which we see increasingly on the feet of Americans today.

It was, however, the discovery of the plants cultivated by the New World aborigines that from the very first produced the most profound impact on both European and American culture, revolutionalizing the food economy and diet of Old World peoples and at the same time laying one of the foundations on which was to rise the distinctive structure of American agriculture. Of the several plants—maize, beans, pumpkins, squash, and others—maize in particular was important from the start, taking precedence over the grain which the settlers had brought from Europe. It became a primary factor in the acculturation of the Englishmen to an American way of life. We need think only of corn on the cob, corn bread, Indian pudding, hominy, mush, grits, succotash, and corn syrup; of breakfast cereals, cornstarch, and popcorn; or of corncob pipes and bourbon, to understand the extent of this Indian contribution to our civilization today.

Tobacco is an equally significant "gift" of the American Indians, symbolized by the once-familiar figure of the "wooden Indian" inextricably linked with the tobacco shop in the nineteenth century. The history and use of it in our culture present a number of features in cultural borrowing at large. Readaptation to the values of the borrowing people is well illustrated. The consumption of tobacco was completely divorced from the ceremonial context in which it appeared among the Indians and became purely secular.

Peruvian bark, now known as quinine, proved highly sensational since it was a specific for malaria. It reached Spain before the middle of the seventeenth century and was soon introduced into the English colonies. In Virginia, Governor Berkeley said in 1671 that whereas formerly one person in five had died of fever in his first year, now almost no one succumbed. When one considers that in this same century Governor Winthrop's famous remedy for ulcers consisted of "one ounce of crabbe's eyes and four ounces of strong wine vinegar," the general state of colonial medicine can be well appreciated, and the reason why Peruvian bark, an Indian herbal, achieved such high fame can be easily understood. Indian medicine was likewise given a boost when, in 1738, Dr. John Tennent was awarded one hundred pounds by the Virginia House of Burgesses for curing pleurisy with Seneca rattlesnake root. As William Fenton well says, when Western medicine met Indian herbalism, the former "was still carrying a heavy burden of medieval practices so that the first few physicians in the colonies were but several centuries advanced from the Indian shaman who selected his herbs thinking of the effect that their appearance might contribute to the disease and guaranteed their efficiency with incantations and feats of magic. Moreover, the average settler had brought from the Old World a knowledge of herbs that in kind was not unlike that of the Indian, but as newcomers they were unfamiliar with New World plants, and although the level of their own popular medicine did not set them above adopting Indian remedies, the Indian herbalist whose knowledge was power was not always a ready teacher." [9] In *The Pioneers,* Cooper pictures for us how "Doctor" Elnathan Todd managed to steal one of John Mohegan's remedies.

Popular confidence in Indian medicine remained strong during the early nineteenth century, when the population was flowing over the Appalachians. The "yarb and root" doctor, red or white, played a prominent role in many communities. In 1813 in Cincinnati there was published *The Indian Doctor's Dispensatory*. Other books followed, including Selman's *The Indian Guide to Health* (1836) and Foster's *The North American Indian Doctor, or Nature's Method of Curing and Preventing Disease According to the Indians* (1838). In a lecture given at the New York Academy of Medicine in 1936, Dr. Harlow Brooks (emeritus professor of clinical medicine, New York University) said:

The Universal testimony of those qualified to judge has been that even within the memory of my generation we have incorporated into our pharmacopoeia and practice a good many practices and drugs of our Indian predecessors . . . . The leading doctor in my boyhood memory, in the district in which my parents settled, was an old Sioux medicine man, whose services were considered by the territorial government so valuable that when his tribe was removed to a reservation

[9] W. N. Fenton, "Contacts Between Iroquois Herbalism and Colonial Medicine," Smithsonian Institution *Report* (1941), 505–506.

he was asked to remain with his white patients, among whom were my own parents. I am sure that much of the medicine I received as an infant and child was derived directly from the lore of this fine, learned, and much respected old man. In those days it was on the service of these men than our pioneers relied for medical help; otherwise, little or none at all was available to the early settler.[10]

What is particularly interesting is not merely the incorporation in our pharmacopoeia of some aboriginal drugs, but the positive attitude towards Indian medicine and charms that has persisted into the twentieth century. For instance, old Seneca families still sell wild flowers and sassafras on certain street corners in Buffalo, and the Pamunkey Indians of Virginia until a decade ago went to Washington every spring to sell sassafras and other herbs. In *Triple Western* (Fall, 1954) there is a short item on "Medicine Man's Wisdom."

The potencies attributed to Indian herbal remedies have had still other manifestations in our culture, an important one being the medicine show. While not all these shows made use of the Indian, most of them did. It has been said that "as a symbol" the native "was as important to the med-show platform as the wooden Indian was to the tobacco shop." It exploited the image that had already been created of him as a "healer." When Chief Chauncey Kills-in-the-Bush Yellow Robe died, eulogies appeared in the theatrical press. Rolling Thunder, the owner of the Kiowa Indian Medicine and Vaudeville Company, commented on these as follows:

It is fine to see this intelligent recognition of the life work of an Indian. Too many people have always thought of the American Indian as next to a beast. There are some who are now learning the truth: that the Indian's drugstore was always the field and the forest, where the herbs he uses in his medicines are gathered as God placed them for him to use, and God gave the Indian the knowledge to gather and compound them. That is why the Indian as a healer has been a success.[11]

[10] Harlow Brooks, "The Contribution of the Primitive American to Medicine," in I. Goldston (ed.), *Medicine and Mankind* (New York, 1936), 87.
[11] Winnifred Johnston, "Medicine Show," *Southwest Review*, XXI (1936), 393.

The authors of *Show Biz* say that "when the Kickapoo Indian Medicine Company went on the block in 1911, after thirty years roaming the American plains and hamlets, it still brought $250,000. At one time, there were 150 medicine shows on the road, all of them featuring one or more Kickapoo Indians." [12] It may be pointed out in passing that at the same time that the image of the Indian as a healer was being exploited in the medicine show, the old image of him as a bloodthirsty enemy was being dramatized by the wild West show that William F. Cody took on the road in 1883 and which in various incarnations and imitations continued until 1931, when the 101 Ranch closed down.

The red man also became involved in another characteristic area of American cultural development in the years before the Civil War—religion. In Spiritualism, the United Society of Believers (Shakers), and the Church of Latter-day Saints (Mormons), the American Indians had special significance for the founders or adherents. According to Shaker tradition, "it was a native of the forest who first recognized the saintliness of Mother Ann. One poor Indian saw a bright light around her, and prophesied that the Great Spirit had sent her to do much good. In another story it is related that when Ann was returning from her eastern mission, she was met at the Albany ferry by a number of Indians, who joyfully cried: 'The good woman is come! The good woman is come!'" [13] What other religious sect in the world has turned to an aboriginal people for validation of the saintliness of the founder? Besides this, some of the Shaker "gift songs" received in trance came from Indian spirits. Once the spirits of a whole tribe of Indians, who had died before Columbus discovered America and had been wandering homeless ever since, turned up at a Shaker meetinghouse, where they were made welcome. As described by an eyewitness, more than a dozen of the Shakers present became possessed by these Indian guests. A powwow ensued. There were yells, whoops, and strange antics. The Indian spirits asked for succotash, which they ate, and after some instruction were sent off under guidance "to the Shakers' heavenly world."

[12] Abel Green and Joe Laurie, Jr., *Show Biz, from Vaude to Video* (New York, 1953), 83.

[13] E. D. Andrews, *The People Called Shakers* ... (New York, 1953), 83.

Although "speaking in tongues" had a long history in Europe as well as in America, one of the striking facts in the early developmental phases of American Spiritualism is the frequency of references to mediums speaking Indian languages and to those who had an Indian "control" or "guide." The names of more than a dozen mediums, men and women and their Indian controls, appear in the *Encyclopaedia of Psychic Science*. Such historic figures as Red Jacket, Black Hawk, and Tecumseh are on the list, as well as spirits with such names as White Feather, Bright Eyes, and Moonstone. What is particularly significant is that these Indian spirits were thought to be beneficent in their influence, especially because of their healing powers, although they often manifested themselves at seances in a somewhat rambunctious manner. As time went on and spirit photography was introduced, some of these spirits appeared in native costume in the photographs.

It would seem that no other American religious sect, with the possible exception of the Shakers, felt such a genuine affinity with the aborigines. While there was no question of borrowing Indian beliefs as such, nevertheless the Spiritualists saw analogies to their own views and practices. One of these was the "shaking tent" rite of the Algonkians of the eastern woodlands (which has been described elsewhere).[14] Into a framework of poles covered with birchbark or canvas a conjurer goes; the tent sways and voices are heard which, however, are usually believed to be nonhuman. An early historian of American Spiritualism, writing in 1870, after referring to some of these rites, says:

Such are some of the phases in which communication exhibits itself amongst a people whom we call 'savage' and whom, in comparison to our more advanced civilization, we may justly call so; and yet, does our knowledge of the occult and invisible forces in nature furnish us with any clue to the mystery of these astounding manifestations or the power by which the unlettered 'savage' can avail himself of a knowledge which all our control over the elements fails to compete with? In a word, the red Indian can do what we can neither explain nor imitate.[15]

[14] A. Irving Hallowell, *The Role of Conjuring in Saulteaux Society* (Philadelphia, 1942).

[15] Emma Hardinge [Emma Hardinge Britten], *History of Modern American Spiritualism* (Independence, Missouri, 1945), 144; (New York, 1870), 487.

This interest of the Spiritualists in the Indian and his ways has
continued down to the present. At Lily Dale, New York, the
summer mecca of Spiritualists, which commemorated its fiftieth
anniversary in 1929, it has been customary to celebrate Indian
Day with parades and dances given by natives from near-by
reservations.

To turn now to the Church of Jesus Christ of Latter-day Saints,
the attitude of the adherents of this indigenous American sect
towards the Indians is in sharp contrast with that of the Spiritualists. According to *The Book of Mormon,* the red men are essentially the degenerate posterity of a rebellious segment of a small
group of Jews who, migrating to the New World before the
beginning of the Christian era, brought with them an advanced
culture. Consequently, it is said that *The Book of Mormon*
supplements the Bible, since it is a history of God's dealings with
remnants of Israel and the Saviour's ministrations among them in
the Western Hemisphere.[16] For in America, the great Nephrite
prophecy has been fulfilled—the second coming of Christ. After
the Resurrection He appeared to a multitude of nearly 3,000
people in Mexico, before a greater assembly the next day, and
after this "he did show himself unto them oft." The occurrence
of the legendary figure of a so-called "white god" with certain
associated attributes among the Incas, Mayas, Aztecs, and Toltecs,
the Mormons interpret as supporting evidence for the historic appearance of Christ in America.

In the Mormon view, the aborigines of the United States were
the descendants of the Lamanites, the "bad" people of the
Mormon epic. Unlike the Spiritualists, the Mormons had nothing
they could look to them for; still, a strange affinity connected them
with the Indians. In Mormon hymnals there are songs about the
red man. In the days before the rise of archaeology or anthropology in the contemporary sense, *The Book of Mormon* was
representative of the speculations that had been going on in
Europe for several centuries about the peopling of the New
World. These earlier theories had to be reconciled first of all with
the account given in the Bible of man's creation and dispersal.
What is peculiar in the Mormon case, however, is the fact that a

[16] Paul M. Hanson, *Jesus Christ Among the Ancient Americans* (Independence, Missouri, 1945), 144.

particular theory of the peopling of the New World was incorporated as a dogma of a religious sect. This could hardly have occurred anywhere but in early nineteenth-century America. The early Mormons easily reconciled their theory with the Bible, but since the sect has survived into a period of American culture when an enormous increase in our knowledge of New World prehistory from archaeological investigations has taken place, a further reconciliation of the inspired history found in *The Book of Mormon* with this new knowledge is now being sought.

Outside the Mormon church, the consensus is that in its nondoctrinal aspects *The Book of Mormon* is derived from a romance written but not published by Solomon Spaulding, a clergyman who left the church and was in business in Ohio by 1812. There he dug into some mounds and became interested in the origin of the extinct people who had erected them. The theory that they were of Jewish origin was not original with him, since it was maintained by many prominent men in this country. If Spaulding's manuscript had been printed in its original form as fiction, he would have anticipated those writers in America who were soon to exploit the Indian in the historical novel. Even when *The Book of Mormon* was published in 1830, it fell precisely in the period when the Indian was assuming great prominence in American literature. Three of Cooper's *Leatherstocking Tales* had met with acclaim by this date, and at least thirty-nine novels published between 1824 and 1834 included Indian episodes.

There was a parallel development in the drama. Barker's *Indian Princess* (Pocahontas), staged in 1808, had a long line of successors. There were at least thirty so-called Indian plays staged between 1820 and 1840 and twenty or more between the latter date and the Civil War. Some of these were dramatizations of the novels of Cooper, Bird, and Simms. The peak in the popularity of these Indian dramas also falls within the period (1830–70) that has been called "the golden days of the American actor." Perhaps the most outstanding example is *Metamora, or The Last of the Wampanoags*, which was in the repertoire of Edwin Forrest for almost forty years. It was played in Philadelphia every year— except two—for a quarter of a century. Forrest had specifically advertised in 1828 for a play in which "the hero, or principal character, shall be an aboriginal of this country." William Cullen

Bryant was the chairman of the committee which selected *Metamora* from the fourteen plays submitted. It proved to be one of the most popular plays of the nineteenth-century American theater. *Metamora* was played even after Forrest's death, and a radio version was broadcast in 1939. During its theatrical lifetime, more Americans are said to have seen *Metamora* than *Abie's Irish Rose* or *Tobacco Road* in the twentieth century.

In poetry, the Indian had appeared as a subject ever since the time of Freneau, but there was nothing that could compare with the initial impact and continuing popularity of *Hiawatha*. It became *the* poem of the American Indian. Before publication in 1855, there was an advance sale of four thousand copies; in five months the sale had risen to fifty thousand copies. It has been said that what was unique about Longfellow's poem was the fact that "*Hiawatha* was the first poem of its kind in America based on Indian legend rather than on Indian history." [17] While true enough, it is clarifying to note that until 1839, when Schoolcraft published his *Algic Researches,* there were no reliable collections of Indian myths or tales on which a poet could draw. It was, therefore, a historical accident that Longfellow came to exploit Ojibwa material; he had no other choice. Paradoxically, Schoolcraft himself published a poem dealing with the Creek Indian wars twelve years before *Hiawatha* appeared. He did not know the Creeks at first hand, while he knew the Ojibwas intimately, his wife being of that tribe. Evidently it never occurred to him to use his Ojibwa myths as the basis of a narrative poem. Thus Schoolcraft epitomizes the force of the traditional literary approach to the use of Indian themes.

Longfellow bore the same sort of relation to Schoolcraft as Cooper did to Heckewelder. Generally speaking, there was no inclination on the part of eastern novelists, dramatists, or poets who selected Indian themes to become acquainted with living Indians of the contemporary frontiers as a background for their productions. Indeed, a volume of short stories, *Tales of the Northwest,* about Indians in the Upper Mississippi region, written by one who knew them intimately, was ignored after its publication in 1839. William Joseph Snelling, the author, had insisted that "a

[17] W. L. Schramm, "*Hiawatha* and Its Predecessors," *Philological Quarterly,* XI (1932), 341.

man must live, emphatically, live with Indians; share with them
their lodges, their food, and their blankets, for years, before he can
comprehend their ideas, or enter their feelings." American writers
were not yet ready for this early call to realism. But for American
readers, a novel entitled *Altowan; or Incidents of Life and Adventure in the Rocky Mountains,* by Sir William Drummond Stewart,
an eccentric Scot, who during the 1830's had spent six years in the
West, was published in New York in 1846. Although the novel was
undistinguished in writing and had some romantic trappings, in
this case the author *had* seen a great deal of Indian life. What
makes the book unique is that one of the leading characters, as
pointed out by De Voto, is an Indian transvestite—a berdache—
and this individual is depicted in highly realistic terms. The
author pictures his behavior and dress in detail, and no doubt is
left about what he was. "I know of no English or American novel
of that time or for many years later that is half so frank about
homosexuality," writes De Voto.[18]

In painting and popular music there was a parallel romantic
tradition. Gleanings from historical documents or tradition were
tinctured by an extremely free use of imagination. It is obvious,
for instance, that the artist who provided the frontispiece for Mrs.
Morton's *Ouabi, or The Virtue of Nature* (1790) knew as little
about Indians at first hand as did the author of this poem in the
Noble Savage tradition. And Benjamin West's painting of one of
Penn's treaties with the Indians, dating from about 1771, offers a
direct parallel to the literary artist who drew on historical documents for his source material.

Part of Mrs. Morton's poem was set to music by Hans Gram the
year after its publication. This composition, the first orchestral
score published in the United States, was entitled *The Death Song
of an Indian Chief,* although there is no evidence that the composer knew anything about aboriginal music. In 1799, a musical
arrangement of *Alkamoonok, the Death Song of the Cherokee
Indians,* reputedly based on a genuine Indian melody, was published and soon became very popular. It had been sung in
Tammany (1794), the first American opera. An eccentric musician,
Anton Philip Heinrich, who died in 1861, was the composer of the
Pocahontas Waltz for piano and is said to have been the first to use

18 Bernard De Voto, *Across the Wide Missouri* (Boston, 1947), 426.

Indian themes in larger orchestral works. The heroine of the big song hit of 1844, *The Blue Juniata,* was an Indian girl, "Bright Alforata."

Actually, it is at this vernacular level that the backwash of the frontier is most clearly discernible in American music of the nineteenth century. This was due to the role the Indian played in the subject matter of folk songs. In one group of songs, the Indian appears "merely as an incidental personality" and the attitudes towards him are vague. In a second group, however, negative attitudes are sharply defined since many songs in this class are long narrative ballads which depict actual frontier conflicts. Folk songs about historic events, "including songs about dramatic episodes in the relationships of Indians and White, have been sung regularly since the earliest days of colonization and have faithfully reflected changing relationships between the two culture groups at least down to the present century when modern techniques for the commercialization of popular songs may have beclouded the issue." A third category of songs reflects a positive attitude towards the Indian varying "from vague references to good Indians or Indians with heroic qualities, to songs and ballads exclusively about romanticized Indians, who are admired for their stamina and other heroic qualities." [19] An anonymous, undated example of America's folk painting, depicting the rescue of John Smith, belongs to this earlier period.[20] The same motif was subsequently as popular in prints as it was in fiction, drama, poetry, and music.

However, in the midst of all this romanticizing of the Indian, a trend toward greater realism developed, particularly in painting. Here and there in colonial times there had been some realistic paintings of the Indians, for example, the masterly portraits of Lenape chiefs painted in 1735 by Gustavus Hesselius (1682–1755). But about 1821, many of the western chiefs who came to Washington on business with the government sat for their portraits. A collection of these became the nucleus of the famous "Indian Gallery." The magnificent reproduction of 120 of these portraits in

[19] Austin E. Fife and Francesca Redden, "The Pseudo-Indian Folksongs of the Anglo-American and French-Canadian," *Journal of American Folklore,* LVII (1954), 241, 394.

[20] *American Folk Art. The Art of the Common Man in America, 1750–1900* (Museum of Modern Art publication No. 19 [New York, 1932]).

a folio edition of three volumes (McKenny and Hall, *History of the Indian Tribes of North America, 1836–44*) gave the eastern public an opportunity to see what contemporary Indians looked like. On the other hand, artists themselves began to go west (Seymour, Rindisbacher, Lewis, Catlin, Miller, Eastman, Stanley, Kane, Bodmer, Kurz), so that greatly enriched images of the natives, the kind of life they led, and the grandeur of the country they inhabited soon became more widely known to those living far removed from the contemporary frontier. It was the author of *Altowan* who induced Alfred Jacob Miller—now one of the most famous of these artists, whose true accomplishments have only become known to the public in recent years—to accompany him west in 1837. Catlin is particularly important, however, not only because he was a pioneer, but because he was a showman. He toured eastern cities in the late 1830's exhibiting his "Indian Gallery," which has been called the first wild West show. It included Indian "curios," featuring pipes, and in exhibition halls he erected a real Crow tepee. Catlin appeared in person and, taking selected pictures as a point of departure, lectured to his audiences about Indian life. He would dress lay figures in Indian clothing and frequently had some Indians on hand to pantomime native activities. Although Catlin was not an anthropologist, his Indian Gallery did mediate to Americans a more realistic type of knowledge about the Plains tribes than had been available. After touring American cities, he took his show to England and the Continent. In 1954, an exhibition of Catlin's work, sponsored by the United States Information Agency, was again on tour in Europe, while in this country Bodmer's water colors were being exhibited.

Even though Catlin "had been there," he had detractors, like Audubon, who challenged the accuracy of his paintings. The same thing had happened to Cooper and Longfellow. The romantic tradition in America was strong, and the application of a purely realistic standard of judgment was, in effect, an attack upon the tradition. Cooper may have idealized the Indian in some respects and erred in many details, but he idealized the pioneer and backwoodsman too. The Indian was enveloped in the romantic tradition and what is interesting is how long he has remained a part of it.

When the dime novel sprang into popularity in the sixties, the
Indians of the Cooper tradition became an integral part of this
literature. In one way or another, Indians play a role in at least
45 per cent of the 321 stories in the original dime-novel series.
Maleska, the Indian Wife of the White Hunter (1860), the first
one published by Beadle and Adams, actually was a reprinting of a
story that had been serialized in 1839. "The death of the dime
novel, if it ever really occurred, was accompanied by the birth of
the nickelodeon, the motion picture, and the radio, which simply
transferred the old stories of cowboys, desperadoes, and Indians to
more dynamic forms." [21] In fact, as soon as the silent cinema began
to flicker, the Indian of the old romantic tradition was in. There
was a screen version of *Hiawatha* as early as 1909, the *Deerslayer*
was shown in 1911, the *Last of the Mohicans* in 1920. And, until
very recently, what Stanley Vestal called the "Hollywooden
Indian" has persisted in that typically American movie genre—
the western.

On the other hand, there was an increasing awareness that
authentic knowledge of the aboriginal cultures was relevant and
desirable in the arts. Perhaps this attitude developed along with
the emergence of a more realistic tradition in American writing.
However this may be, I think that the publication of Edna Dean
Proctor's *Song of the Ancient People* in 1893 represents a transi-
tional case. While it is in the high romantic tradition, there is an
appended commentary to this poem by F. H. Cushing (1857–
1900), a pioneer anthropologist who went to the Southwest in
1879 and lived among the Zuñi for five years. He says he can bear
witness to the poet's "strict fidelity of statement, and attempt to
show, as one of the Ancient People themselves would be glad to
show, how well she has divined their spirit." The volume was
illustrated with realistic aquatints made by Julian Scott in the
Hopi country. No other Indian poem had ever been offered to the
public with such an aura of authenticity about it—it was bound
in buckskin with a design taken from Southwestern pottery on the
cover.

The inauguration of genuine Indian themes in American concert music is ordinarily attributed to Edward MacDowell, whose

[21] James D. Hart, *The Popular Book. A History of America's Literary
Taste* (New York, 1950), 156.

Indian Suite was first performed in 1896. But where did he find such themes? He was not a frontier boy. He entered the Paris Conservatory at the age of fourteen and did not take up residence here until he was twenty-seven. The fact is that MacDowell exemplifies a repetition of the same kind of relationship to the source of his thematic material as was noted in the case of Cooper and Longfellow. He got them from Theodore Baker, the first trained musician to go into the field and study Indian music at first hand. Baker, a German, visited the Seneca Reservation and the Carlisle Indian School in the summer of 1880, offering the results of his analysis to Leipzig University as a doctoral dissertation. But he was not a composer, nor was Alice C. Fletcher, whose monograph on Omaha songs (1893) initiated the study of Indian music in American anthropology. However, two of the songs she collected, *Shupida* and the *Omaha Tribal Prayer,* undoubtedly have been among the most widely circulated examples of authentic Indian music in American culture. Together with three other Indian songs, they appear in *Indian Lore,* a pamphlet in the Merit Badge Series of the Boy Scouts of America. In the past six years, approximately forty-seven thousand copies of this booklet have been printed. Scouts who aspire to the merit badge in Indian lore must be able to "sing three Indian songs including the Omaha Tribal Prayer and tell something of their meaning." Since 1911, there have been 18,719 American boys who have won this distinction.

Following the lead of MacDowell, other composers began to make increasing use of Indian themes, though only a few made direct contact with the reservation Indians. Among them were Burton, Cadman, Farwell, Jacobi, Lieurance, Arthur Nevin, Skilton, and Troyer, who found native music interesting to them, because as Skilton has said, "many devices of the ultra modern composers of the present day have long been employed by Indians —unusual intervals, arbitrary scales, changing tune, conflicting rhythm, polychoral effects, hypnotic monotony." [22] Indian songs were harmonized and arranged for performance by white musicians; Indian themes were handled freely in the composition of original works, much in the same way that Longfellow handled Ojibwa myths.

[22] Charles S. Skilton, "American Indian Music," *International Cyclopedia of Music and Musicians* (New York, 1939), 48.

In the field of operatic composition, despite the popularity of other compositions of Herbert and Cadman, neither the former's *Natoma* (1911) nor the latter's *Shanewis* (1918) became established in operatic repertoire. Some compositions based on Indian themes have received high acclaim in the repertoire of orchestral music, others as popular songs. Skilton's *Indian Dances,* along with Mac-Dowell's *Indian Suite,* were among the twenty-seven compositions of twelve American composers which had the greatest number of performances in the United States during the seven years following World War I. Jacobi's *String Quartet on Indian Themes* was selected to represent American music at the International Festival of Contemporary Music at Zurich in 1926. Elliott Carter's ballet *Pocahontas,* presented in New York in 1939 (and later developed into a suite for orchestra), received the Juilliard Publication Award the following year. Cadman, who went to the Omaha Reservation in 1909 with Francis LaFlesche, an Indian anthropologist, wrote one of his most famous songs that year, *From the Land of the Sky Blue Water.* It vied with *The Rosary* in popularity. He likewise wrote two operas on Indian themes. *By the Waters of Minnetonka* (1921), composed by Thurlow Lieurance, who had visited the western reservations as early as 1905, has had a phenomenal success. At mid-century, it appears in the Victor Album *Twelve Beloved American Songs* along with *The Rosary* and *A Perfect Day.* Nor should commercialized popular songs of a lower order—some Indian in name only—be forgotten. Among those composed early in this century were *Navajo* (1903), *Tammany* (1905), *Red Wing* (1907), and *Hiawatha's Melody of Love* (1920), to say nothing of *The Indian Love Call* (1924), and *Ramona,* a hit of 1927.

In the early years of this century, some American poets, like the musicians, sought out the Indians, and those of the Southwest became a focal point of interest. These were the same people that Edna Procter had written about. They had been the subject, too, of a novel, *The Delight Makers* (1890) by A. F. Bandelier, said by Alfred L. Kroeber to be "a more comprehensive and coherent view of native Pueblo life than any scientific volume on the southwest."

A few American painters (Sharp, Phillips, Blumenschein) had also discovered the Southwest before the opening of the twentieth

century. Blumenschein's graphic commentary on the acculturation
process, which shows two Indians mounted on merry-go-round
horses, had appeared in *Harper's Weekly* in 1899.

Among the poets who became interested, Mary Austin soon
took the lead. She became the key figure in the use of Indian
material for literary purposes, and her extremely positive attitude
toward the cultures of the Indians influenced many others to seek
inspiration in their art. She characterized her *Amerindian Songs*
as being "Re-expressed from the Originals." Some of these first
appeared in *Poetry* (1917), along with comparable interpretations
by Frank S. Gordon, Alice Corbin Henderson, and Constance
Lindsay Skinner. Mary Austin wrote plays and stories, too. She
seems to have moved from a romantic primitivism to a more and
more realistic handling of Indian themes, as exemplified by her
play *The Arrow Maker,* produced on Broadway in 1911, and her
One-Smoke Stories (1934), one of her last books. Nor should the
fact be overlooked that four anthologies containing translations of
American Indian songs and poetry have appeared in this century
(George W. Cronyn, *The Path of the Rainbow,* 1918 and 1934;
Nellie Barnes, *American Indian Love Lyrics and Other Verse,*
1925; Margot Astrov, *The Winged Serpent,* 1946; and A. Grove
Day, *The Sky Clears,* 1951).

In the twentieth century, the Indian has also reappeared in
American plays, particularly in the work of the regional dramatists. While the setting is frequently the historic past, the problems
the native faces in the acculturation process are sometimes drama-
tized. Both *Strongheart* (1905) and *Cherokee Night* (1936) are
examples of this theme. In prose fiction, we also find that anthropologists, inspired by Bandelier and the stories collected in Elsie
Clews Parsons' *American Indian Life* (1922), entered the field.
Laughing Boy, a Literary Guild book of 1929, by Oliver LaFarge
and *Hawk Over Whirlpools* by Ruth Underhill (1940) are outstanding illustrations. In *America in Fiction,* the authors call attention to the fact that "now that he is on reservations, not a military foe, and generally not an economic competitor, the Indian is
a subject of great interest, so much so that more fiction has been
written about him in recent years than about any other ethnic
group except the Negro. In many works of fiction, he has been
given central prominence, his cultural complex has been detailed,

and much attention has been paid to his problems of adjusting himself to the dominating civilization that surrounds him." [23] Their bibliography lists thirty-seven novels or collections of stories published between 1902 and 1947. "Where once we had melodrama about the Indian with his bloody tomahawk," they say, "now we have clear-cut realism." Whatever the art form may be, what is striking is the more intimate acquaintance with contemporary Indians that informs the work of the painter, musician, poet, dramatist, or novelist who has drawn upon aboriginal cultural forms or used the problems of the Indian for his thematic material.

Finally, it seems to me that among these more recent influences, the impact of the Indian on modern anthropology should not be omitted. The social sciences as they have developed in the United States during the past half-century have attained an unusual prominence in American culture. Among these, anthropology in its modern form was just getting under way about the time the frontier closed. It was in the 1890's that Franz Boas began to teach at Columbia University and to train students in field work. Boas was a specialist in studies of the American Indian and a majority of his early students followed in his footsteps. Indeed, practically all the chief authorities on North American Indian ethnology, archaeology, and linguistics have been American. A historical accident? Of course. But that is the point. It is only recently among the younger generation that more attention is being devoted to peoples in the South Seas, Africa, and Asia. But it was the study of the Indians, and the problems that emerged from the investigation of the Indian as a subject, that gave American anthropology a distinctive coloring as compared with British, French, and German anthropology. Recently an American psychologist has remarked that "if the word 'anthropology' were presented to a sample of psychologists in a word-association test, I would venture 'culture' would probably be the most popular response, with 'Indians' a runner-up." [24] The presumption, no

[23] Otis W. Coan and Richard G. Lillard, *America in Fiction. An Annotated List of Novels that Interpret Aspects of Life in the United States* (3d ed., Stanford, 1949), 161–162.

[24] M. Brewster Smith, "Anthropology and Psychology," in *For a Science of Social Man. Convergences in Anthropology, Psychology and Sociology*, ed. John Gillin (New York, 1954), 39.

doubt, is that these hypothetical responses would be those of *American* psychologists.

The more detailed and reliable accounts of native Indian cultures that have emerged from the field work of American anthropologists have made possible a more objective appraisal of the values inherent in the aboriginal modes of life. To those who look at the record, the Indian no longer appears as either a noble or ignoble savage. He has moved into a clearer focus as a human being. Like our own, his traditional cultural background and historical situation have determined the nature of his experience and made him what he is.

Viewing the panorama of our colonial and national history as a whole, I have referred to many diverse aspects of our culture— speech, economic life, food habits, clothing, transportation, medicine, religion, the arts, and even a social science—which have been influenced by our relations with the Indians at different times and in differing ways. Some of these influences have been mediated directly, others indirectly. Contacts with the Indian on the frontier have by no means been the source of all of them.

In summing up, we may ask: how deeply have such influences penetrated our culture? To what extent are our relations with the Indians one key to our differentiation as Americans, not only culturally but psychologically? Constance Rourke once wrote, "The Backwoodsman conquered the Indian, but the Indian also conquered him. He ravaged the land and was ravaged in turn." Phillips D. Carleton, concluding his comments on the captivity literature, writes: "it emphasizes the fact that it was the line of fluid frontiers receding into the West that changed the colonists into a new people; they conquered the Indian but he was the hammer that beat out a new race on the anvil of the continent." [25] Carl Jung, who has probably analyzed more persons of various nationalities than anyone else, thought he could discern an Indian component in the character structure of his American patients, and D. H. Lawrence asked whether a dead Indian is nought. "Not that the Red Indian will ever possess the broadlands of America," he said and then added, "But his ghost will."

In America we faced the Indian on receding frontiers for a long period; but outside the frontier there was the shadow of the

[25] Phillips D. Carleton, "The Indian Captivity," *American Literature*, No. 15 (1943), 180.

Indian. This shadow is still upon us. We still mouth words and idioms that reflect intimate contacts with the aborigines of our land. We still make use of plants originally cultivated by them. We wear derivative forms of the footgear they wore. We have collected objects made by them in our homes and in our museums. Our artists have found inspiration in their artistic modes of expression. We constantly see the Indian sweep past our eyes on the movie screen. He persists in our historical novels and westerns. In 1954, *The Leatherstocking Saga* reappeared, compressed into one handsome volume. We Americans have seen the Indian come and go on the commonest national coins we have fingered. The first Bible to be printed in colonial America was in the Indian language, John Eliot's translation of the Old and New Testament into an Algonkian tongue. Over the generations thousands of American men have belonged to the more-than-a-century-old *Improved Order of Red Men*. American anthropologists have labored most industriously to provide more and more authentic information about aboriginal modes of life and the influence of American culture on the Indian. The Indian has never been rejected from the American consciousness. Perhaps his shadow upon us is even disappearing—he has become a part of us: in the *Dictionary of American Biography* will be found side by side with other famous Americans, Pontiac and Tecumseh, Blackhawk and Osceola. In 1931 a brief popular biography of Osceola—only a few pages in length—was printed at Palm Beach; it was entitled *Osceola the Seminole. Florida's Most Distinguished Historical Character!* And it is said that more statues have been erected of Sacajawea than of any other American woman.

Now that the frontier has passed, our children discover the Indian in the comic books, as well as in the library. They are familiar with Cooper's tales in *Classics Illustrated*. Indeed, there appears to have been a marked increase in number, variety, and quality of children's books about Indians published in the last two or more decades. There are biographies of Indians famous in our history as well as historical romances. The stories of famous white captives have been retold; there are excellent books on Indian crafts and simplified but accurate accounts of tribal life, besides well-written stories which center around Indian children as major characters. Nevertheless, the average American is by no means aware of all the ramifications of Indian influence upon our culture. Perhaps the Red Indian ghost D. H. Lawrence saw here and what Jung discerned in the character of his patients provide clues to an aspect of the American ethos that invites deeper scrutiny in the future.

SELECTED READINGS

Arbaugh, G. B. *Revelation in Mormonism, Its Character and Changing Forms.* Chicago: University of Chicago Press, 1932.

Chamberlain, Alexander F. "The Contribution of the American Indian to Civilization," *Proceedings of the American Antiquarian Society,* n.s. XVI (1905), 91–126.

Clark, Barrett H. (ed.). *Favorite American Plays of the Nineteenth Century.* Princeton, N.J.: Princeton University Press, 1943.

De Voto, Bernard. *Across the Wide Missouri. Illustrated with paintings by Alfred Jacob Miller, Charles Bodmer, and George Catlin.* Boston: Houghton, Mifflin, 1947.

Fairchild, Hoxie N. *The Noble Savage, a Study in Romantic Naturalism.* New York: Columbia University Press, 1928.

Hallowell, A. Irving. *Culture and Experience.* Philadelphia: University of Pennsylvania Press, 1955.

———. "The Impact of the American Indian on American Culture," *American Anthropologist,* LIX (1957), No. 2, 201–217.

Howard, John T. *Our American Music; Three Hundred Years of It.* 3d ed., rev. New York: Crowell, 1946.

Johannsen, Albert. *The House of Beadle and Adams and Its Dime and Nickel Novels. The Story of a Vanished Literature.* . . . Norman: University of Oklahoma Press, 1950.

Jung, Carl G. *Contributions to Analytical Psychology.* New York: Harcourt, Brace, & Co., 1928.

Keiser, Albert. *The Indian in American Literature.* New York: Oxford University Press, 1933.

Lawrence, D. H. *Studies in Classic American Literature.* New York: T. Seltzer, 1923.

Lawton, George. *The Drama of Life After Death; A Study of the Spiritualist Religion.* New York: H. Holt, 1932.

Mencken, Henry L. *The American Language.* 4th rev. ed. New York: A. A. Knopf, 1936.

Orians, G. H. *The Cult of the Vanishing American: A Century View, 1834–1934* ("Bulletin of the University of Toledo"). Toledo, November, 1935.

Pearce, Roy H. *The Savages of America. A Study of the Indian and the Idea of Civilization.* Baltimore: Johns Hopkins University Press, 1953.

Peckham, Howard H. *Captured by Indians; True Tales of Pioneer Survivors.* New Brunswick: Rutgers University Press, 1954.

Pickard, Madge E. and Buley, R. Carlyle. *The Midwest Pioneer, His Ills, Cures, & Doctors.* New York: H. Schuman, 1946.

Quinn, Arthur H. *A History of the American Drama from the Beginning to the Civil War.* 2d ed. New York: F. S. Crofts, 1943.

Rourke, Constance. *American Humor; A Study of the National Character.* New York: Harcourt, Brace, & Co., 1931.

————. *The Roots of American Culture and Other Essays.* New York: Harcourt, Brace, & Co., 1942.

Shook, C. A. *Cumorah Revisited; or "The Book of Mormon" and the Claims of the Mormons Re-examined from the Viewpoint of American Archaeology and Ethnology.* Cincinnati: Standard Publishing Co., 1910.

Snelling, W. Joseph. *William Joseph Snelling's Tales of the Northwest, with an Introduction by John T. Flanagan.* Minneapolis: University of Minnesota Press, 1936.

Spaeth, Sigmund. *A History of Popular Music in America.* New York: Random House, 1948.

Sper, Felix. *From Native Roots; A Panorama of Our Regional Drama.* Caldwell, Idaho: Caxton Printers, 1948.

Stewart, George R. *American Ways of Life.* Garden City, New York: Doubleday, 1954.

————. *Names on the Land.* New York: Random House, 1945.

Vestal, Stanley. "The Hollywooden Indian," *Southwest Review,* No. 21 (1936).

Wroth, Lawrence C. "The Indian Treaty as Literature," *Yale Review,* XVII (1928), 749–766.

Index